THE
VONNEGUT CHRONICLES

Illustration by Peter J. Reed.

THE
VONNEGUT
CHRONICLES

Interviews and Essays

Edited by
PETER J. REED
and MARC LEEDS

Contributions to the Study of World Literature,
Number 65

GREENWOOD PRESS
Westport, Connecticut • London

Library of Congress Cataloging-in-Publication Data

The Vonnegut chronicles : interviews and essays / edited by Peter J. Reed
and Marc Leeds.
     p.   cm.—(Contributions to the study of world literature,
ISSN 0738–9345 ; no. 65)
  Includes bibliographical references and index.
  ISBN 0–313–29719–3 (alk. paper)
    1. Vonnegut, Kurt—Criticism and interpretation. 2. Postmodernism
(Literature)—United States. I. Reed, Peter J. II. Leeds, Marc.
III. Series.
PS3572.05Z895   1996
813′.54—dc20   95–4670

British Library Cataloguing in Publication Data is available.

Library of Congress Catalog Card Number: 95–4670
ISBN: 0–313–29719–3
ISSN: 0738–9345

First published in 1996

Greenwood Press, 88 Post Road West, Westport, CT 06881
An imprint of Greenwood Publishing Group, Inc.

Printed in the United States of America

The paper used in this book complies with the
Permanent Paper Standard issued by the National
Information Standards Organization (Z39.48–1984).

10 9 8 7 6 5 4 3 2 1

Contents

Preface

This book has its origins in a Quad City Arts program in 1989 which featured Kurt Vonnegut as its "Super Author in Residence." The Arts Council of those four cities (Davenport and Bettendorf, Iowa, and Rock Island and Moline, Illinois) annually promotes a week-long festival celebrating an artist who is featured in appearances and honored in other supporting events. One of the events that accompanied a number of appearances by Vonnegut himself was a panel presentation by a group of six academics, five of them professors of English and one a painter and art instructor. Their papers were duplicated and hurriedly presented together in a single paper-covered, spiral-bound collection that looked enough like a book to plant a seed. Why not make a book?

The bond between the members of that group and a couple of other Vonnegut devotees of long standing, Asa Pieratt, a Vonnegut bibliographer and collector, and Bob Weide, who was filming a documentary on the author, grew strong during several days of following Vonnegut from one appearance to another, sharing his company when his commitments permitted, and swapping Vonnegut trivia and countless jokes. The man himself was our bond. He arrived after a harrowing, weather-delayed journey, exhausted and bleak. The pessimism of his mood at that time showed in some of his talks. But as always he drew overflow audiences, and he warmed to them and drew energy from them. In his later performances his audiences were enthralled, and he thrived on the rapport. With us he was charming, patient, loving, and enormously funny.

Naturally, the seven original papers remained far short of a book, especially of the kind that we now sought to make—not just another critical commentary but a tribute to an admired friend. The two of us who set about creating the book wanted one that seemed appropriate to Vonnegut's own fiction and his social role. That meant a collection that would be at once available to a general readership and critically sound for the academic audience, a collection, in fact, that like his own fiction diminishes the distinction between the culturally elite and the popular. To this end we sought contributions from both the older generation of critics who helped to bring critical recognition to Vonnegut's work and the younger commentators for whom Vonnegut is an established figure at the core of postmodern culture. We also included three conversations with Kurt Vonnegut in which he discusses his work and his worldview. These conversations, spaced over the last fifteen years, contribute to the collection's attempt to reflect on the broad span of Vonnegut's career. Finally, the bibliography attempts to bring up to date the existing listings of writing by and about Kurt Vonnegut, so that readers may further pursue their enjoyment and understanding of this author.

We began with the working title *Kurt Vonnegut at 70/40*, aiming at a 1992 publication when Vonnegut would be seventy years old and his first novel would have been published forty years previous. Working with a group of contributors and sharing editorial duties among people separated by half a continent demonstrated emphatically the wisdom of Saul Bellow's words from *Henderson the Rain King* that "nothing runs unmingled." The succession of upheavals, illnesses, opportunities, distractions, and demands experienced in the lives of the small group of people who contributed to this volume could itself be the stuff of Vonnegut fiction. So we missed Kurt's seventieth, but we are here at last.

Acknowledgments

We gratefully acknowledge the generous assistance and friendship of Kurt Vonnegut. Obviously the contributors to this collection were inspired by their delight in and respect for his work. He has patiently submitted to our interviews, generously offered help, particularly in granting quotation rights and the use of his graphics. Joe Petro III of Lexington, Kentucky, the artist who has collaborated with Kurt and silk-screened the paintings (which were originally done on acetate) has been generous with access to his studio, photographs, and expert commentary.

The organizers and staff of the Quad Cities Arts Festival, in particular the Director, Leslie Rasmussen, earn our thanks for prompting the occasion from which this project originated. The editors must also acknowledge the patience of the contributors who have born with our many delays. Paul Baepler took a supportive interest in this project throughout, as well as contributing more than his share to the compilation of the bibliography.

Peter received assistance from the Graduate School and the College of Liberal Arts of the University of Minnesota, and wishes to acknowledge particularly the support of Dean Julia Davis. Marc is especially appreciative of Jerry Holt, Robert Forrey, Jim Flavin and Marcia Tackett of Shawnee State University for their constant support and focus, as well as student assistants Angela Campbell and Leslie Carver whose early work on the text proved invaluable.

We are also indebted to Jude Grant, the original production editor of the text, and Catherine Lyons who took over the task with Jude's great enthusiasm and added her own wise counsel. Cynthia Harris graciously brought the book into the Greenwood fold, and what author doesn't have a soft spot for their acquisitions editor?

Our telephone bills not withstanding, we developed a strong friendship and deep respect for the other's unique abilities. Thank you Mr. Bell for the gift that keeps on ringing, and a similar thanks to all the anonymous Internet gurus who unknowingly assisted our efforts.

More than anyone else, we wish to thank our wives Maggie and Saralyn. They put up with large phone bills and absentee husbands. We've been blessed with partners who indulge our whims, encourage our self-fulfilling pursuits, and remain our truest advisors. Not to be overlooked, Marc's daughters Marisa and Whitney often had to wait for their turn at the computer, to say nothing about simply waiting for their dad to finish everything. At least he didn't take the computer on vacation as he did with the last book.

Introduction

The Vonnegut Chronicles celebrates the career of Kurt Vonnegut and his nearly fifty years as an active, publishing author. His first short stories appeared in 1950; his first novel, *Player Piano*, in 1952. Since that time he has published almost fifty short stories (most gathered in two collections), thirteen novels, three collections of nonfiction, two plays, and a teleplay. At this date, all of his novels are still in print. That fact, and simply the length of his career, is remarkable. Few other major American authors have remained active over such a long career, and even fewer have retained their popularity and a market which has kept their books in print.

Throughout this long career, Kurt Vonnegut has remained one of the shrewdest commentators—and often harshest critics—of American society. He began by challenging the complacency of the Eisenhower years, warning against its faith in technological progress and its bland postwar "can do" assurance. He watched the Kennedys with admiration of their panache and humor, and about their reenergizing the country, but with doubts of their faith in bright young men and charisma. Though he obviously disliked Nixon and his henchmen, he did not gloat over their fall at Watergate but rather lamented the fate of the country and the threat to its Constitution. In the years since, he has deplored the economic plight of the nation, with its creation of an expanding underclass and an indifferent plutocracy, its soaring debt and foreign takeovers, its collapsing culture and indifference to impending apocalypse by overpopulation, ecological destruction, or nuclear disaster.

For almost half a century, then, Vonnegut has remained one of the most important chroniclers of American life. His message is often one of foreboding, yet it is rarely gloomy, for Vonnegut extracts humor out of even the direst of circumstances. In this he follows the traditions of great American social satirists like Mark Twain and H. L. Mencken, or its comic cultural critics like Will Rogers, W. C. Fields, and Bob and Ray. It is this stance, with its detached, ironic observation of the society while standing firmly within its traditions, that gives

Vonnegut his value. Who better fills the roles of observer, commentator, judge, and even pardoner of American society through the last quarter of its history? For his cultural commentary alone he is surely marked out for an important place in American letters.

Beyond that, however, there remains the Vonnegut who tells good yarns, who spices his novels with comic plots seemingly tossed off with ease, who makes us laugh, who liberates adolescent impulses in us, who spurs our irreverence and asks the unaskable questions. "Spring is the mischief in me," says Robert Frost, and it is something like that, along with conscience and responsibility and compassion, that Vonnegut stirs in his readers and that saves him from becoming didactic and pedantic.[1] He consistently has found a response in young audiences, frequently for his message but more often for his freshness, for the liberating daring of his approach. His happy recklessness in the Bokononist lexicon of *Cat's Cradle*; the childlike drawings of *Breakfast of Champions*; the recipes of *Deadeye Dick*; the recurrent Tralfamadorians; or the general willingness to question, to invert, to debunk, all these radical traits that together characterize what we sum up as "Vonnegutian," have charmed and amused the youthful and the young at heart.

But for the Second World War, which in fact supplied the material for two of his most successful novels and contributed to others, Vonnegut's literary career may well have been even longer. He was an active journalist in high school and college, contributing regular columns to the *Shortridge Daily Echo* and the *Cornell Sun*, showing the enthusiasm and discipline that may well have pointed toward a career. After the war, while doing graduate study in anthropology at the University of Chicago, he again worked as a reporter, and his first job was as a public relations writer for the General Electric Company. Was writing in his genes? His mother is known to have attempted short-story writing in the thirties, largely with the aim of increasing the family income. Perhaps that influenced him. His grandfather and father were both architects, and Kurt himself has always shown great interest in the graphic arts. (He has been exhibited in New York; his drawings have been silkscreened onto posters and T-shirts; and his self-portraits now adorn the dust jackets of two books written about him.) These forebears read widely and loved books, played music, and pursued other arts. That artistic eclecticism shows in Kurt Vonnegut's interests as well as within the chosen medium for which he is most famous.

The love of the arts that surrounded Vonnegut from his early years might be viewed as supporting a proclivity to become a writer, but there are other influences in those early years that help to explain why, when he did become a published writer, he would be perceived as an unusual one. In the first place, those paternal ancestors who revered the arts favored training in the sciences. His older brother, Bernard, was trained as a scientist, and followed a notable career as a physicist. The expectation was that Kurt would follow in that tradition, and when he went off to Cornell it was to study biochemistry (at which he professes ineptitude). The scientific way of viewing events colors his reactions to his experiences in the war (his favorite way of accounting for the firebombing of Dresden is that it was an experiment in the creation of a firestorm), and is nourished by his employment at General Electric. In his fiction, however, his expression of the scientific perspective is more often negative reaction than positive exposition. Yet that perspective remains a constant presence in his fiction, and not simply in those works that, rightly or wrongly, have been characterized as science fiction. In the works so characterized, his vision of technologically advanced societies appears more often dystopian than utopian, and the same seems generally true for his views of such advances in the world around us. But for Vonnegut, the inclusion of scientific theory or the technology of his society is as natural as allusions to the flora and fauna of England were to Shakespeare.

While the scientific background influences the distinctive nature of the worldview in Vonnegut's fiction, there is little doubt that the early experience in journalism shapes its form, its sound and texture. Vonnegut's beginning point in narrative is to get the facts out, to be succinct, brisk, and attention holding. In his earliest works he shows a marked tendency to keep himself or a narrator or any specific location for the narrative voice out of the story. Only later do surrogates, narrators, and first-person intrusions emerge, often in intricate patterns but sometimes with a directness that appalled literary sophisticates (namely the vociferous objections of some critics to such interjections as "so it goes" or "hi ho"). Vonnegut is capable if not of "purple prose" then of lyricism or poetically introspective passages, but it is a spare, clipped, declarative prose that invites puns on "curt" that typifies particularly his early style.

Other circumstances that contribute to Vonnegut's choice of subjects and how he has presented them include his growing up during the Great Depression and his family. While, he says, his family never went hungry or shared any of the dire distress that afflicted so many in the thirties, he saw the consequences around him. That has influenced his views on economics and politics ever since. He saw the impact of unemployment on his father and of reduced social aspirations on his mother. The psychological effects wrought on them, especially of his mother's subsequent suicide, left their marks, and these, too, emerge in the fiction. At the same time, the depression produced an antidote in the great comedians of the time, and Vonnegut has long revered and sought to emulate their models. He was seven years younger than his brother, five years younger than his sister, and thus very much the baby of the family. He speaks of finding that the best way to gain attention at the table was to make the family laugh. Presumably (and clips from family film tend to support this) he often made himself funny by playing on his being the youngest, by making childishness comic. It is a technique he never left, frequently applying a kind of adolescent naivete to complex social situations or accepted commonplaces to demythologize or to debunk them.

These incurred characteristics account for much that is distinctive about Vonnegut's fiction, and consequently about his place in American letters and his acceptance by both the literary establishment and the general readership.

Paradoxically, some of those characteristics that have made him popular with the latter have generated restraint within the former. This is not simply a matter of the long-familiar issue of Vonnegut's having been classified as a science fiction writer in his early days and consequently not considered deserving of serious attention. That attitude persists in some quarters, though less and less is science fiction, or the use of science fiction elements in other genres, deprecated by academic critics. Rather it seems to be a more general sense in some quarters that Vonnegut is out of the mainstream. In part it is those uniquely "Vonnegutian" qualities that account for this. Might it not be that there is a literary establishment that tolerates, even approves of social dissent, but is intolerant of violence against perceived traditional views of what constitutes "literature"? For example, Jonathan Swift is generally viewed as the classic exponent of the satirist's art. His "Modest Proposal" is outrageous in social terms but has been revered as an exemplum of sophisticated satire for generations. His works containing four-letter words, however, have shocked even his admirers and have been pushed to the margins as "the problem of Swift's scatology." Something similar may hold true for Vonnegut. In the 1982 interview contained in this collection, for instance, Vonnegut speaks of a reviewer who called one of his works "tasteless." Even some of those who have sought to censor his books from school classrooms or libraries, have tended to focus on his use of particular epithets rather than subversive ideas.

Kurt Vonnegut, then, continues to occupy a somewhat ambiguous place in American letters. Widely read and recognized; remaining in demand as novelist, essayist, and speaker; enjoying an international reputation; taught in classes from high school to graduate school; and the subject of a growing body of literary criticism, he nevertheless still seems denied unqualified acceptance as a dominant figure at the center of the literary scene. One might well ask, indeed, whether anyone is accorded such unequivocal elevation today. Even those who seemed to have been so acknowledged in the recent past—Hemingway, Fitzgerald, or Bellow, for instance—stand somewhat rockily on their pedestals today. Vonnegut's career has spread over a period of cultural upheaval, where the prevailing social contexts in which any narrative has been viewed have undergone dramatic changes. Beginning as an iconoclast in the sedate Eisenhower years, he became a rallying voice in the turbulent Vietnam War era, to emerge once again as a voice of conscience and civic responsibility in the acquisitive eighties and nineties. More narrowly within the context of literary taste, however, he has written into periods where his own radicalism, in form and content, was surpassed, and where civil rights and women's rights and gay rights and multiculturalism have each raised social consciousness with their own discourses that have in turn impacted on the literary mainstream. In the midst of such flux, this white midwestern male has had to yield some of his hold on the avant garde, while remaining too experimental, too free thinking and too "tasteless" for the conservative establishment. In this situation he remains acknowledged and respected by many audiences, but frequently with that degree of reservation or hesitancy that distances one seen as not quite part of the group.

The remarkable thing is how often, over that long career, Vonnegut has preceded successive movement voices in calling attention to social issues. While he has not written a "feminist novel" or an "African American novel," for instance, his fiction repeatedly has been ahead of its time in addressing the social issues that have given timelessness to those discourses. At the heart of his social views is the admiration of speakers for the oppressed such as fellow Hoosier Eugene Debs or Sacco and Vanzetti. That compassion for those who are economically deprived, and therefore socially and psychologically victimized, easily extends to concern for specific groups. As early as his first novel *Player Piano* he decries the roles that women of that era were forced into, becoming perfect company wives or molded by glossy magazines into becoming, as Ed Finnerty says of Anita Proteus, something that could be replaced with stainless steel and foam rubber. *Breakfast of Champions*, the novel that is a watershed in many respects, represents perhaps his strongest condemnation of race relations in America, not just in identifying the past use of slaves with the reduction of humans to robot status, but in attacking a society which by discrimination keeps a large body of men from employment and then copes with that by housing them in ever-increasing, inhumane prisons. *Breakfast of Champions* and the nearly contemporary play *Happy Birthday, Wanda June*, return to issues of women's status very forcefully, though Vonnegut's most emphatic treatment of the subject comes later in *Bluebeard*. Topics such as ecology, postcolonialism, and the treatment of what has been called the "third world," animal welfare, or what might be grouped in a school civics course as "citizenship and public ethics" have been constant motifs throughout his career. In many instances his views were at first taken as the eccentricities of an iconoclast, only to become subsumed into mainstream thinking as the times caught up with him.

The fourteen essays in this collection seek to chronicle Vonnegut's career as it moves through changing times. They celebrate the joys of reading his fiction, as well as exploring its richness and explaining some of those less apparent complexities that give it its depth. Most are written by academics, including scholars recognized as leading authorities on Vonnegut and contemporary trends in American fiction. The writers are an international group and include contributors from Hungary, Germany, and Britain as well as the United States. Their essays are intended to combine interest and readability for a broader audience along with critical worth to more serious scholars. In general the essays either focus on the later work of Vonnegut or are retrospectives that reevaluate aspects of his literary career. Some confine themselves to commentary on an individual work, particularly in the case of the later novels about which relatively little has been written, but most are interested in the ways Vonnegut pursues a theme or a technique, the ways his mind works both in the construction of the novels and in the ideas embodied within them. Others talk more broadly about

Vonnegut's interaction with his audience, both as a writer and as a speaker, and one addresses the particular circumstances of his being a German American.

The poet W. H. Auden, mourning the death of W. B. Yeats, laments "The words of a dead man . . . modified in the guts of the living."[2] Too often a writer's words are modified by his or her critics while he or she is still alive. To give Vonnegut a chance to speak for himself in this collection, we have included three conversations with him recorded over the last decade and a half. The earliest, with Peter Reed, occurred in Vonnegut's Manhattan home in 1982. Zoltán Abádi-Nagy's longer and richly probing interview took place in 1989. The 1993 conversation with Reed and Marc Leeds occurred in convivial circumstances in the home of Ollie and Billie Lyon in Lexington, Kentucky. (Ollie Lyon had been a public relations writer with Kurt Vonnegut at the General Electric Company in Schenectady, New York, at the time that Vonnegut achieved his first publishing successes.) In their differences in tone and circumstance, and spread over the latter period of Vonnegut's career, these conversations provide some interesting insights into the author's own thoughts on his methods and accomplishments.

Finally, we have appended a bibliography that attempts to extend the listing of works by and about Kurt Vonnegut previously published. In particular, we have noted the two excellent and comprehensive bibliographies compiled by Asa Pieratt, Jerome Klinkowitz, and Julie Huffman-Klinkowitz—musts for any serious Vonnegut scholar. Where the latter of these ends, the present bibliography takes up, with the intention of giving any serious reader of Vonnegut who wishes to learn more a start on where to look.

Quite obviously, no book on a living, active author can be conclusive. Kurt Vonnegut continues to write, though he confesses that he finds writing more difficult now and that it comes more slowly. Nevertheless, the editors of this collection have worked with the constant awareness that their subject might beat them to it with the publication of another book, something that as friends and admirers they would applaud but as would-be editors of an up-to-date book they would forgo. There is an encouragingly large body of serious critical work on Vonnegut's fiction in existence now, and any new contributions can only be viewed as taking their places in that canon. They will be, to use Vonnegut's own image, like tiles in a mosaic. The assessment that this collection attempts will only finally be accomplished by that body of critical evaluation that seems to grow year by year. In recent years Vonnegut has spent more time making drawings that he has taken to autographing with a cartoon self-portrait in profile. It seems to reflect a comfortable sense of himself, touched with self-deprecating whimsy but affirming "here I am," and that seems like a good place for any artist to have reached in the later stages of a career. We hope that this collection, with its mix of perceptions and perceivers, helps to provide others with an identification of the essence of Kurt Vonnegut.

NOTES

1. Robert Frost, "Mending Wall," *American Poetry*, ed. Karl Shapiro, Thomas Y. Crowell, N.Y.: 1960) p. 115.

2. W. H. Auden, "In Memory of W. B. Yeats," *Chief Modern Poets of Britain and America,* Vol. 1; *Poets of Britain,* eds. Gerald DeWitt Sanders, John Herbert Nelson and M. L. Rosenthal, 5th edition, Macmillan, New York, 1970, p. 370.

Chronology

1848	Clemens Vonnegut, Sr. (1824–1906), the author's great-grandfather, arrives in the U.S.A.
1913	November 22. Kurt Vonnegut and Edith Lieber, the author's parents, marry in Indianapolis.
1922	November 11. Kurt Vonnegut, Jr., born Indianapolis. Siblings Bernard, born 1914 and Alice, born 1917.
1928–36	Attends Orchard School, Indianapolis.
1936–40	Shortridge High School. Works on the *Shortridge Daily Echo*, a student newspaper, as a reporter, columnist, and editor.
1940	Enters Cornell University, to major in biochemistry. Writes for the *Cornell Sun*.
1943	March. Enlists in U.S. Army as a private. Enrolls in training courses at Carnegie Institute and University of Tennessee.
1944	May 14. Mother commits suicide.
1944	December. The Battle of the Bulge. Vonnegut captured on December 22, while serving with the 106 Infantry Division as a battalion scout.
1945	February 13–14, Dresden bombed and 35,000 inhabitants killed. Vonnegut and fellow POWs take shelter in underground meatlocker, the basis for *Slaughterhouse-Five*.

1945   April. Soviet troops occupy Dresden. Vonnegut liberated and later returns to United States. Receives Purple Heart.

1945   September 1. Marries high school sweetheart Jane Marie Cox.

1945–47   December 1945. Moves to Chicago. Enters M.A. program in anthropology at the University of Chicago and works as reporter for Chicago City News Bureau. M.A. thesis rejected.

1947   Joins his brother, Bernard, at the General Electric Company Research Laboratory in Schenectady, New York, as a public relations writer. Begins writing short fiction.

1950   Vonnegut's first published fiction, the short story "Report on the Barnhouse Effect," appears in *Collier's* on February 11.

1951   Leaves GE to pursue writing professionally. Moves to Provincetown and later West Barnstable, Mass.

1952   Vonnegut's first novel, *Player Piano*, published by Charles Scribner's Sons.

1954   *Player Piano* published in paperback by Bantam as *Utopia 14*. Engages in various work to supplement his income, including teaching at Hopefield School, freelance advertising copy writing, and opening a Saab automobile dealership.

1957   October 1. Father dies.

1958   Sister Alice dies of cancer the day after her husband, John Adams, is killed in a train crash. Kurt and Jane adopt three of Alice's four children (Tiger, Jim, and Steven Adams), adding to their own three children: Mark, Edith, and Nanette.

1959   *The Sirens of Titan* published by Dell.

1961   Collection of short stories, *Canary in a Cat House*, published by Fawcett.

1961   *Mother Night* published by Fawcett (actually appeared in 1962).

1963   *Cat's Cradle* published by Holt, Rinehart & Winston.

1965   *God Bless You, Mr. Rosewater* published by Holt, Rinehart & Winston. Begins two-year appointment at the Writers Workshop, University of Iowa.

1967–68   Guggenheim Fellowship. Visits Dresden to research *Slaughterhouse-Five*.

1968   *Welcome to the Monkey House* (short stories) published by Delacorte/Seymour Lawrence.

1969   *Slaughterhouse-Five* published by Delacorte/Seymour Lawrence.

1970   January. Visits Biafra shortly before its collapse in war with Nigeria. Literature Award from National Institute of Arts and Letters. Teaches creative writing at Harvard University.

1971   October 7. *Happy Birthday, Wanda June* (play) opens in New York, and runs until March 14, 1971. Published by Delacorte/Seymour Lawrence in 1971.

1971   Anthropology department, University of Chicago, accepts *Cat's Cradle* as an M.A. thesis and awards degree. Moves to New York. Separates from wife Jane.

1972   March 13. *Between Time and Timbuktu*, ninety-minute television play based on characters and situations from Vonnegut's fiction. Published the same year by Delacorte/Seymour Lawrence with introduction by Vonnegut, though in a letter to Marc Leeds (November 15, 1989), Vonnegut clearly denies authorship. "It is what it is, and doesn't belong in the canon of my work anywhere since the idea of doing such a thing *did not in the least originate with me. (Vonnegut's emphasis.)* I was so lacking in passion about what people were doing with my ideas within the demands of their own art form that I didn't even protect the title of a short story of mine, 'Between *Timid* and Timbuktu.' In small dictionaries, the word between Timid and Timbuktu is Time."

1973   *Breakfast of Champions* published by Delacorte/Seymour Lawrence.

1973   Awarded honorary L.H.D. by Indiana University. Appointment as Distinguished Professor of English Prose, City University of New York, replacing Anthony Burgess.

1974   *Wampeters, Foma & Granfalloons* (essays, interviews, etc.) published by Delacorte/Seymour Lawrence.

1975   Elected Vice President of the National Institute of Arts and Letters.

1975   *The Eden Express*, by son, Mark, published by Praeger Publishers. Recounts Mark's breakdown in 1972.

1976   *Slapstick, or Lonesome No More!* published by Delacorte/Seymour Lawrence.

1979   October 11. Musical adaptation of *God Bless You, Mr. Rosewater*, produced by his daughter Edith, opens at Entermedia Theatre, New York.

1979   November 24. Marries Jill Krementz, photographer and author.

1979   *Jailbird* published by Delacorte/Seymour Lawrence.

1980   *Sun Moon Star*, (Christmas story about the Creator of the Universe coming to earth as a baby), by Vonnegut and Ivan Chermayeff, illustrator, published by Harper & Row.

1980   October. One-man exhibition of his drawings at Margo Fine Galleries, New York.

1981   *Palm Sunday: An Autobiographical Collage* (essays, letters, etc.) published by Delacorte/Seymour Lawrence.

1982   *Deadeye Dick* published by Delacorte/Seymour Lawrence. *Nothing Is Lost Save Honor* (two essays, "The Worst Addiction of Them All," and "Fates Worse Than Death"), published in hardback by Nouveau Press for the Mississippi Civil Liberties Union, Jackson, Mississippi.

1982   December 15. Adopted daughter Lily Vonnegut born.

1985   *Galápagos* published by Delacorte/Seymour Lawrence.

1987   *Bluebeard* published by Delacorte.

1990   *Hocus Pocus* published by Putnam.

1991   *Fates Worse Than Death: An Autobiographical Collage of the 1980s* (essays, reviews, etc.) published by Putnam.

Part I

INTERVIEWS WITH VONNEGUT

A Conversation with Kurt Vonnegut, 1982

Peter J. Reed

For the following informal interview, Peter Reed met with Kurt Vonnegut in his Manhattan home. It took place in the autumn of 1982, a time when Vonnegut had been treated roughly by some reviewers who had not been favorably impressed by the group of novels from Breakfast of Champions *to the then newly released* Deadeye Dick.

R: I've spoken about the artificiality in breaking up your work into segments or periods, but I wanted to ask about the shape of the fiction overall. . . . It is common to see the works, the novels, as breaking up into six and four, or for people to talk about the works up through *Slaughterhouse-Five* and what's come since. Do you have any fear of that yourself?

V: No, that's legitimate. All that annoys me about arbitrariness is that history is divided up into decades, you know, so I am a sixties person. Just what the hell was I doing in the seventies and eighties? You know, people feel that. So time is cut up into sausages—decades now. You're asked, "What do you expect the eighties to be like as compared with the seventies?" But in terms of my personal life, you're absolutely right: I had a sense of completion, of the mission accomplished with *Slaughterhouse-Five*, and after that I had to start a new business, a major new business, that was all. That was closed out, and that was satisfying to me, and that was more than I ever expected to do with my life. That was more writing than I ever expected to get published. And so I was quite contented.

R: Did you really have a feeling from the start of working toward saying something about Dresden or getting that thing written *down* or written *out?*

V: Well, I had a certain sense of architecture of what my career might be and a suitable ending for it was *Slaughterhouse-Five*. You know, it's like the last two lines in a Shakespearean sonnet. They are not necessarily a culminating idea, they're a very appropriate ending to something. As far as the endings of any linear work of art, a piece of music or an opera or play or novel, they in fact are over with two-thirds of the way through. I've said this before. The remaining third is saying, "Sorry, you can go home now. 'Good-bye' is really about all we can do for you, and it *is* late."

R: You're almost talking about this in the same terms that you talk about life, or some people's lives, in *Deadeye Dick*, where somebody's life is virtually over and this is the story of a posthumous kind of life.

V: Yeah, well, it's absurd, this idea that your life is a story, except that careers are structured that way. In business, if you stay with General Electric, then your life is going to be a story and it will be over when you're sixty-five. You'll start by making a little money and then if you work hard you make more and more and more, and it just grows, and life is a story—and then it does make sense as a story. A business is able to structure life that way, but a writer isn't able to do that. I think that *Slaughterhouse-Five* would've made a very appropriate end for—how many books did you say, six?—because they're all about abuses of technology. And what about the ultimate abuse short of Hiroshima?

R: Certainly, at the end of each novel is some sort of an apocalypse or destruction—ice-nine or a bombing of Indianapolis or something like that—that makes it look as if the Dresden thing is inevitably coming all the way through the first six.

V: What you're doing is, you have to let your subconscious do a lot of the work or you simply won't fill the pages and . . . well, you can see it if you try to write a sonnet again.   Suddenly as you're just juggling the rhyme scheme or the metric scheme and all that, an idea will appear and become more and more insistent until the last two lines are inevitable. You know that only one couplet would do. So a body of work starts implying things about itself, and that can seem to a writer like a sort of tin-horn triumph, you know: "This is really gonna wow 'em, this last couplet—or this curtain line."

R: That's interesting because that implies that you're very much aware of form in your individual novels not just in each group. But if, when you're writing a novel, you work anything like the way you're talking about writing a sonnet, that implies a very strong sense of the *form* of the novel, not necessarily as the starting point, but as a sort of guiding principle, rather than the message or something you want to say *in* the novel. Does it?

V: Yes, but you load the thing. For instance, I might say almost everything I personally want to say on the first page, and meanwhile we have to produce a book. And as far as delivering messages, I almost insert a telegram anywhere I like, and meanwhile there's this bribery to the readers to keep going which is a plot and jokes and all that. Yet, a perfect structure that builds to a great curtain line is *A Doll's House*. That play has gone on five minutes and you know what's wrong with that marriage. There was a hell of lot of marriages and mistreating women that way. Samuel Beckett might have got rid of it in three minutes, and the rest is running sort of a high-level cabaret because the people have come out of their houses, you know, and gone to a lot of trouble to get to this thing. But he said it almost instantly, and this is true of *Babbitt*. In five pages, the first five pages—it's been awhile since I've looked at *Babbitt* but I'm almost sure this is the case—there's the innocent barbarism of badly educated Americans in the Middle West. This portrait had never been drawn before, of what Americans really look like and what they sound like. And Lewis has done that in the opening pages of *Babbitt* and the rest is that then he had to become an entertainer. So this sort of thing goes on and on and on, but I think people are mistaken about moralizing novels that build and build and build and finally the point is inevitable. I think the point is very often made five pages in, and surely by two-thirds of the way through. There must be a point in *A Doll's House* where Nora has said everything she says, before she finally goes. I'm sure she's said it somewhere before in another way, but an awful lot is sopping up people's time and giving them their money's worth, and you indeed do that, because you make good use of that time if you're a good writer, and you do give them good value, but as far as any moral instruction or any special new idea you wish to introduce to the reader, you've done it almost instantly.

R: In your interview with Robert Short that came out right about the time of *Breakfast of Champions*, you said that people might be more and more dissatisfied with your writing from this point on. You were saying how difficult it was to get going again after *Slaughterhouse-Five,* and that readers might be more dissatisfied because there would be less narrative and more didacticism or editorializing. Do you think that's been true?

V: I don't know. I suspected that that would happen. A guy had interviewed me for Pacifica Radio WBAI and I was just telling him in the interview I in fact could be didactic, and if I wanted to do it, I would. And his advice was, "Don't be, that would spoil it all." So my response is screw it, you know, I'll be as courageous as the armory painters or radicals in painting and in music. It's my life and I operate in an Adam Smith market, and if people don't like what I write there's no money comes in. So it's utterly fair, it seems to me, to take my chances on that open market with whatever I choose to do next. The first six books were careful pieces of work. Now it's pretty much coloring within the lines, and having done that much I wanted to fart around, and Philip Guston, the painter, you know, started painting in an entirely different way, and so I decided to do that. It seems to me I'm wildly experimental.

R: I think so.

V: And the critics who hate me never acknowledge this at all.

R: That's right.

V: That is, if there's some experiment that's going on, or if they see a radical way to do things, they act as though I have made some boneheaded mistake.

R: It seems to me, if we are talking about the same thing, that they cannot even talk about it as an experiment that failed, they don't even talk about it as experimental. That is extraordinary to me.

V: What really does it for them is that my books really don't look a hell of a lot like other people's books.

R: No, that's right. Now that's one thing that I wanted to ask you about. *Breakfast of Champions* got probably the least favorable reviews when it came out and yet I find myself looking back at that and being more and more interested by that book, and every once in awhile I exchange a letter with Jerry Klinkowitz and it seems the same thing is happening to him. It's not any particular conscious choice or sitting down and saying, "Gee, that book interests me," it's just that in continuing to poke around I keep coming back to that one. Do you have any special feeling about that or any changed feeling about that book from about the time that it came out?

V: Well, I've tended to respond to critics. I am not able to achieve the proper frame of mind to dismiss them as idiots, because they're educated and I know they are thinking about something and they have learned things in college, and all that, so I'm interested in them and I don't want to offend them to the extent I have. I just don't want them that mad at me, and I have to suspect that maybe they're right. The whole idea of the armory show excites me very much . . . a marvelous historical event and I was encouraged by that, and it's good. I tend to do things that look like books, you know, they're still in the same old frames and all that, and they're rectangles and all, but they don't look like the books people have seen before. Turns out this isn't a very heavy financial sacrifice or anything else, except it really pisses off the critics, some of them. I'd say it pisses off half of them, I guess. I am mystified why people get so goddamn mad at me, but people got terribly mad at Duchamp, you know, for *Nude Descending a Staircase;* they just couldn't stop talking about it. But it's an explosion in a shingle factory, and I think the training of critics has given them old standards which they're not able to abandon. They're not able to look at a book that doesn't look like other reputable books.

R: Deadeye Dick has picked up a couple of bad reviews and most of the others have been good. There seems to be great division. It seemed to me the number that don't like it is smaller.

V: I protest too much, but *Time* was dismissing me in about three paragraphs.

R: Oh yes, that was a rotten review.

V: I called up *Time*, but it was an unsigned review and I can't just say," Tell me who this man is and where he went to school and how old he is," you know, "because I'm curious." What I said about *Love Story* and those ferocious attacks on Erich Segal, you know, is it's like attacking a banana split or something. They get so goddamn mad, and the only reason they get so goddamn mad, I think, is the amounts of money that come my way. I think it seems to them an unjust society that someone who does what I do could get rewarded.

R: Well, given the point you were making about the critics having a traditional frame of reference with which to look at these things, one of the things that I think is the most interesting about *Deadeye Dick* is that on the surface it looks more conventional than the three before it. It seems to me, though, that this is one of the most experimental that you've done, but I think on the *surface* it looks more conventional.

V: What, putting recipes through the whole goddamn thing? People treat this as the most obvious, dumb idea that anybody could have, you know, "Oh, how tiresome," and all that, and I think it really worked. I think a swell way to celebrate life, really, no matter how bad it gets, is to think about food, and that was my intention. I got a lot of goddamn credit for that.

R: Did anything trigger that idea, particularly, inspire that?

V: Well, I tried it once.

R: The recipes?

V: Yes, I mean, he [Rudy Waltz of *Deadeye Dick*] was a cook and all that and so I wanted him to forget his troubles and start talking about how to make sauerkraut and I tried it several ways. Of course he spent years farting around trying this and that and sticking it in and taking it out—it seemed to work very well.

R: The device itself reminds me a bit of the calypsos in *Cat's Cradle*. The other thing that was interesting was the way you seem very interested in how language itself, just the very fact of putting the record of something that happens into a sentence, almost necessarily changes that event; if not the language and syntax, just the very words themselves can do that. It's like the Haitian, the Creole, use of only the present tense that you show in *Deadeye Dick*. There's a great fascination in both of those books [*Deadeye Dick* and *Cat's Cradle*] with how words themselves change the thing, as if the thing itself has no separate existence.

V: It was true of Creole, close enough, that they speak almost entirely in the present. They have other tenses but they don't use them. I got this when we were down in Haiti. "What does your father do?" "My father is dead." "I like him" (laughter). But there's some people who won't laugh at that, who won't even enjoy it, and my goodness . . .

R: Well, you seem very interested in emphasizing the fact that fiction *is* fiction, and at one point in *Deadeye Dick* you say, roughly, "This isn't history, it's fiction, and anybody who reads it as history is going to get into trouble." It seems to me that one of the aspects of your experimentalism is that emphasis on the fictiveness of fiction itself.

V: One thing that I've just instinctively worked on, and one thing I've instinctively avoided as comforting the reader about his class or his education or whatever, is using jokes that only those that have been to Harvard would truly appreciate. Even the *New Yorker* has stopped doing it now. But it used to be that in a short story somebody would walk into the house of a stranger, and this poor son-of-a-bitch of a stranger had money but, you know, oh my God, he had Swedish modern furniture, he had a print of van Gogh's sunflowers on the wall, and this person was characterized by his possessions. He had done all these klutzy things. And then the host is going to be cordial and all that, and brings out this very expensive bottle of wine, which is totally inappropriate as an afternoon drink. All these mistakes are made, and the storyteller knows who his audience is and wants them to come right along with him and judge the taste of this man. Edith Oliver reviewed *Happy Birthday, Wanda June,* for the *New Yorker* and she said it was tasteless. I didn't know her, and I was finally introduced to her a couple of years ago and I said, "You know, you just really startled me when you called a play of mine tasteless." And she said, "Oh dear, did I? I hope not."

R: Did she ever go on to explain what she meant by that?

V: I know exactly what she meant. It's that the *New Yorker* reader and the *New Yorker* staffer happened to have certain standards of interior decoration and food, and I'd gone outside those limits. So that was her tip to the readership of the *New Yorker:* "This is in fact in bad taste and we don't often say that."

R: It's funny the way that happens. It's like what I've read of a couple of instances where people have been banning the books or trying get them taken out of the schools. The surprise is always less that somebody is trying to do that than *why* they are trying to do it and the grounds they choose. Of all the things you could talk about, that you think they might be worried about, it's always something silly that seems a violation of average American decorum.

V: You're often advised by local lawyers now, too, because there's been a hell of a lot of litigation, and the book banners know now that they can expect to be hailed into court, maybe, and the lawyers will help them to say the right thing. And the first time a reporter asks them, "Why in the world did you do this?" they will mention community standards. You know, "This might be suitable for some communities, but not for ours."

R: One thing I've used a number of times in classes is that self-interview film you made for Films for the Humanities, you remember, I think that must have been made in about, what?

V: Eight years ago, I would think.

R: I think that's a nice interview and it's always good in classrooms, and one of the things that's interesting in teaching books is to let the students—and this seems particularly true with you—see the man and hear the voice.
(Interruption)
R: Well, I was going to ask you about one thing I think was particularly interesting. We were talking about *Breakfast of Champions* and that whole business of setting *Deadeye Dick* back in the world of *Breakfast of Champions*. I think that's a fascinating idea. What led to that? What in particular did you have in mind in doing it, and what led you to do it?

V: One critic for *Philadelphia Magazine* wrote a very angry piece. His name was David Slaven and he said this book was more revenge against Indianapolis, which I would never forgive. Anyway, he said that this was about Indianapolis, and he's never seen Indianapolis, and I wasn't kidding when I said it was about Kokomo or Troy, New York, or a town of that size which can't really support a cultural center. Hell, Indianapolis had an important symphony orchestra when I was born there. And I knew two sculptors and many, many painters who were all making their living there, and it had a rich cultural life and a university and all of that. Slaven was so wrong that Indianapolis is like what I described, but Kokomo really is. And other than that there were a whole lot of things going on in what I showed happening to Midland City, like the indifference of our government to the closing down of these towns. Like Terra Haute: The last business just closed down there—Columbia Records closed down its plant there permanently. You know this place has got twenty-seven churches, it's got a railroad yard, it's got all this, and it might has well have been neutron bombed, and so there was that analogy in mind. And then there's the indifference of our thinkers to our taking casualties, you know, talking about "manageable casualties." Fifty million people, I believe, is an acceptable figure now. And so obviously there is this indifference, and I swear I'm right that if a neutron bomb did go off accidentally in Terra Haute, it would be on the news for about three days because the feeling is that these people weren't really of any importance.
Anyway, there are all these things that bothered me. I spoke about it in Terra Haute, about a society of people who matter and who don't matter, and Americans have taken this to heart. That is, we have superstars who very much matter and then everybody else is completely expendable. I think a very sad thing is going to happen this winter. I think all these people, families, who've been living in cars for several months now, I think they're going to kill themselves in great numbers. And it's very American to blame yourself, to think it's your own damn fault. I saw that growing up during the Great Depression, everybody blaming themselves even though something, almost geological, some enormous catastrophe had wiped out the factories, brought all the business to a halt. Might as well have been the new ice age and yet everybody on the edge of this huge sheet of ice, creeping down from Canada, blamed himself . . . it was his own damn fault.

R: I'm surprised at the lack of anger against the government or against the White House for the way things are going. It's almost as if people feel that it's just some economic disease which has afflicted the world and there's nothing people can do.

V: Yes, but look at me; I'm doing all right, I really am. What the hell's the matter with all these people out in Marion, Ohio?

R: Yes, well, that's another thing I was going to ask you about, in terms of finding things to motivate your writing and to keep you writing or that you want to write about. In one of the interviews you talked about needing something from outside to get you going again and at that particular time you didn't feel there was much happening that was prompting you to write. It seems to me that in the last couple of books, with references to Sacco and Vanzetti and the Sermon on the Mount and current economic concerns, that you're finding more and more in terms of the economic or socioeconomic or however you want to describe that.

V: Actually I can remember when our culture was so small, you know, that an educated person had to know only about fourteen art objects in order to conduct a conversation about culture with somebody else. It'd be the "Mona Lisa," Beethoven's "Fifth," *Hamlet,* probably *Moby Dick*, and so forth, and we had this very small cultural package that all of us carried having gotten through high school in this country, and it enabled us to talk about culture to anyone. Of course, this has been vaporized now; nobody has issued this little package or agreed to limit the conversations to that. So I've been trying to crystallize a few things. Like, let's all be able to talk about the Sermon on the Mount (I mean if I were cultural dictator), let's have that part of the package because it's so influential as a typical outrage in America, the sort of miscarriage of justice that's possible, because of ruling class conspiracy and xenophobia and so forth, let's keep the Sacco and Vanzetti thing alive. I thought it was reason enough to write a book, political reason enough to write the book, just to talk about Sacco and Vanzetti again.

R: Do you have a feeling that there is no shared culture or that there's very little left of a shared culture, there are lots of single issue groups or splinter groups or PACs of one kind or another, but they're not like ribs off a spine, they're all somehow floating.

V: Well, they're class related too, I think. I've seen a little of this very thin veneer of international culture we have on the East Side related to the United Nations, because there are diplomats and there are rich Americans who entertain diplomats. There are also Iranians, you know, and they're all "cultivated." I mean, there's the Ambassador to the United Nations from Upper Volta. I haven't met him, but I'm sure he's capable of discussing Picasso, Mozart, perhaps not a romantic composer—Vivaldi—and there are all these clues as to what level of society you belong to, the international society you belong to. There are those works of art that are admired today—what is interesting is Borges is part of that. Borges! (laughs). So's Samuel Beckett. It's like clothes—there are subtle ways that people dress that those who know will be able identify the school a person went to.

R: So we've got some separate streams of culture within . . .

V: People have done that whimsically anyway. Who was it?—some sociologist divided society into the upper-upper class, the middle-upper class, the lower-upper class, and then there were nonclasses, and he also described what would be hanging on their walls. And he was right, he was dead right, and it was possible to do this fifteen to twenty years ago.

R: It's not very popular to talk about class in American society. I mean, it's a cliché to talk about class in English society because it's so old and so visible. But in *God Bless You, Mr. Rosewater,* you really talk about American society as a class society and not just as haves and have nots. There are multiple stratifications, and I don't think many American writers have shown that.

V: Well, there was Sinclair Lewis, the first American to win a Nobel Prize in literature, and he seemed to his colleagues such a barbarous writer. He was not a member of the National Institute of Arts and Letters, which is what we have for an academy, and after he got the prize they begged him please to join. But he was dealing with the sociology of our society and he does it beautifully. I don't know when *Babbitt* was published—1920, you think? Anyway, Babbitt has some friends over who are poorer than he is, and they're patronized, and after they leave, the Babbitts discuss how these people betrayed their lower-class origins in various ways, certain mistakes they've made throughout the meal or the dumb things they've said. Then the Babbitts are invited over to dinner with an old family in town and they make all these mistakes and become very clumsy and all that. So this *is* a class society, but you can be wonderfully mobile in it.

R: Yes.

V: I mean, you can go literally right up to the top, as Delorean did. He was a street kid, and he simply got all the apparatus identifying him as belonging to the topmost of our class.

R: It's not a mobility that is as universally available as myth would have it, though, is it?

V: Well, swindlers certainly understand it almost immediately. "You know the first thing I do when I get out of prison? I'm going to go over to Brooks Brothers and buy a suit."

R: Well, let's see. One thing I was going to ask you about is the sort of thing that you did in *Jailbird,* where in the index you've got that mix of historical facts and verifiable events with stuff from Kilgore Trout's fantasy stories. Fact and fiction are mixed up together and they're in there with the same right and they're part of the same world. Is that part of an attempt to explode American history, American culture, American society, and put it back together again in a new combination where it can be reseen, as it were?

V: Yes. The joy of discrediting the printed word is that anything can be taken as absolutely fact. But it was almost like concrete poetry or *poesie concrete,* or whatever it is. You know, you cut things up at random and glue them together. And I got the idea because I cited the Society of Indexers [in *Cat's Cradle*], whose headquarters is in England, and they wrote me and asked if I would speak to them, saying I was the only person who had ever made an indexer a character in a book.

R: Like *Cat's Cradle.*

V: In *Cat's Cradle,* and this had not escaped them, and would I please come over and talk to them. I had this beautiful, whimsical British correspondence on this—very nice manners and slightly submerged and flimsy through the whole thing and very elegant, and I couldn't do it? But then they gave me a subscription to the *Index,* and this index was from all over the world. And then I decided, well, this is a profession, and these people are proud of what they're doing and they do have contempt for people who do it badly, those amateur jobs of no service to the reader at all. So I asked Dell if they would please hire an indexer and find out how much it cost to have this book indexed, just find one of these people that does this. So they did, and then the juxtapositions became quite marvelous, so you know they are a very easy way to make a comic work of art. So all I did was say "Do it," and that's what came out.

R: I couldn't remember ever seeing it before but I wasn't certain that it had never happened, but yes, that was wonderful. Another minor thing I was going to ask you is that in a couple of the novels now you've had scenes, like in *Slapstick* and *Deadeye Dick,* with lots and lots of candles, lots of candlelight. I was very intrigued by that. Is this part of making the book sort of a birthday present to yourself?

V: I don't know . . . candlelight is so beautiful if you turn out all the lights anywhere and light candles, it's . . . well grown-ups can't see it, but children can believe it. It's as if the house is full of fairies or something.

R: Well, I thought that was a lovely lyrical passage in *Deadeye Dick* where you describe the candlelit house and the fancy uniform and all that. It's like a scene right out of *The Nutcracker Suite* or something like that maybe, right?

V: Well, I think I was a little disappointed. I got a book on uniforms, and the most elaborate uniform in recent military history, people agree, was the Hungarian lifeguard, which has a rather colorless name associated with it—I wish they could have thought up something better than that. But the uniform is really something.

R: Have you started another book?

V: Yes, I've started *Galápagos*, and then what I was just reading was what Melville said about his visit to the Galápagos Islands. I've read almost all of what Darwin has written and it's interesting to me that this is the only theory of evolution and the only thing that modern man has to cling to, I think, as an idea that has been generated by science and that modern man can understand and build his life around and all that. It has been a substitute for the Bible for a lot of people who have been willing to find it reasonable to put their faith in a theory of evolution and call it God. Everybody has to put his faith somewhere, and it turns out this is the major receptacle in our civilization for faith. So the Galápagos Islands is one place where Darwin just really could not believe that God has done all this—you know, why would he make thirteen sorts of finch for one environment or three separate species of land tortoise for islands just a few miles from each other? That is, God had just really created more forms of life than makes sense out there. But anyway, what's interesting now is that the scientists are beginning to question it more and more and more, because the fossil record does not bear out evolution as described by Darwin. At the same time, they're not about to go public with this because they'd give aid and comfort to all these religious fundamentalists who want to go all the way back to the book of Genesis. And this is a comical situation where the scientists are having to keep their voices down as they discuss what really did happen. Apparently there would be *sudden* changes—that's what the fossil record does show. But the scientists themselves were as pigheaded as the fundamentalists in a way, in that they would not let go of Darwin and kept insisting, and do continue to insist, that if we dig enough and keep digging in deeper and deeper and deeper, sooner or later we'll find all these gradual transitions when in fact they don't seem to exist. Anyway, I'm playing with that, and then it's rather like a ship of fools where there is this religious fundamentalist who says he's going into the lion's den and he's going to go look at what Darwin saw and he's going to see if it shakes his faith in the Biblical story of creation, and there are other people along. Jill and I, we were in the Galápagos Islands two weeks, three weeks. . . .

R: I heard an interview on the radio the other day—two guys who've made a film about the Galápagos, and they were talking about the problem with some of the animals that have been brought in more recently.

V: Rats, goats, cats, dogs, and mice.

R: He said something that astounded me about one of the small islands that had very little fauna but most interesting flora. They took two female and one male goat there in 1963 and within fifteen years they had 60,000 goats on that island. It used to take nine hours to hack your way to the top and now you can walk up there in forty-five minutes. And the park ranger has shot 40,000 goats in the last fifteen years.

V: Yes. Well, of course the reason Mexico looks so terrible is because of goats. Poor people really like goats because they require no care, but they destroy the ecology. I heard a scientist talk about looking for the original tobacco plant that the Indians found and domesticated. The Indians upgraded tobacco plants considerably before white men got here, but they went looking for the original tobacco plant in Central America somewhere, and goats had eaten up the whole area where they thought tobacco had originated. And they finally found it growing on a cliff so steep that goats could not get up there, but they did find it. They're terrible animals. I went into Baja in lower California on a mule trip and they had destroyed that whole peninsula there. Everybody has goats and they turn them loose every morning.

Serenity, Courage, Wisdom: A Talk with Kurt Vonnegut, 1989

Zoltán Abádi-Nagy

The man who opened the door of his Manhattan house for me on that hot summer day of August 8, 1989, was tall, slightly bent, slim and brisk—the full physical reality of the hitherto detached, bodiless face of the photographs I had seen. He was wearing a short-sleeved blue shirt, unbuttoned at the top; grey slacks; and casual shoes. Our meeting also added color to the face previously known in black and white: suntan; grizzly moustache and eyebrows; brown, curly hair.

He is a chain smoker. Not infrequently, throaty, hoarse bursts of laughter exploded behind the smoke screen, and his eyes glanced at me angrily and piercingly as he warmed to a subject. He kept pushing his reading glasses to the top of his head in agitation.

The follies and contradictions of the world animated him with passion, and wherever he sensed nonsense, he charged upon it with smoldering wit and stinging, sarcastic ridicule. His "what if" thought experiments exercised a galvanizing effect on him.

Otherwise his manner was quiet, cordial, modest, and unceremonial.

A: I feel that the prayer on Billy Pilgrim's office wall in *Slaughterhouse-Five* is central to your philosophy of life: "God grant me the serenity to accept the things I cannot change, courage to change the things I can, and wisdom always to tell the difference."

V: In the Soviet Union they imagine that I've made up that prayer. It's the prayer of Alcoholics Anonymous in this country. It was apparently part of a sermon on Cape Cod, and it struck somebody so right that he started passing it around. Alcoholics Anonymous picked it up but it certainly makes sense no matter whether you're an alcoholic or not.

A: It seems you made it your own philosophy of life.

V: I would think so. It's recognizing limitations. One of the troubles with the post-World War II era is people throwing off all restraints to grab as much as they can—sexually, in terms of property, or whatever—as though we all owed it to ourselves because we had conquered this great monster Hitler. There is absolutely no restraint about consumption, about many other things. Billy's prayer recommends restraint, accepting restraint with good humor.

A: Not all of your characters are synthesists like Billy is. In many cases, one or the other aspect of that prayer seems to be predominant. The "serenity to accept things I cannot change" called Beatrice Rumford, the Tralfamadorians, Bokonon, Kilgore Trout and Dwayne Hoover and Rudy Waltz to mind.

V: Yes. This is what they must do in order to survive because they cannot overcome whatever they get.

A: In other cases the main aspiration is "to change the things I can." This is the courage of Dr. Paul Proteus, Winston Rumford and Malachi Constant, Eliot Rosewater, Wilbur Swain, Walter Starbuck and Mary Kathleen O'Looney, Mary Hepburn, Circe Berman and Rabo Karabekian.

V: They had a pretty good idea of what they can change and what they can't change.

A: Some others do get confused, though, as for the "wisdom always to tell the difference." Howard Campbell of *Mother Night* got confused somehow about the difference—played a dangerous game with it anyway.

V: When I started that book, I talked to several people who had been in intelligence during the Second World War, who had been spy masters in fact, and recruited secret agents. They all told me that any successful spy must be two things: one, he must be a double agent—he must work for both sides or he's doomed—and, two, he is schizophrenic. He is not well. Only a sick person could do it.

A: It is Billy Pilgrim whose philosophy seems to boil down to the dialectics of freedom and restraint: for man to achieve meaningful freedom, a recognition of limitations is imperative.

V: What I'm working on now is a book about a Vietnam vet. It's in the year 2000. He's resigned his commission in disgust after the war. He is sick of humanity's delusions of grandeur, the idea that we have a very important mission here on earth, that we are here to do something terribly important, and if we don't do something terribly important—driving Communism out of South Korea or whatever—we will have failed. This is a disastrous way of thinking. We have a mission now to carry our great intelligence into outer space, which is a preposterous idea. Sending all this meat? We are bankrupting ourselves just sending it to the moon. We're not going anywhere. We're much too large to travel anywhere.

A: Will the new book bring old characters back?

V: I don't think so. It will bring Kilgore Trout back in because this is the subject of a short story he's written, which somebody comes across in a magazine. What's obvious to him is that germs are going to make the trip if anybody's going to make it. If life is going to spread out to all the dead stones in the universe, it's not going to be Earth, it's not going to be William Buckley, it's not the president of the MIT, one of these huge animals. It's going to be germs.

A: "Germs" probably in more sense than one?

V: Well, it would be in order to be tiny enough and durable enough to make the trip.

A: So in the very physical and biological sense. I thought it was again the moralist, the satirist speaking here.

V: Oh, no. I'm talking about very practical matters. It is not believed that humanity's destiny is to go populate other planets. This is crazy!

A: Are there any scientific theories that support your germ theory, or is it your personal view?

V: We don't need any theories. It's just obvious to me that only germs can make the trip. We're going to get hit from time to time by meteors, which cause a big splash on the Earth's surface, and maybe some of that stuff will get sufficient velocity to keep going into outer space, or maybe we'll be struck a glancing blow by a meteor and it'll pick up some gum. That's the only way life is going to get spread out to the rest of the universe. And yet the science fiction writers foresee the time, as Arthur Clarke does in the book called *2001*, when we're almost there.

A: On the other hand, there is the theory that the sun will expand again and devour the Solar System . . .

V: I suppose it will.

A: . . . and . . . mankind should try to escape in time in some direction.

V: Why "mankind"? Are we such glorious creations? That's what I'm complaining about. Oh, we are such beautiful animals, with magnificent brains. It comes down to how important we are, and how unimportant everything else is. It's just like elephants being proud of weighing as much as they do. Yes, we've huge brains, and so what? This is certainly a glory of creation: it created Auschwitz, created the Roman games, created crucifixion as a punishment. We should send this out to the world and into the rest of the universe? It's ridiculous to think that we are the peak of evolution, that evolution has tried to produce such terrible farts as we are. Ronald Reagan? This is to be exported? It's so glorious and so beloved by God that we must send these creatures, no matter what they weigh, we must find transportation to send them to Mars?

A: Let us use the transportation of our brains to send us back to the galaxy of worlds you create in your fiction. It seems to me that up to *Slaughterhouse-Five* either/or worlds struggle to obliterate or replace or manipulate each other: technological progress versus moral control in *Player Piano*; human purpose versus galactic indifference in *The Sirens of Titan*; ideologies and spies against each other in *Mother Night*; sense versus nonsense in *Cat's Cradle*; wealth versus samaritrophia in *God Bless You, Mr. Rosewater*. Attitudes of acceptance and rebellion are externalized in different characters. But beginning with *Slaughterhouse-Five* the dichotomy of acceptance versus change is moved inside, as it were, and becomes an internalized dilemma for one single character: for Pilgrim in *Slaughterhouse-Five*, Trout and Hoover in *Breakfast of Champions*, Swain in *Slapstick*, Starbuck in *Jailbird*, Waltz in *Deadeye Dick*, Hepburn in *Galápagos*, and Karabekian in *Bluebeard*. Was it a conscious change on your part?

V: What I do is tell stories. If you have to be rational, you can't do it. It would take your whole lifetime just to write a paragraph. In order to go faster than that, to complete a novel in three years, say, which is how long it takes me to write one, you can't be rational. So it's all instinct; it has to be instinct. It's like skiing: if you have to think, don't do it. It is a function of the critic to perceive things in the work. I'm not an architect. You can't work like an architect where you make a blueprint and then build it.

A: You never contemplate a work once it's done?

V: You have to. I might be a Catholic. I would have a certain outlook. Or I might be a loser, or a Jew, or whatever, and I would have this religious heritage. I do have a religious heritage.

A: What is that heritage?

V: It's freethinking. I am what used to be called a freethinker. It was originated largely in Germany and was brought over here by German immigrants including my ancestors, who were self-educated people, well read, and also very good businessmen. They were Catholics. They got over here before the Civil War, my first ancestors, before there was a Statue of Liberty. They came over here as Catholics, and they read Darwin, who was published over here in about 1870. He said the Bible can't be true. So they left the church. As for resignation, obviously there can't be an afterlife, or it seems highly improbable—so okay, we'll accept that, that's all right, this is enough, it's something anyway; the idea of being rewarded or punished in the afterlife is absurd. So this is just as powerful a message to me as the Trinity would be to a Christian, or the story of Abraham to a Jew. This is my religious heritage, and I believe in it as strongly as a member of any religious group does because that's how I was raised. And the resignation? If this life is enough, okay, I don't want an afterlife. I can easily do without it. God doesn't need anything. By definition he must have absolutely everything he could need. So the highest service is to the community.

A: Would this resignation, this heritage and intellectual attitude have anything to do with life viewed as a puppet show?

V: For life to be a puppet show there must be a puppeteer. I don't think there is one. I think we're puppeteers with each other.

A: Once you referred to your first six novels as puppet shows.

V: They are because I'm working on them. But I don't think that life is a puppet show.

A: In *Breakfast of Champions*, you talk about the chemical mechanism of the human body making us puppets in one sense.

V: Oh, it does, without doubt. But I think it's random how that operates.

A: It's the social side of it that is important.

V: That we can control. We try.

A: That's again Billy Pilgrim's prayer, the central idea. And that's *Slaughterhouse-Five*. But the next book, *Breakfast of Champions*, seems to express the idea of man as a machine more fully than any other work of yours before, although one expected you to opt for characters with more free will since you do say "no more puppet shows" in that very same book. Isn't there a contradiction in *Breakfast of Champions*, in this regard?

V: I suppose there are all kinds of contradictions. This is fiction, not a thesis. People object to my works of fiction as being too close to theses anyway. This is really fiction. I'm obviously selling something. I love to inject ideas or little known facts of history in a book. I've been a teacher. I enjoy telling younger people things they don't know. I'd love to tell that, for instance, I spoke at the University of Texas in Austin a couple of months ago. Are you aware that Texas has lived under the flag of Mexico as one part of Mexico?

A: I am. We visited Austin and San Antonio not long ago.

V: Texas then became an independent republic. Do you know why they fought the Mexicans, these terrible, dark-skinned, greasy Catholics down there?

A: History offers some reasons but you are probably better informed than I am.

V: History has not offered the big reason. The Mexicans told these Anglo-Saxons who settled down there in what was Mexico, "You can't have slaves."

A: I didn't know that.

V: Nobody knows it.

A: How did you find out about it?

V: I opened up the *Encyclopedia Britannica*.

A: Then there must be some people who know.

V: They certainly have not talked about it. So from the stage of Austin I asked them if they knew who Austin was, because the city is named after a person. He was a Quaker who owned slaves. Now there was a deeply religious man. It's deeply ethical, isn't it?

A: Written history can be manipulative. Earlier you said we must try to control social life. Yes, I think your books do urge us to try to control as much as we can. But I also notice a streak of pessimism concerning controllability: In the end Dr. Proteus has to realize that the Ghost Shirt Society's was not the way to change things; Constant dies on his way to a community "where a white man was hanged for the murder of an Indian"; stupidity and irresponsibility do destroy San Lorenzo; Eliot Rosewater, who, in his view of some social problems, is saner than the sane, is mentally ill, and does become comically isolated. And soon after we have had a Billy Pilgrim, who, in spite of all the existential catatonia, is a more successful changer of things than most of those who had gone before, we have Trout and Hoover succumbing to a sheer deterministic view.

V: My training is as a scientist. I was trained to be a biochemist, and I eventually—after the war—studied anthropology. So I've never studied literature. My brother is a distinguished physicist. He's ten years older than I am, will be seventy-five this month. I've spent more time with his science friends when I was growing up than I did with literary people. Scientists often perform experiments in their heads. If they haven't got the apparatus, if there is, in fact, no way to experiment with the sun or with clouds or with something so enormous, they can still, in their heads, try and think through the results of an experiment which can never be performed—guess how it would come out if they had infinite resources? So what I will do in a book is take a premise, as in *The Sirens of Titan*: suppose there were somebody who needed us to do something down here . . . and this person is trying to steer us. Of course, that's a premise of religion: that there is such a creature, who needs serving way up there. So I would perform that experiment in my head: suppose there were somebody. Or, in *Breakfast of Champions*: suppose we were all robots in fact and run that out. These are scientific premises for experiments which can never be performed anywhere but in my head. How about this premise: suppose a man met Hitler when he was young, down and out in Vienna, was about to give up and this other young man gave him a grubstake so he could get going again. What if, what if, what if? I myself don't know what the "what if?" is. But what about the "what if" now? I've invented a fictitious valley in upstate New York. It's like the Finger Lakes at Cornell University. There are a whole row of long, narrow lakes that run north and south. I invented another one. On one side of it is a very expensive college for rich kids who can't get into any other college because they are learning disabled in some way; they're dyslexic. This was founded shortly after the Civil War. They have always kept it down to about 300 students. The parents are very grateful. Their children, who hadn't been able to get into Harvard or Yale, get in here and get some kind of education because they're going to be owning huge parts of the United States whether they can read and write or not. They may not be morons; they may be learning disabled. On the other side of the lake is what starts as a work camp for city kids who've been in trouble with the police. This is 1870 or so. By the time my novel begins, the school on one side of the lake has a bell tower with carillon. It's got a skating rink; it's got a sailing fleet; it's even got a bowling alley. It's got its dormitories. Each student has a room of his own. There are suites with fireplaces; there is an ice cream parlor and all that. Still with 300 students, from some of the richest families. The whole Western Hemisphere is sending its learning disabled kids up here. On the other side is this prison started as a work camp, which was to reform children by giving them fresh air and letting them chop wood, and take cold showers. Ten thousand. And they all break out. The lake is frozen.

A: The thought experiment here is . . . .

V: To see what happens.

A: You told an earlier interview that you don't know how a novel is going to end. But you probably know the main thrust, where it is going, if not how it exactly will close.

V: I know what the trouble is going to be.

A: I don't want you to give this particular story away.

V: I mean in any story. That something very bad is going to happen. Beginning writers don't have enough courage to make something bad happen to their characters. They're too polite. They think their characters are real. You take the great Maupassant short story, "The Pearl Necklace." Here are two very nice, lower middle-class people. He is a civil servant, and she is from a nice family, too. But their families have lost all their money. So they know rich people but they can't give parties themselves and they can't have nice clothes. They are invited to a ball, the great ball that everyone wants to be invited to. Classmates of both of them know that they're good people. There is nothing wrong with these people at all, they are darling, they're not in vain. She finally—she doesn't have much in the way of clothes or anything—borrows a string of pearls from a very rich friend. They go to the dance, they have a swell time, and they fall in love with each other all over again. And what's the worst possible thing that could happen? She loses the pearl. Isn't that a mean author who would do that? In every book of mine something perfectly terrible has happened. In *Deadeye Dick* the kid's father is a gun collector. . . .

A: And the kid kills a pregnant woman.

V: You know, I did that. I didn't kill anybody. But I fired a rifle, out over Indianapolis. I didn't hit anybody as far as I know.

A: Did it have an awful effect on you psychically?

V: I never told anybody about it until I was an adult. I cleaned that gun and put it away.

A: If you didn't kill anyone, what was it that frightened you in the experience?

V: That I was such a person. That I could be that silly. Because it was silly. I had no intent. The gun was an abstract thing. It wasn't aimed. It was just very easy to fire.

A: The gun was a birthday present, or you sneaked out with one of your father's guns?

V: No, I was trusted with all my father's guns, since I was well trained in gun safety.

A: When I asked that question about the more deterministic and pessimistic Trout and Hoover after an active changer like Billy Pilgrim (he speaks out against atrocities and wars), I thought that perhaps something happened between *Slaughterhouse-Five* and *Breakfast of Champions* that darkened your view.

V: I don't know. That's what I wrote next.

A: Kilgore Trout does say in that novel, by the way, that "Everything was necessary." How does this relate to the main idea in the same book, that cultural cleansing is possible and one culture can be replaced with another?

V: I think what he meant about that was that everything does have a cause. And once it has happened, there's no taking it back.

A: So it's not a fatalistic philosophy; it is simply causal thinking.

V: Again, it's acceptance. Jung said one time that Nature can't make a mistake, that Nature defines itself as it goes along. You can never argue with it. We're part of that, presumable the hydrogen bomb is part of that, as is the pollution in the world and all that if Nature can't make a mistake. The planet dies. Why? That's what Nature did.

A: So "everything was necessary" may sound fatalistic but you didn't mean it that way. If what you mean is that there are causes, it can translate—to put it in social terms—into an imperative for us to try to recognize causes so as to be capable of changing the things we can.

V: Yes.

A: To say that "everything was necessary," or as in *Slaughterhouse-Five*, that the moment is structured the way it is, and to mean by these that everything does have a cause, is one thing. To say that everybody is right is another. That's exactly what "chrono-synclastic infundibulum" means in *The Sirens of Titan*.

V: It's just fun. Don't forget that my training is technical, and it once involved a lot of mathematics. And mathematics comes up with absurd conclusions, improbable, unlikely accidents due to the interrelationship of numbers. So there's an awful lot of whimsy in mathematics. Mathematicians don't take themselves as nearly as seriously as the *New York Times* does. These are playful people.

A: In your preface to *Happy Birthday, Wanda June*, you referred to yourself as someone living in a chrono-synclastic infundibulum. Would not the cultural cleansing accounted in *Breakfast of Champions*—the two works are very close in time—contradict the idea that everybody is right?

V: It's a whimsical idea. They're often jokes. Part of this is that I don't want to argue anymore. One of the climaxes at the end of my new book is that the narrator has been a teacher, first at the very expensive college, and then he is fired there for pessimism for speaking out against the Vietnam War, although he is a West Point graduate. He is finally fired for depressing the students. The only job he can get is across the lake. It is where they need a teacher so he moves over there. He survives the prison break. One of the people, who is on the board of directors—"the board of trustees of the college," it's called, by these 10,000 prisoners crossing the frozen lake, swamping this little campus, and holding people as valuable hostages—so one of them is a right-wing idealogue, an American conservative who has his own TV show, and invites all sorts of people who disagree with him on. After the break he has the other viewpoint character come on, too, as the other guest, and they discuss the prison break. The viewpoint character is supposed to shed light on the prisoners' attitudes, what they had in mind. This show took place as the great summing-up after the surviving convicts were rounded up. I'm going to say in the book that both said "blah blah blah."

A: How far into the book are you?

V: I'm just finishing it now.

A: Has it got a title?

V: No, so I mean these goddamn talk shows: "blah-blah-blah-blah, blah-blah." I refuse to write down any more of this: what one person says, what the other person says. Everybody is right. Of course, they're not.

A: How did you develop the idea of the chrono-synclastic infundibulum, the mathematical point where all opinions harmonize? Is there a concrete influence there? A mathematician's?

V: No, it's just a witticism that occurred to me, a mathematical witticism.

A: How about the Bokononian lingo in *Cat's Cradle*? Some of these linguistic innovations are suggestive of their meaning. Granfalloon suggests to me "grand fallacy/lunacy/balloon." Thus it is expressive of something that is false or meaningless.

V: Yes.

A: Duprass (karass of two) probably means "two-press"-ed together?

V: Yes.

A: Is this the way you conceived them?

V: I didn't think too hard about them. I don't suppose I spent more than ten minutes coining any one of those words. Karass is a basic unit that God uses in order to do His work, and they're very hard to detect, and they're spread all over the world. This word was off a mailbox on Cape Cod as I have a neighbor named Karass, which is a common Greek name.

A: What's funny is that karass is homophone with "caress," and the latter brings the Bokononian rite of caressing soles to mind. One wonders if the word—an actual name, as you have just said—has something to do with the Bokononian rite, too?

V: Sure. It sounded right. It had that. It may still have that. That's what I am calling it.

A: How about "zah-mah-ki-bo," which means "fate." Did it have anything to do with your interest in Africa?

V: No. I made it up.

A: And Bokonon's name?

V: I don't know how I made it up but I did.

A: This was the linguistic aspect. As for the concepts themselves, are all of them your own original contribution to social anthropology, or, were there any of them that were inspired by philosophy, anthropology, social psychology?

V: Of course, the attitudes of social sciences. It's interesting that Saul Bellow is a product of the same anthropology department that produced me at the University of Chicago. It's a very small but reputable anthropology department. Both of us were unable to make any field trips as we were a little too old, and we had families. You must be young in order to take the summer off or to take a year or two off. And neither one of us could afford it or spare the time. So he made up the field-trip in his most amusing book, *Henderson the Rain King*. He totally invents Africa. He's never been there. I made up a Haiti. I hadn't seen it at the time. But I have seen it now. These two frustrated anthropologists, who were never able to go out into the field. Each one of us invented a field trip anyway.

A: Whether you write an antiutopia as in *Player Piano*, or a sociophilosophical allegory as in *The Sirens of Titan*, or stage a world disaster as in the satiric anthropology of *Cat's Cradle* or in *Slapstick* or in *Galápagos*, science fiction technique comes easy for you. But once you remarked that it was easier to write realistic fiction.

V: It's more difficult to write science fiction because you are having to do two things at once. It's to hold the reader emotionally: to present scenes which will make the reader want to laugh or cry, or love or hate—you must manipulate the reader that way or he will stop reading. At the same time what's going on must make sense scientifically. *Galápagos* had to be responsible in terms of the theory of evolution, the situations; I had to be faithful to the theory of evolution. It is an artificial construct, incidentally. It's playing a game and holding the reader's attention at the same time. It was very hard to do. But if you just deal with the breakup of marriages and the death of a newborn baby and the father and son reconciling after hating each other all their lives, that's all you have to do. That's enough, nothing else has to go on. It is also a lot easier if you're not funny. You don't have to build jokes.

A: We will have to speak about the jokes. But remaining with science fiction a little longer, once in an interview you expressed your totally justified view that science fiction technique does not harm the seriousness of an artist. What are your criteria for the seriousness of an artist?

V: I'm a freethinker, and I think the highest service we can perform is to the community. Of course, Hitler believed that take and Mussolini believed it and Stalin. But we disagree as to how best serve the community.

A: And what is it that makes good science fiction?

V: To make people think intelligently about science and what it can or cannot do. That's what we must do now. And you get this nitwit, uneducated Ronald Reagan who imagines we could do all sorts of impossible things. This great invisible bubble.

A: Once you also said that if you had been in the position, you would have awarded H. G. Wells the Nobel Prize. I assume that the reasons you would have given to support such a decision have just been given.

V: Yes, he was trying to educate people about science, what its implications are, what its limitations are. We must know that. We are going to spend so much money on this absurd bubble!

A: Apropos of science fiction the worlds presented in your novels are often apocalyptic. Is this your way of pricking bubbles?

V: Yes, it's a way of saying God doesn't care what becomes of us, and neither does Nature, so we'd better care. We're all there is to care.

A: Back to the jokes then. There is a sentence in *Mother Night* that says, "This is a hard world to be ludicrous in." Does it follow that this is a hard world to be a humorist in?

V: Yes, because so many people are humorless and so they think you're stupid or foolish. When I lectured in Sweden at Uppsala, I addressed an intellectual hall. After I was through, this one man stood up and was just outraged, and said, "You know, with the world in such a condition that it is now, how can you sit up there and make jokes?"

A: Sounds like John Gardner's idea of moral fiction.

V: Yes, maybe so.

A: In your "Self-Interview" you refer to your books as "mosaics of jokes," and when interviewers ask you about the jokes, you always say that what makes a good jokester is being the youngest member of the family at the dinner table, i.e., there is no other way to call attention to yourself. But that granted, there must be more to the making of a humorist. Perhaps something in the brain chemistry? Or in the genes?

V: Yes, I think so. I speak of humorless people as having a moral flaw, and that's not fair. It's just like regarding it as a moral flaw that someone can't sing. An awful lot of humorless people come into this world, and they make very good Nazis.

A: And power is humorless anyway. Were there jokesters in the family?

V: Yes, there's an awful lot of funny things we've said. I said somewhere that I was glad my parents were as funny as they were. They said extremely funny things, often. But I was so sorry that they were as unhappy as they were—and they were desperately unhappy. Humor is a way of dealing with unhappiness and at least they were able to do it that way. One thing that's in *God Bless You, Mr. Rosewater*, is that Eliot Rosewater is listening to *Aïda* here in New York and suddenly starts shouting at the end that they mustn't try to sing in this tune because they're using up oxygen much faster. When I was a kid, Father used to listen to the opera every Saturday afternoon. And it still goes on, practically from the earliest days of radio an opera was broadcast every Saturday afternoon. This was out in Indianapolis. My father said about the last scene in *Aïda*, "You know, it would last a lot longer if they wouldn't try to sing it." That's really a very funny thing to say.

A: You learned how to make jokes from radio comedians. What is it they taught you?

V: Timing. Jokes are very short. That's one reason it's so hard for me to write books, because jokes use up very little space since you really can't string out a joke very long. I started writing an essay for another book, just an autobiographical book on humor and how jokes do work. One thing I talk about is that danger must be present, a subject that's troubling. Sex is such a subject. To start with the dirty joke: Everybody is uneasy, nobody feels entirely comfortable or confident about his or her sexuality, and that causes biological changes, just the fact that the subject of sex is brought up. Or take children's jokes: "Why does the chicken cross the road?" You know what the answer is: "To get to the other side." A very simple joke but it caused a biological reaction on your part because you think I'm testing your intelligence, and the whole school feeling comes back. And again, the teacher has called on you when you were least expecting it, and you get a biological response. And then you have to get rid of the adrenalin that's been generated by the mention of the troubling subject by laughing. Or you can get rid of its by crying. These are convulsions of two different kinds throwing it out. Now there are comedians who are absolutely not funny at all. I certainly notice them. Bob Hope is such a one. He never mentions a subject which is troubling yet he is thought to be a comedian. But he is most popular when there is a war going on. He is going as close to the front as possible, as during the Second World War. Everybody adored him. He would be on the deck of a battleship, out the North Sea somewhere. Or he'd be behind the lines on some Goddamned island when everybody was already in danger.

A: Diverting attention . . . ?

V: No, they were so full, so ready to laugh.

A: Full of tension . . .

V: From the tension. As they could hear the guns. Here's the funniest man in the world. All he had to say was "Hello," and everybody was capable of laughing.

A: In the *Paris Review* you said you regard yourself as a technocrat of stories. Stories have their own mechanics and "they can be tinkered with like Model T Fords."

V: In order to hold the reader's attention.

A: Yes, your works are satiric parables full of challenging ideas dramatized in intricate ways. But then how does one understand your statements like, "I let the old ghost use me when he feels he can," or that yours is "a shaman's way of writing?" The technocrat of artistic creation on the one hand and a totally instinctive way of writing on the other.

V: We have to have them both going.

A: Your "mosaics" are made of a "a whole bunch of tiny chips; and each chip is a joke," as you say. This has led some people to the unwary conclusion that you have no sense of structure. Robert Coover for example . . . sees you as Mark Twain incarnate: playful technique, no sense of structure.

V: I would hope that there is a structure. The only reason we would want structure is to keep the reading. The reader insists on structure; otherwise, I think, we'd all gladly do without it.

A: You say about writing that you "have to be entertaining while you do it," because it's "annoying." What's annoying?

V: I think it may be an error there. It's annoying that you have to be entertaining, or the reader would stop.

A: Does that mean that, as opposed to the Aristotelian view—which says that a literary work must both educate and entertain—you think that the story *per se* is supposed to educate the reader, and it is only in order to be able to do that that entertainment is additionally provided?

V: It has to be integrated, or the reader will stop reading.

A: Should we attribute a sequential significance to recurring details in your different works, or such details should not be interpreted sequentially? For example, Tralfamadorians in different novels; Rumfoord, Trout in different novels.

V: No, they should be read individually. The novel is instinctive, it's putting something in or leaving it out.

A: James Lundquist speaks about your characters being Protean men. I find it fascinating in this context that the main character of your very first novel is called Proteus. Is this your view of survival and of the possibility for the character to reinvent himself? Many selves in the same person, and the most important ones protected by being hidden?

V: In order to survive we must be Protean. Think of the germs again. As we sit here, a generation of germs has lived and died. But a human generation is very slow thing. To respond to this or that damned fool invention or to the hydrogen bomb or to the destruction of the ozone layer we must change, and chances are we can't. It's like these huge tankers, which are cruising all over the world, and it takes them about three miles to change course. For humanity to change course now is to stop consuming as much as it does.

A: Dr. Proteus has periodic depression. He seems to be a prototype of the Vonnegutian character in this sense, too. I don't just mean all the depressive cases from Paul Proteus to Billy Pilgrim's catatonic stupor or Hoover's depression and so on. There are a lot of personality problems of different kinds; there is much abr ˉmal psychology in psychopathic and sociopathic personalities. Why?

V: Because that in fact is the human experience.

A: I think that much of that mental illness is sheer social psychology.

V: Yes, but you have seen a lot. It's very common.

A: Yes, it's the social experience that makes it easy for us to realize that when Billy Pilgrim is "a listless plaything of enormous forces," his catatonia does, indeed, reflect on those "enormous forces"—that is to say, the times are pathological and therefore pathogenic.

V: Of course, they are. Look at all the Polish people who are responding now: economically, to help Poland's place in the world economy; in manufacturing, because they're really not very good at it; in merchandising, I have no idea in what shape their agriculture is, I know that their coal is of very low quality, which nobody else wants to buy. So they've got a hell of a lot of problems that no amount of will or enthusiasm or interviews with him in Gdansk will solve. We met in a cathedral not far from the shipyard. He's an electrician and had just come off work. This is a very real competitive industry, building ships. And they're not very damned good at it. They haven't got the machinery; they haven't got the skills. The will toward freedom is wonderful; and toward economic justice and all that, but they've got a hell of a problem with how to build ships that somebody else wants to buy.

A: So mental illnesses are functional, aesthetically, in your works. You are playing the satiric game others—Heller, Kesey, Percy, Pynchon—are playing, too: who is sane, so-called sane society or the nonconformist sensitive, who is branded "insane" by the "sane."

V: That's a literary cliché, it goes back a long way. I think we—all the ones you named—are willing to identify those who are sane and those who are not, and to make that diagnosis on the basis of the results of the person's life, whether a person has produced great unhappiness for others or in fact has enhanced lives.

A: Besides the aesthetic functions that mental illnesses fulfill in your fiction, there may be a biographical side to the coin. There were very serious psychological crises and catastrophes in your immediate family. Your mother committed suicide; your son had a breakdown once. You have had depressive periods yourself. This may have been autobiographical about Dr. Proteus in Player Piano.

V: Sure.

A: You still have depressive periods?

V: Yes. Not as severe.

A: Once you mentioned that suicide was at the heart of *Breakfast of Champions.* You also said that it is a promise not to commit suicide. Did you ever consider suicide seriously?

V: Of course, as the child of every suicide does. It's just another way to solve problems to a person who's been close to someone who's committed suicide—which is one reason not to commit suicide, because it makes others think; "Well, here's way to solve my problem." If this is one option and a reputable person has done it, and many reputable people have done it, then maybe that's the way I should solve things, too.

A: We are less than a year away from 1990. If memory serves, you published your first story in 1950, almost exactly forty years ago. I am sure you do have a clear sense of where American fiction was going in these past four decades.

V: Technology again. It is to write a contemporary novel without taking into consideration that goddamn machine, television which is principal teacher here, and all these people who are writing novels about fathers and sons finally making peace, a baby dying, about divorce and all that, and totally ignoring this very powerful character, television, who's in the house all the time. What this machine has done? One, it killed the magazines because the advertising agencies found out that money was much better invested in television than it was in magazines. So the magazines I wrote short stories for died. We used to have hundreds of short-story writers. I was one of them. So the short response to the technology. . . . Another thing this machine has done is to make people less patient. It used to be that you have a play, for example, where the curtain goes up and the maid says, "Oh, yes, the master is in Brazil, trying to get back his gold mine, and the daughter has just come back from Wellesley, where she's been kicked out, and she's love with this gigolo," and so forth. You can't do that any more. You must begin with action, with movement. Something's going on. We'll find out halfway through the play what the hell the problem is. But if you start slow today, they'll just change the channel; they get up and leave the "theater" and go get a drink. Presumably it's desensitized us. This very bloody stuff on television, that's all that seems to hold the attention of an audience now. Or that's what the advertisers believe. They may be mistaken. There is all this response to technology, and it has very little to do with any other big social changes.

A: The way TV influenced fiction is that . . .

V: . . . it killed the outlets for printed fiction.

A: The Vonnegut oeuvre of 1950–1990 has obviously been shaped by world events and by events shaping America. Dresden, Watergate, other things. They are all there in your works. But are there any less obvious ways in which events shaping your personal life shaped your works?

V: I would suppose so but I have never subjected myself to psychoanalysis to dig out what these events might be. I would say this, in very quick order. In college I was told by my father to be a scientist or nothing, as my brother had been. I was not gifted this way, so I was always at the bottom of my class although I understood the spirit of what was going on. So I was in the process of flunking out of college. I got pneumonia. I recovered from that. I went into the army. My mother committed suicide. I was sent overseas. I was captured and I saw the bombing of Dresden. All this in a space of about four—hundred days. And this is failure, failure, failure, failure, failure, failure. It's a very ordinary human experience to lose, to get bad news instead of good, to accept it somehow. That is the ordinary human experience: defeat. Libraries are just full of stories of victories, something almost no one has experienced. Who do you think our greatest playwright is, far greater than Eugene O'Neill? (Eugene O'Neill died of drink, of course, bad enough that he did that.) Tennessee Williams choking on a bottle cap and all alone. And Herman Melville unappreciated during his whole life. Defeat is the ordinary human experience, not victory. We can expect it, be prepared for it and not be humiliated by it.

A: This sense of defeat may have contributed to the black mood of the much-anthologized, so-called black humor Vonnegut stories and excerpts from novels. I am aware of your aversion to being referred to as a black humorist and do regard you as a satirist primarily, since what you expose are mostly human stupidity and social abuse and these are not beyond human control. But disregarding the problems with the black humor label now, there was this black mood of a whole generation—laughter based on disappointments and fears, to use your own definition of "the biggest laughs" from the *Playboy* interview—a mood which is gone from the American novel of the 1980s. What, in your view, caused the black mood to subside?

V: The fact that television and the magazines say it has subsided. The only evidence that it has subsided appears on magazines: "The New American Marriage"; "The Return to Religion"; the blah-blah-blah. They've got to get out an issue every week, and people believe this.

A: Where we get the sense of defeat, is postmodern fiction, the existentialist fiction that comes after the Second World War.

V: We are defeated. It turns out we won almost nothing for humanity in that war. As a Hungarian you must have some sense of how little Hungary got out of it.

A: The postwar experience certainly added to the Hungarian resourcefulness in strategies of survival.

V: Yes. So they're notoriously pessimistic and so are the Austrians, as the cheerfulness of all those people through the Austrian-Hungarian empire is pretense. And that is also where black humor came from. "Galgen humor" did not come from Germany, from Sweden, from Scandinavia. It came from the southern tier, but north of Italy. The resignation of all those terrible black jokes, that's where black humor, "galgen humor" came form. Freud wrote a whole essay on it. Yes, the Hungarians are resourceful, but I think that part of their cunning comes from their awareness of how bad things are. You can make a real fool of yourself saying the situation isn't as bad as it really is. If you know how bad it really is, then you can behave appropriately.

A: The Hungarian sense of humor is certainly illustrative of the Freudian theory—humor as an outlet for the pressure that results from repression. As a Hungarian, I find your interest in that part of the world very exciting. I know that you are well informed, even concerning the plight of Hungarian minorities living in some of the other East Central European countries.

V: That whole area is interesting to a whole lot of us and not particularly Hungarians. I have some friends of Hungarian descent. We're quite interested in Gypsies, and we used to think of them in connection with Hungary more than any other country. I don't know why. I guess you have more Gypsies than any other country.

A: Yes, we have a lot of Gypsies. If the answer to that "why" is not the worldwide popularity of Hungarian gypsy music, then it probably is that Gypsies are, in fact, mistakenly called "Hungarians" in some Western European countries. The reason for that is that the Gypsies—who had come from India—reached Hungary and settled there first, in the fifteenth to sixteenth centuries, and migrated to Western Europe from Hungary and some other Central European countries. Western Europeans misidentified them as "Hungarians," "Bohemians," or whatever country they were coming from. But Gypsies aside, there is a good number of Hungarian names and references to things or people Hungarian in your works. In *Galápagos*, for instance, Mary Hepburn's paternal grandfather was a Hungarian horse trainer. He changed his name to Michael Boone so everybody thinks Mary is related to Daniel Boone. (She is, but on her mother's side.)

V: A close friend of mine is the son of a Hungarian horse trainer so I just pulled that out of my memory.

A: Have you ever been to Hungary?

V: No, never.

A: Do you plan to?

V: I've certainly been invited sometimes. I've been told what a beautiful city Budapest is. I would like to see Budapest at least.

A: To come back to the Vonnegut oeuvre: To what extent have your works been shaped by the inner logic of an *ars poetica?*

V: My family has always been in the arts since it's what we've done best: architects, painters, musicians. It's the way we've been able to make our livings ordinarily. My brother is an unusual sport, a mutation. So we have no vocabulary to go with what we do, we simply do it.

A: It's interesting that your brother can be regarded a mutation from the point of view of family history yet your father wanted you to go in that direction too, to move away from the family tradition.

V: He pitied himself, my father did, as an artist, that the artist didn't have a chance, that they're all weak. He told me to be anything but an architect.

A: Do you distinguish stages, periods, patterns of some sort when you think of your works, something else than what we talked about earlier, i.e., the pre-Dresden-novel phase and the post-Dresden-novel phase?

V: No, that's for critics to do.

A: Would you regard any of your works a typically sixties novel?

V: *Player Piano* was a cult book during the sixties, along with *One Flew Over the Cuckoo's Nest, Catch-22,* and probably *The Catcher in the Rye.* There was this little library that many of the hippies had. Hippies, I think, liked the idea of a "karass" in *Cat's Cradle*, an idea I don't take seriously except intellectually. I think scientists on opposite sides of the earth can work together and cooperate.

A: A typically eighties novel? Is there such a thing at all?

V: I don't know what it would be. Much younger people who are responding to the eighties are writing those. I'm part of the generation of 1922 and that's it. We have a large number of writers—myself, James Jones, Joe Heller, Norman Mailer—who were all born in 1922.

A: In your 1973 Stockholm P.E.N. address you said that writers are "specialized cells in a single, huge organism, mankind." According to the *Playboy* interview, they are "evolutionary cells" in the social organism, introducing new ideas, and responding symbolically to life. Does American fiction fulfill that function today?

V: Yes, if we knew where to look. The problem is that such books aren't particularly popular, usually. It's very hard to get the attention of the American public unless you're a person of as great importance as Jacqueline Kennedy or an ex-president or something like that. Then people will be interested in your ideas.

A: In one of the novels you say that to hate America is as silly as loving it.

V: It's much too big to think about. Everybody is here. We are the world. And I think it's quite a failure. I think that it's admirable and envied because of its great natural wealth.

A: Your critical view of American society reminds me of the hippies you mentioned a minute ago. What do you think of the counterculture now, when you look back at it from a perspective that a distance of two decades provides?

V: It was very unfortunate, because they were right about so many things, that drugs coincidentally were involved. The drugs were very bad news it turns out. I liked a lot of the music; I was glad that everybody was singing and dancing, as I think people should be encouraged to do that. And people should be loving and they should be pacifistic and they should worship the earth and respect it, but God dammit the drugs arrived at the same time.

A: How do you regard the American youth today?

V: I think they're deeply discouraged. The yuppies, these supposed materialists, I think, are worried about themselves and the shallowness of their happiness.

A: In *Breakfast of Champions* you told Trout that you were cleansing yourself "for the very different sorts of years to come." Did these past two decades turn out to be "very different sorts of years?"

V: Not particularly, no.

A: The "place" where you have been living, figuratively speaking, is probably "Edge-City" ever since the first novel. The "center" is . . .

V: . . . what television and what the magazines and what the *New York Times* says the news is. This is what we're supposed to look at today. The hostages, say, we're not going to think about anything but the hostages for the next week.

A: What's the secret of staying "as close to the edge" as you can "without going over?"

V: I don't know how you would keep from going over. That's a health matter. How do you not catch a cold? Nobody knows.

A: Do school committees still burn your books?

V: Not for a long time, no. Again and again there's a lawsuit where the censors are defeated.

A: As we entered the decade of the 1980s, your major fears were that a third world war and ecological disaster were inescapable and that at least a nuclear plant was to blow up soon. We did have nuclear accidents (Chernobyl, for one) and have every reason to worry about ecology: the global greenhouse effect, the ozone hole, oil spills (Alaska, for one). But as for the third world war, we have Gorbachev and glasnost . . .

V: Yes, the news is very good that way.

A: So how much better or worse off are we, on the threshold of the new decade of the 1990s, than we were when we entered the eighties?

V: What we're talking about is middle-class Europeans when we say things are looking pretty good for us. We're not Sudanese, we're not Ethiopians, we're not Zambians, we're not Bangladeshesi and we're not Mexicans. So yes, the news is very good.

On Art, Writing, Fellini, and *Time Quake*, 1993

Peter J. Reed and Marc Leeds

This conversation with Kurt Vonnegut took place on Sunday, October 31, 1993, at the home of Ollie and Billie Lyon in Lexington, Kentucky. Ollie Lyon had worked with Kurt Vonnegut at General Electric in Schenectady in the late 1940s when both were public relations writers and Kurt was striving to publish his first short story. Vonnegut was in Lexington at Ollie's instigation to help raise funds for the library of Midway College. He had designed posters, silkscreened by Joe Petro III, a Lexington artist, which were sold, autographed, and also used to advertise his appearance on the following night, Monday, November 1. That occasion saw another performance of his combination lecture–reading–stand up comedy show "How to Get a Job Like Mine."

Questioners in this very informal interview were Peter Reed and Marc Leeds, professors of English at the University of Minnesota and Shawnee State University, respectively, with Ollie and Billie Lyon providing hospitality and joining in the frequent laughter.

R: In the last couple of novels you have used a roughly similar kind of narrator—an older man reflecting on life. So you have gone over to using first-person narrators more than you had been in the earlier ones, and I wondered if there was any particular reason for doing that or any reason you feel more comfortable doing that?

V: I was prevented from doing that for a long time because I came up through journalism really. And it used to be, until Tom Wolff came along, that you goddamn well kept yourself out of the story, you know, and if you had turned in a story where you intimated that you, yourself existed, you caught hell for that. A story is a gadget and for one reason or another—and it's almost trial and error—it will turn out that this particular story is better told from an omniscient point of view or from first-person point of view. And this is a result of experiment. John Irving does this. He writes his books in the first person. I guess he can bring his emotions to this. But then he puts it in the third person. But so much of it is simply technical because the story is finally a gadget. And for one reason or another, it will work or it won't work. But the options are fairly limited and quite well known. And point of view is one.

R: These narrators in the recent novels, they are involved in an almost accidental guilt. They're almost blundering victims and go through a kind of punishment and increased sensitivity. Do you feel in these last three novels that you have an evolving hero-figure or protagonist?

V: Yeah. I think it's completely organic. It's just what came up in the garden. I've been interested in teaching how to write a story and helping other people write their stories, as I did when I taught at Iowa.

R: A long time ago on the Films for the Humanities film interview that you did, you talked about the way you write and at that point, you said there are people who are swoopers, who do the whole thing and then go back and rewrite, whereas you tend to write one page at a time and correct it. When you think you've got that right, that's page one and then you do page two. Do you still do it that way?

V: Yes, I do. As a matter of fact, I've set a premise for myself which turns out to be so promising that I have to live up to it, have to respond to it properly, or forget it. The last five years, I guess, have gone down the toilet, but I've been trying to make this thing work. But two days ago, I was on chapter 3 and I stopped and had to go back. As I've said, there are no second drafts for me. But thousands upon thousands of failed pages have been thrown away. When I teach storytelling, I am likely to give the conventional advice that writers write about what they know, and start with a fascinating character worth following. But I myself start with a fascinating situation rather than a character, and I don't know from experience what will come of it. Each story is an experiment at the frontier of my understanding. What if all economically useful work could be done more cheaply and satisfactorily by machines than by human beings? That's *Player Piano*. What if there were actual, detectable creatures looking down on Earth, and, like gods we have imagined, are governing many of our actions, and have very specific missions they hope we'll carry out for their sake? That's *The Sirens of Titan*. What if there were an expensive prep school for the privileged on one side of a beautiful lake and a maximum security prison on the other. That's *Hocus Pocus*. I throw away pages when they aren't adequately responsive to the situation. The past three years or so have gone into the wastebasket because a premise, the start of the experiment is so wonderful, so thought provoking, that I am maybe too old and tired to do it justice. Physicists and mathematicians commonly die while working on problems they have yet to solve.

R: One reason I thought about that technique again was because in *Hocus Pocus*, you talk about that novel being written by the fictional writer on a whole series of itty bits of paper, and then they've been pieced together in an order. When you look at *Hocus Pocus*, it looks like something that could hypothetically have been written in lots of little pieces. Then you go back and reordered it. But you didn't write it that way?

V: I think so, sure, because I might go from page one to page two and so forth, but I'll take another shot at it, particularly if it isn't working, and make all sorts of adjustments.

R: So you can move those bits around?

V: Yeah, and I avoid a computer, although I own one, because it makes it all seem too easy to think of this or that and then push a button and the machine goes *rrrrrrrrrr* and you've made a few changes. I spoke at Cheltenham at a literary festival there two weeks ago, and I spoke about myself because they asked me to. But I said that I was a child of the Great Depression and, roughly, the class of 1922, the military class of 1922 which would include Heller and Mailer. And to us a job has always been a job. If you got a job, there would be a party and everything. Then about midnight, somebody would ask what the job was. Ollie's a member of that generation, and, hell, we both ate shit at General Electric as public relations men. Very good ones, I must say. We were good at our jobs. I just felt that I lucked out, really. I found something I could make money at. I was making money off the magazines. I was a very highly paid magazine writer. At one point, we decided to hold down the price of my stories so they'd buy all of them instead of just saving them for the anniversary issues. But anyway, an enormous amount of opportunism here is just surviving.

R: How does that feel, looking back on that short–story writing? Because you were selling a lot of stories to very good magazines. Did you get the feeling, doing that, that you were a commercial success without your name being noticed? Or do you think your name was known to a lot of magazine readers?

V: No, because I had become part of a gang and you don't want to let go of that. That is, I recommend everybody do this. And there are a whole bunch of us writing for the *Saturday Evening Post* and *Collier's* who were regarded as corrupt and shallow or whatever, as compared with the people who were writing for the *Atlantic Monthly* or for *Partisan Review* or for the *New Yorker*. Actually, the magazines that I wrote for, *Collier's* and the *Saturday Evening Post*, published more Faulkner than anybody. Published more of Fitzgerald than anybody.

R: Looking back, I've got photocopies of some of those stories now and it looks like you had good illustrators and everything.

V: Oh, Jesus, they got as much as we did. Ray Bradbury is a good friend of mine now. We both came through that. At that time, it seemed to us that the *New Yorker* was responding to the sensibilities of its subscribers, as middle–class people on their way to lower upper middle-class, and dealing with their problems. We were, frankly, trying to be entertaining and really working at that or dealing with more general subjects.

R: The same is said about the origin of the novel in England, and it has been said cynically that the novel was to teach middle–class women which fork to use first. A lot of your stories, it seems to me, have those kinds of settings about the country club or something, got that same kind of social function almost.

V: I guess that's true. General readers have a great curiosity about what goes on at country clubs. That was the secret ingredient of the Jacqueline Susann novels, and her successes is that they are etiquette books, among other things. If you suddenly get a lot of money, what do you say to a duke? If the maid talks back to you, what the hell do you say to her or what do you do about it? What kind of drapes do you have?

R: Your newest book, *Hocus Pocus*, is rather like *Galápagos* in that you've got this combination in there of evolution except it's not evolution in the Darwinian sense. It's a social sense—a combination of a succession of accidents on the one hand, mixed with fixed hereditary qualities on the other. Where do you see the balance between those two things?

V: Well, you heard me talk about this book before it ever existed and so did Marc. I think that when we were in Iowa together, I was talking about it. What I had started with is the sort of thing my brother, the scientist, starts with, that is, a premise. You set up a situation and look at what is going to happen out of the situation. You have a private school on one side of the lake and a prison on the other side and what was likely to become of that, and that was the tension. And the Vietnam War didn't have that much to do with it or anything else but that original premise. I've talked about how my brother and I do very much the same sort of thing because he's an experimental atmospheric scientist and what he does is, he puts a bucket of water over the door and tells Mother Nature to come in. And see what she does! He agrees we're in the same line of work; but I will take a premise like that: If there's a school for rich kids on one side of the lake and a prison for people born poor on the other side, what is going to happen? Then, of course, that kind of situation does happen, too. It's happening around us now.

But what I've been working on now—which has turned out to be impossible, I think—"that way lies madness"—is with these people having to deal with the universe when it hesitates between expanding or shrinking. It hesitates between going back for a big family reunion and then making a big bang again. So what it does is, it shrinks only ten earthling years and then decides to go on expanding again. Well, the consequences of this are that everybody has to do exactly what he or she did from 1991 to 2001. This is an experiment that I'm performing in my head and it turns out to be *so* complicated that to do it justice, after farting around with it, the responsibilities that I've saddled myself with are just enormous. When free will kicks in again on February 13, 2001, which is when the time-quake struck and sent everybody back to 1991, everybody in a moving vehicle is expecting this thing to go on steering itself where it should go for the past ten years. They think about whatever they want, and they're hanging onto the steering wheel and doing everything they did the first time through, but they're expecting to go on automatically. So the population of the earth, in the first hours after free will kicks in, is reduced by 5 percent. Pedestrians will not get out of the way, expecting their bodies to do what they've been doing for the past ten years.

R: This is when the contraction begins?

V: No, after it's all over. All of a sudden, when the universe goes on expanding, it gets back to February 13, 2001, in the afternoon in New York City. A fireman is holding onto the steering wheel of the fire engine and blowing the sirens and everything, but this thing has been steering itself for the past ten years during the reruns. It's suddenly plowing into pedestrians and everything, and they don't get out of the way as they can see this damn thing coming. It is so complicated.

L: I thought you shelved it.

V: Well, I did, but I started over again. But the actual consequences of free will kicking in again when nobody expects it, you know, everybody just completely . . .

R: So it's a little bit like the movie in *Slaughterhouse-Five* that you show forward and then backward.

V: Yeah, but it's much more complicated.

L: It's interesting that you're starting at that date. Going back to February 13, in the past it has a biographical explanation as the firebombing of Dresden and in the fiction as Billy Pilgrim's death date.

V: It does, but that's just trivia. It's not all that important. I had to pick some date. I picked to rerun the last ten years because it makes the storytelling so much simpler. These are events the reader can keep in mind.

R: I wanted to write something about the perpetual motion machines in *Hocus Pocus*, and I don't know quite how to phrase it, but it sounds as if in the philosophical sense, you find them beautiful but futile. It reminded me of at one point in the Quad Cities speaking tour when somebody, a student in the audience, asked you a question about whether you thought with all your social questioning and your trying to wake people up to things that were happening, whether it would ever do any good. And you gave an answer that reminded me of Camus, of saying that it's absurd and futile but you've got to do it anyway. These perpetual motion machines, which are beautiful, remind me of that idea.

V: Well, they're so appealing. You almost want to help the guy build one, and to say, "Why don't you do this or why don't you do that?" But all of this is so recent. I was going to give a speech at Cheltenham about Fitzgerald and Hemingway, and I didn't for one reason or another. I didn't get back to Cheltenham. But I realized that they're roughly as old as this century. So when they were twenty-two, it was roughly 1922. Everything goes so fast. Only fifty years earlier, slavery was legal in the United States of America. That's no time at all. Right now, in 1993, the Holocaust is longer ago than that for us. Fifty years would put us back into that era. It all goes so goddamn fast. I think how compressed history is now. The extraordinary events happening within virtually the lifetime of one person or two persons.

L: Since the collapse of the Berlin Wall, I've been reading a lot of material, reaching to construct parallels between what Europe was like at the beginning of the century with what it is now with everybody split off into nationalistic or tribalistic factions.

V: When I studied anthropology at the University of Chicago, under left–wingers, they loved the Soviet Union for preserving all the tribal traditions . . .
[Here a recording problem.]
V: Why the hell couldn't they have sent me an engineer instead of an English major? Same trouble we had last time. . . . Do you know John Casey? He was a student of mine at Iowa. He's a stammerer. His father is a prominent politician, but John is a stammerer and he interviewed me like this: Whoever had to tttttranscribe it would bbbbblow her fucking ggggourd!

R: You were teasing me about deconstruction the other day on the phone. There are people who talk about you as a deconstructive fiction writer in that you have deconstructed Dresden and deconstructed war in the sense that you demythologize things. Do you like that term or not?

V: The people who say that have been formally trained in one way or another to think literature is one thing and not another. And the sort of person who would get a job as a critic for the *Washington Post* or the *New York Times* or *Newsweek* or *Time* has been taught about what is a book and what isn't and has been given a responsibility of keeping barbarians from the gate.

But I have one friend of mine, a friend of Ollie's, too, Phillip Martin, a guy from Cleveland who finally wound up living in England after working for the State Department. He said one time that my work had everything but originality. And we're still friends. I think it's true because I've been inspired by people who write unconventional books. Most strikingly is Voltaire. Is *Candide*. It's a book that thick. And a lot of the writing of Swift and so forth. I find people who teach literature tend to avoid them pretty much. But Hawthorne was quite radical and so I'm in part of the mainstream of radicalism. I watched a writer be interviewed on PBS some nights ago, and he is writing stories about his growing up in the South. And I'm sure they're exquisitely done and I think a lot of people feel that this is what books are supposed to do. My books deal with much more public issues. Part of it would be, I think, because of my seeming rootlessness. As I said, I'm not anything. I'm a public school product from the Middle West. I'm a German on top of that. But it seems to me that I'm writing all the time about things which are really going on right now. Tomorrow night in my speech, I'll talk about what computers are doing to us right now. That's of no concern to a writer who writes about growing up in a particular time and place.

R: That originality charge seems ridiculous to me. There are lots of ways in which you're technically original, but even in that of subject matter I think you were not exclusive but you were one of the first writers to put that emphasis upon social and technological issues. And your thinking about that is certainly original.

V: Yeah, but I can trace my lineage, which is to Orwell. And to Zamiatin and to H. G. Wells. And these people have all been considered outside the mainstream. But the heritage is, in fact, a long one. And that is we're just not real writers, which is what the writer's union in Moscow said about Solzhenitsyn: This man is not a writer.

L: I'm sure you heard that Fellini passed away this morning.

V: Yes. Wow.

L: I was listening to National Public Radio, and they were talking about the fact that, in Italy, apparently, they call Fellini "The Magician." His combination of the real and the bizarre was only, could only be described as Felliniesque, and then there were other things that came along afterwards and by comparison were also called Felliniesque. And that makes me wonder what Vonnegutian means to you.

V: Well, I'd be honored to have practically the same thing. It's sort of an opportunism, a wide-awake opportunism. And it occurs in filmmaking, you know, we're just coming out in the street, and you see a person with a wonderful face as Fellini did. He'd see somebody with a face and say, "You've gotta be in my movie." And I've been awake when I'm writing, and you're suddenly seeing a wonderful opportunity presenting itself. If I were writing about my experience growing up in a particular time and place, I wouldn't be that wide open to accidents and so forth. There's an opportunity to do something extremely funny. You just get lucky.

I think about growing old. I think I have a very nice run here. I'm having a lot of trouble now and I just feel probably I've run out of luck. That's all right. You know, I'm like Joe Namath who can no longer pass into a crowd.

R: When you say you feel as if you've run out of luck, do you mean that this most recent book is hard to do?

V: Yeah, I'm not up to it. I've set myself a problem that either I'm just not bright enough to solve or I'm not energetic enough to solve. But again, as a child of the Great Depression, I don't regard this as a very serious matter. You take lots of jobs and they poop out or you're not up to them or whatever.

You want to hear about my new book? What I've written is really very pessimistic. There's a Kilgore Trout story in the middle of this thing I keep trying to work. Since receiving the news of the death of his only child, his son, in a shipyard in Sweden in 1975, he's never submitted anything for publication. He's written all the time and thrown it away. The story he writes is called "The Sisters B36," and this is merely coincidence because this is a family name of a planet and a crab nebula. It's just coincidence. But there are these three sisters. One is a painter, one is a writer, and one is a scientist. And the painter and the writer are beloved by everybody and the scientist is regarded as very boring because all she wants to talk about is science, and nobody's interested, so she is secretly envious. She's a hypocritical woman, and she's the bad sister. She's envious of the popularity of her sisters. So she invents television. Up to that time, schools and parents have been devoted to teaching their children to respond elaborately to very minimal cues. The arrangements in the case of the writer sister, of twenty-six symbols, arranged in various ways, plus ten numbers, are used to paint the most elaborate verbal pictures. And education consists of the teachers not only teaching people how to pick up the words there but of asking, "Can't you see the man on the horse? Can't you see the volcano erupting? Can't you see this? Can't you see that?" That goes right along with literacy. And so the bad sister invents television, and imagining becomes completely unnecessary. And the television replaces everything that goes on in your own head. The teaching of imagination. So all anybody has to do is turn on a switch and you don't have to search for it in the head at all. There it all is. It's in color with professional actors. It's produced at the cost of millions of dollars with music underneath it and everything else. So this is a complete replacement of everything the imagination does. We come into the world with a computer which is a tabula rasa. It can be programmed to do anything. And up to the time that the wicked daughter invented television everybody had to learn to entertain themselves by developing imagination circuits. It's become unnecessary. The good sisters and the bad sister are all old ladies. They're on the Planet Booboo and people are looking at what the two good sisters did and wondering how on earth anybody could have been thrilled or responded at all to such minimal cues. Little black marks on paper. Or some dabs of paint on a flat surface. They can't imagine why anybody else got off on this, and then the wicked sister goes on to invent barbed wire, the machine gun, and the atom bomb. And it's all right with everybody. Because the only two people on the Planet BooBoo who can imagine the consequences are the two good sisters.

But anyway, I think it's really going to happen. I really think people are going to learn to do without the imagination circuits and I think they are what English departments have taught. Because you've harangued the people while they aren't picking up these very minimal signals, again twenty-six letters, ten numbers, and eight punctuation marks. You're haranguing them all the time. Imagine how Madame Bovary felt. Why did she fall in love with this fool? What was her husband thinking when he cut the Achilles' tendon in the village idiot and all that? They wouldn't be able to see it if you didn't harangue them the same time you were teaching them how to read. I think that's going to stop.

L: I'm finding I'm having to instruct them what to look for. They already have lost the cues on what to look for.

V: There's an amount of pressure that's brought on every student to imagine while reading. Because that was going to be the principle source of entertainment. Or to look at a painting. Fifty-three strokes at the most. I'll tell you what was worth a trip to England. We went to the Tate and they had the first big show of Eakins and, Jesus, he was good and they are finally acknowledging that he is. And what's so interesting about that show—I've seen a lot of Eakins stuff—is these portraits of middle–class Philadelphia people or upper class Philadelphia people. They told Eakins they would pose for him without realizing what he would see. But to see old people, family businesses have gone, things about their business have gone wrong, sons have gone off to war. . . . Finally over there, they're admitting that this American, this Philadelphia guy, is really good. And we also took in Freud's show. It was very depressing. He himself complained about these paintings that they are so ugly. They're all together in one place and he couldn't stand to look at them. But this Eakins thing is beautiful.

L: Getting back to the early novels, the women were mechanical and reactive. In the second half or particularly in the last three or four books, the women are very well accomplished as well as very nurturing. What do you think accounts for that shift?

V: Well, it's partly that I'm a child of my times, I think. It's probably completely responsive to what was going on.

   I taught at Iowa '65 and '66 in the Writer's Workshop. They admitted unqualified women for social balance and electricity in the classes. The stories they submitted as compared to what the men were submitting were inferior. Now it's reversed. I'd been back to Iowa before we went there together. The women were so excited and had tons to write about and the men were quite demoralized and had become what the women were.

L: I want to know who you're reading these days.

V: I'm liable to read anything. It could be an old book. We are swamped with a number of artists equivalent to the population of Florence. Not just renaissance artists, but just everybody living in Florence. A friend of mine out there, Sid Solomon, who is an old timey painter, who painted for the WPA and all that and was an artist in the Army and everything, said that in the thirties, he knew personally or knew of every artist in the United States. I, myself, have two daughters who are painters. There are so many that we can never begin to deal with it.

   You can go back to what literature used to be. It was just something you did with no hope of reward. It was a social act. Like cooking. You didn't expect to make your living that way.

   Again, you get back to feudalism. I think a state of that size is congenial. I've told people if I were a young writer now, I wouldn't get married because I couldn't support a family, and I'd go to Chicago and I'd tie in with one of those neighborhood theaters there. What's going on in local theaters is wonderful. I was on a committee for the American Academy of Arts and Letters reading all these beautiful play manuscripts that will have the life of a junebug, and that will be the end of it. But there are these wonderful, brief, artistic moments people are creating and they're just going to have to be satisfied with that because there's so much really interesting art around. Including my prints, may I say!

Part II

ESSAYS ON VONNEGUT

The Responsive Shaman: Kurt Vonnegut and His World

Peter J. Reed

One of the most remarkable features of the career of Kurt Vonnegut is its length. He has been publishing widely read fiction, either short stories or novels, for forty-five years. Few major American writers can match that longevity, or boast at such a point in their careers that all of their novels remain in print. This publication record, and the numbers attending his public speaking engagements, are testimony to the enduring relationship between Vonnegut and his audience. Perhaps as we pause to reevaluate Vonnegut it is worth considering not only the responses of his audience to his work but also what is integral to that, namely his response to the people that constitute his audience or, in short, to the society in which he lives. For Vonnegut is more than the social commentator who inflates social issues in his fiction for added relevance. He has spoken of himself as "a kind of shaman" who responds to the world around him and draws his energy from it, and also as a satirist in the tradition of Voltaire. In both these roles of shaman and satirist, Vonnegut's interaction with the world of his audience is essential and not merely elemental.

In recent years his shaman role has been most obvious in his nonfiction writing. Such pieces as "Requiem: The Hocus Pocus Laundromat" (1986)[1], "War Preparers Anonymous" (1987), or essays in *Palm Sunday* (1981) and *Fates Worse Than Death* (1991) demonstrate clearly why Vonnegut might call himself a shaman due to his quasi-religious moral commentary on contemporary society. In his 1976 interview with Robert Short, Vonnegut noted that after *Slaughterhouse-Five* (1969)[2] his writing would become less fictive and increasingly didactic (300). Such direct, personally stated commentary (as opposed to implied, briefly interjected, or fictionally cloaked commentary) first appears in the prefaces or introductory chapters to his novels after the addition of the 1965 "Introduction" to *Mother Night* (1961). It would be easy to conclude that this is the point at which he begins to address directly social issues that heretofore have been embedded, with whatever degree of transparency, within the fiction. What is more easily overlooked, however, is Vonnegut's beginnings as a writer. When examining his writing in high school and college, one is struck by the fact that though both Shortridge High School and Cornell had ample outlets for "creative writing," Vonnegut was writing journalism. His columns for the *Shortridge Daily Echo* and the *Cornell Sun* were written in response to what he saw going on in their respective communities. They may become anecdotal, even fictional, in the course of conveying their social commentary, but clearly the young Vonnegut felt a stronger impulse to write in response to behavior he observed around him than to fabricate stories. This impulse seems to have remained with him. In the film "Kurt Vonnegut: A Self-Portrait," he again observes that he needs something to react to, noting that while living on the Cape his long walks provided little creative stimulation whereas his morning outings in New York invariably make him mad at something. Vonnegut may have provided us with a model, in fact, with the Kilgore Trout of *Breakfast of Champions* (1973), who repeatedly observes something, responds to it as a phenomenon of human behavior, theorizes from the particular, then weaves a story around his generalization as a kind of illustration.

If Vonnegut is a shaman, though, he is an irreverent one, with laughter in his passionately moral voice. These characteristics were recognized by his early readers. It has become traditional to trace the beginnings of Vonnegut's popularity back to an underground audience consisting largely of students who passed his books around in the mid–1960s. The first academic critics to applaud him, such as Leslie Fiedler in his essay "The Divine Stupidity of Kurt Vonnegut," delighted in him because he *did* work in popular modes. The merging of critical respect and popular acclaim reached a peak at the start of the seventies after the publication and film adaptation of *Slaughterhouse-Five*. The times were right, of course; that text's antiwar theme was in complete accord with the moods of youth and academe. Vonnegut became something of a cult figure, a guru in the eyes of many of the young, as well a writer firmly established—at least among his contemporaries. The first books on Vonnegut joined the flow of articles, manifesting his stature in the world of academe as well as in popular culture. All this success produced some inevitable reaction. Even Vonnegut's life seems to have been in flux, as his marriage ended and he shifted from novel to play to novel again, eventually producing the then–controversial *Breakfast of Champions*, and some fiercely negative criticism began to appear.

Perhaps most conspicuous among the negative assessments of Vonnegut was the review of *Slapstick* (1976) written by Roger Sale that appeared in the *New York Times Book Review* on October 3, 1976. Sale is an intelligent and articulate spokesperson for the kind of pejorative criticism that, while not predominating, has sometimes been leveled at Vonnegut, especially in academic circles. An examination of Sale's characterization of Vonnegut's shortcomings might lead us to an assessment of his durable strengths.

First, Sale asserts: "One thing I resist in Vonnegut's books is that they seem formulaic, made of interchangeable parts. . . . Once Vonnegut finds what he takes to be a successful character, motif or phrase he can't bear to give it up, and so he carries it around from novel to novel" (3). Second, Sale objects that "all his novels flit about in time as pointlessly and arbitrarily as Billy Pilgrim does" (3). Third, Sale objects to Vonnegut's audience. "His appeal, so far as I can see, is to the slightly laid back, rather dropped out, minimally intelligent young." Vonnegut is "an ideal writer for the semi-literate young who are slightly too hip for *Jonathan Livingston Seagull* or *The Little Prince*"(20). Related to this point, Sale argues that the main reason for Vonnegut's appeal to this audience is that his "easy, sentimental cynicism leads him into endless parading of the dumb notion that life isn't much good in America because we're all stupid, unloving or both. . . . He offers the great assurance that there is nothing worth caring about" (20).

This leads Sale to a fourth point. Vonnegut's novels are replete with frivolous phrases that reveal a lazy flippancy about serious matters: the dismissive grunt of "so it goes," "and so on," or "hi ho." "Vonnegut had so much fun sprinkling 'so it goes' all over *Slaughterhouse-Five* and 'and so on' throughout *Breakfast of Champions* that he couldn't bear to leave *Slapstick* innocent of such confetti. [*Slapstick's*] 'Hi ho!' thus, is not just a bored grunt that disclaims all responsibility for having to look at something; it is a gesture of contempt for all writers who are willing to be responsible for their creations; for all readers who long to read real books; for anyone whose idea of America is more complicated than Vonnegut's country of interchangeable parts full of poor people with uninteresting lives"(20).

Sale's fifth and final point of contention is that Vonnegut's books never pose hard questions, never struggle with difficult issues, and have instead just become formulaic.

We can consider these points, as I said earlier, with the hope that denigration will reveal strengths. To begin, the charge that Vonnegut is a formulaic writer may be true to an extent, but two things should be said about that: First, most writers are formulaic, in the sense that an economy of method exists in their using and modifying techniques or reiterating themes; second, if it is true that Vonnegut is a formulaic writer, it is only superficially so. The opposing argument, that Vonnegut in fact shows great variety in both the subject and the construction of his novels, seems far more true. When one considers, for example, how he goes from an Orwellian anti-Utopian novel in *Player Piano* (1952) to a space opera in *The Sirens of Titan* (1959) to an entirely nonscience-fiction, first-person self-examination by a spy cum war criminal in *Mother Night*, one sees that these may be formulaic in the sense of fitting established generic modes, but that they show Vonnegut's variety in form and theme. If one looks at the way *Player Piano* is constructed with a central narrative, also initialed "P.P.," namely the story of Paul Proteus, around which are woven the "H" subplots of Hacketts, Hagstrohm, Halyard, and Haycox, and then at the continuous straight-line episodic narrative of *The Sirens of Titan*, it becomes apparent that these structures are not first and foremost formulaic. Contrast the dark, tragic *Mother Night* with the light, comic *Cat's Cradle* (1963) which follows it, and one sees great variety in tone. The novels written since *Slapstick* (1976), following Sale's review, extends even further the range and variety evident in Vonnegut's work.

As for Sale's charge that Vonnegut's novels flit "about in time as pointlessly and arbitrarily as Billy Pilgrim does," there is nothing any more pointless and arbitrary about the journey of Vonnegut's Pilgrim than there is of John Bunyan's, and several of Vonnegut's protagonists follow carefully plotted mythic journeys. His plots, beginning with *Cat's Cradle* and *Slaughterhouse-Five*, are often presented with the disjointedness that is characteristic of postmodernism, but Vonnegut's uses of time and space are seldom arbitrary or pointless. They afford new perspectives; they emphasize connections, disconnections, or mere coincidence; and, as James Lundquist has observed, they contribute an element of humor to ideas that might otherwise be unpalatable (86–87). So when, for example, in *Slaughterhouse-Five* Vonnegut "flits" from the destruction of Sodom and Gomorrah to Hiroshima to the Tralfamadorians' ending the world with an explosion of their flying saucer fuel, we know he is placing the bombing of Dresden in a context that makes its unique horrors all the more terrible for their having a place in a continuum of self-inflicted disasters. Or consider another humorous flitting in time and space: In *Slaughterhouse-Five* Vonnegut says, "When a Tralfamadorian sees a corpse, all he thinks is that the dead person is in a bad condition in that particular moment" (27)—this in a novel that describes the destruction of a city and the incineration of perhaps 100,000 people. So, the personal experience of mass slaughter juxtaposed against the perspective that death is nothing more than being in a bad condition in a certain moment provides an eloquent contrast. Possibly the humor about death helps the reader contend with the horror, but more likely it underscores the absurdity of such slaughter emphasizes that the Tralfamadorians' seemingly ludicrous explanation is no more absurd than any official, or logically intended, explanation.

In response to Sale's criticism of Vonnegut's semi-literate and slightly laid back audience, I would be inclined to question the validity of both the technique and the assumptions behind this criticism. The kind of audience Sale describes does not sound like one that makes an author enduringly popular, though it might explain fads; and if I were to characterize my impression of Vonnegut's audience based on just as much hard information as Roger Sale has, I would attribute to it a much more varied composition in age, literacy, and motivation than he suggests. Sale's related point, though, that Vonnegut offers an "easy, sentimental cynicism" and "the great assurance that there is nothing worth caring about," needs more thought. It must be conceded that Vonnegut is sometimes sentimental, frequently cynical, and often gives the *appearance* of ease. But this is one of the criticisms of Vonnegut that was addressed in the *New Republic* on September 22, 1979, by a former student, John Irving. Irving notes that John Gardner makes a very similar criticism of Vonnegut. Gardner has suggested that Vonnegut slips away from the moral issues, lacks commitment and concern for his characters, and that this makes his writing slight. Gardner feels art is "essentially and primarily moral—that is, life giving—" and here Vonnegut fails (quoted in Irving 44).

Both Gardner and Sale, then, criticize Vonnegut for a cynicism that gives up on life. Perhaps a superficial reading of "hi ho" and "so it goes" deflects them from the observation that Vonnegut keeps on being *bothered* that so much in life *does* make him feel cynical, that he keeps on trying to cheer, trying to inform, trying to affirm, trying, even, to preach. This larger persistence underlies the surface dismissiveness and, in fact, gives it meaning, as we shall see when we come to those "frivolous phrases." Surely his continuing appeal for "human decency" is moral and life giving. Surely his having Chrono in *The Sirens of Titan*, after one of the most blighted childhoods conceivable, return to say, "Thank you, Mother and Father, for the gift of life," belies a defeated cynicism (312). And surely the whole point of the remarkable journey of Melody at the end of *Slapstick* is designed *precisely* to transcend the cynicism of Wilbur Swain's narrative, to create a new Miranda who really can discover a "brave new world" in Prospero's shabby old one.

Those "frivolous phrases" Sale complains of also offend John Gardner, who complains of "the seeming cold-heartedness and trivial mindedness of his famous comment on the American fire-bombing of Dresden, 'So it goes,' a desperate, perhaps overcensored attitude mindlessly echoed by the turned-off and cynical" (quoted in Irving, 44). There's that turned-off, laid-back, cynical audience again! But as I argued twenty-five years ago when writing about *Slaughterhouse-Five*, to label that phrase as detached or dismissive or trivial is to miss its point entirely. It seems to me that the whole intent is to make it *appear* trivial; until by the very persistence of its repetition and the sharp disparity between its seeming flippancy and the poignancy of the deaths so punctuated that the effect emerges as one that emphasizes compassion and exasperation. Similarly, in a January 13, 1973, piece in the *New York Times* called "Thinking Unthinkable, Speaking Unspeakable," Vonnegut asserted that America has cultivated a mercenary warrior class in its midst. "We have made our soldiers ghastly by giving them ghastly things to do. Too bad" (31). And he ends with this society's most ubiquitous and annoyingly flippant phrase; "Sorry about that." Once again the impropriety of the catch phrase is stark and calculated; it effectively reverses on itself so that the hackneyed suddenly recovers it literal meaning, and we are not only made to feel Vonnegut's conviction that this *is* too bad and that he *is* sorry about it, but also to recognize that the situation is one we have been dismissing with the scant attention those phrases typically imply. The frivolousness, then, is not in Vonnegut but in his world, in us. Vonnegut suggests that our easy attitudes toward war and militarism might seem to imply that we *do* in fact feel nonchalance about death and destruction.

Sale's final, and potentially most weighty point, is that Vonnegut disdains responsibility to struggle with the difficult questions. John Gardner again pointed out a related flaw, suggesting Vonnegut hedges moral affirmations. Yet Vonnegut's moral certitude is often remarkable. Take, for example, the passage near the end of *Mother Night* where he speaks through the morally ambiguous Howard Campbell:

"There are plenty of good reasons for fighting," I said, "but no good reason ever to hate without reservation, to imagine that God Almighty Himself hates with you, too. Where's evil? It's that large part of every man that wants to hate without limit, that wants to hate with God on its side. It's *that* part of every man that finds all kinds of ugliness so attractive" (181).

And surely few writers have taken public stands on so many moral issues as has Kurt Vonnegut.

Probably Irving is right in suggesting that Sale and others are misled by "the childlike availability of his prose, its fast and easy-to-read surfaces" (41). Sometimes this simplicity, when applied to complex issues, shows us our failure previously to have considered the possibility of other perspectives. Sometimes it makes us wonder if we have not missed the obvious all along. Frequently the almost impishly adolescent tone helps strip ideas of false reverence. The contrived naivete of the description is frequently Vonnegut's device to defamiliarize the familiar or to deconstruct the official myths created to obscure the true nature of events. In addition, there is the general point that Irving makes in response to Sale:

Why is "readable" such a bad thing to be these days? . . . As someone who, like Roger Sale, "has struggled many hard hours with the semi-literate young," I am more often gratified by a writer who has accepted the enormous effort necessary to make writing clear. Vonnegut's lucidity is hard and brave work in a literary world where pure messiness is frequently thought to be a sign of some essential wrestling with the "hard questions." Good writers have always shown that hard questions must also be posed and answered cleanly and well. It is as if Roger Sale—and he's hardly alone; I use him as an example of many—is championing a literature for second-year graduate students, a literature dependent on interpretation. (42)

The interesting thing is that the best response to Sale's criticism was already in print before he made it. In a review of the reissued *Mother Night* published in the *New York Times Book Review* for February 4, 1973, Doris Lessing spoke of Vonnegut's responsibility in not flinching from the complexities of difficult moral questions. She says:

The force of Vonnegut's questioning is such that one has to sit down to think, to define degrees. . . . He makes me remember . . . that when Nazism was not stopped, but flowered . . . into the expected and forecast war, how soon our judgments became swayed by the horribleness of what was going on. . . . Good and Evil became polarized into Us and Them and quite forgotten was the knowledge that the war could have been prevented if our governments had wanted. What Vonnegut deals with, always, is responsibility: Whose fault was it all—the gas chambers, the camps, the degradations and the debasements of all our standards? Whose? Well, *ours* as much as *theirs*.

This is so, that is, provided you can believe in responsibility at all—it is here that Vonnegut is moral in an old-fashioned way. He does take full weight of responsibility, while more and more people are coming to see humanity's slide into chaos as beyond our prevention, our will, our choice. The strength of Kurt Vonnegut, Jr., derives from his refusal to succumb to this new and general feeling of helplessness. (35)

For Doris Lessing, then, Vonnegut's fiction does not offer only "easy, sentimental cynicism" or "the great assurance that there is nothing worth caring about."

What I hope this contention with Roger Sale serves to illustrate is that the reverse of his claim is true: that Vonnegut is intensely and directly involved with his audience and is bringing it to face (and bear) the hard questions of its times. One register of his success may be that Vonnegut continues to be in demand as a novelist, with his sales still high and all of his books still in print. Not that popularity necessarily denotes thought-provoking influence, but sales do suggest that while Vonnegut's social commentary is frequently topical, it also apparently transcends merely short-term appeal and remains relevant. Another register is the continuing demand for him as an invited commentator on various social issues and as a speaker. He is being clearly identified as not merely provocative and entertaining but profound. He is known for his original insights and the courage and honesty to declare them, and he is even thought of as something of a moral beacon in our murky times. In this respect it appears that the judgment of time, of successive generations of readers, leans toward validating his role as "shaman."

Earlier I claimed that the origins of Vonnegut's particular mode of interaction with the world of his audience are evident in his early journalism. It has always seemed to me that his apprenticeship in this medium has received too little attention. It might go far toward explaining many characteristics of his writing as well as of his working methods. Vonnegut's writing for the *Shortridge Daily Echo* is not always easy to identify, but there are strong clues to his authorship of some columns. Notable are the "Bull Session" columns of 1939 and 1940, which are usually signed "Ferdinand" (from *Ferdinand the Bull*) or some variant of that name. Often these columns, like the other contributions that may be his, are concerned only with the high school social world. Sometimes, however, a more serious note emerges. On September 29, 1939, the page 2 editorial (he is listed as the paper's "2nd Page Columnist" on Tuesdays) contains a strong antiwar statement. Another page 2 editorial (September 26, 1939) contains a brief comment on Hitler and the invasion of Poland. After Vonnegut becomes an editor, the paper carries an editorial titled "Mutual Apathy and Propaganda," which talks of the dangers of propaganda, our vulnerability to it, and its success in the Axis countries (April 30, 1940). So while both Vonnegut and his high school audience viewed him as a light commentator on social happenings and as a humorist, serious subjects also emerged to which he would later return. It is equally noteworthy that while Shortridge had a fiction club, and much poetry and fiction was published by the *Daily Echo*, Vonnegut seems to have had no part in this. He was the journalist, his writing coming mostly in response to events in the school's social life and sometimes to national affairs.

At Cornell, Vonnegut's seventeen "Well All Right" columns in the *Sun* were also mostly light-hearted commentaries on campus life. His first column in this series (April 22, 1941), however, is an interesting foretaste of the Vonnegut of

Mother Night. It tells of meeting on a bus a recruit who is full of enthusiasm for his new military training, including bayonet drill, and who yearns for some real Germans to practice it on. The column concludes:

He hates Germans—all of 'em.
    We were going to ask him what he had against Beethoven but we decided that we probably wouldn't get a very good answer.

His third column is hardly serious but turns to the war again in addressing the draft's impact on fraternity finances. His next column, "Finding the News in the News" (May 22, 1941), returns to the serious issues focusing on one that has never ceased to preoccupy Vonnegut: censorship. He discusses the pro-British biasing of news about the invasion of Crete and the suppressing of reports of anti-British riots in Malaya. "You must weigh the FACTS you have found—and you may not have found many—yourself. Don't let your newspaper do it for you. . . . We must know the shortcomings of the British—and of ourselves—as well as of the Germans" (4). These columns are thoughtfully resistant to much jingoism of the times—not that Vonnegut was alone at this date in his resistance to American entry into the war. His column of October 13, 1941, "We Chase the Lone Eagle and End Up on the Wrong Side of the Fence," brings this conflict of public feeling to the fore. Vonnegut wrote a staunch defense of Charles Lindbergh, questioned the motives of America's going to war, and again chided (Howard Campbell–style) the American male's propensity for finding a target for unqualified hate. It is a strongly stated column, and draws a disclaimer from his editor. Pearl Harbor settles these issues for Vonnegut, at least in a practical sense, and in his last column (May 4, 1942) he is facing up to going into the army as a private. In sum, the *Cornell Sun* illustrates again Vonnegut's tendency to write in direct response to events in his world around him. Many of the columns are primarily entertainment oriented, even if satirical, but the ones I have noted, especially the Lindbergh defense, address serious issues and reveal Vonnegut's willingness to take moral stands against popular opinion. In the late 1930s he was already opposing uncritical thinking, jingoistic patriotism, capitalist–dominated foreign policy, and censorship, all of which become hallmarks of his later work.

    To trace the pattern of the inclusion of world and national events in all of Vonnegut's fiction and to show how so much of his writing seems to be triggered by responses to them would be tiresomely redundant. Let me confine myself to a selection of illustrations from the fiction since *Breakfast of Champions*. That novel, of course, is replete with such direct social commentary since it commences with the statement, "I have no culture" (Vonnegut 1973, 5), and goes on to document America's lack of a coherent, humane culture. A specific point of interest is the considerable space devoted to the black convict Wayne Hoobler and his experiences in prison. At the time Vonnegut was deeply concerned about prisons and prison reform in the country as a result of the involvement of his friend, Tom Wicker, in the negotiations that ended the Attica prison riots of 1971.

In *Jailbird* (1979), Vonnegut's starting point is the Watergate affair, and he draws many real-life characters into his plot. There is satire in the participants' turning crime into profit by writing books and in conveniently timed rebirths to religious fundamentalism. Vonnegut's creation of the RAMJAC Corporation, owner of everything, makes comment on the wave of mergers, takeovers, and conglomerate formation then sweeping the country. Vonnegut puts this accumulation of such vast wealth and power in the context of America's newly growing population of homeless and working poor through the characterization of the (seeming) bag-lady, Mary Kathleen O'Looney. *Jailbird* looks back to the early days of union formation in the United States, to the depression and the left-wing politics which flourished in the thirties, and to the House Un–American Activities Committee and McCarthyism of the fifties. This provides a historical context for Vonnegut's commentary on labor law, the distribution of the nation's wealth, and social justice. His response to Watergate, then, far transcends that particular event. Notably, it reaches not just to those who have lived through Watergate but also to those generations who can remember Roy Cohn and Joe McCarthy or the Great Depression or even Sacco and Vanzetti.

Galápagos (1985) makes reference to a wealth of contemporary material. A third world war is triggered by a worldwide economic collapse brought about by overwhelming third–world debt. But when humans (except the few survivors on the Galápagos Islands) are exterminated it is by a virus that obviously invokes the contemporaneous shock over the spread of AIDS. The book's theme of human evolution seems to grow from the creationism-evolution controversy raging in the country's schools and courts. The seeming supremacy of Japanese technology is introduced in the form of Zenji Hiroguchi, inventor of the computers Mandarax and Gokubi, which themselves seem to comment on the headlong evolution of microcomputers as well as, in their names, seeming to echo the contemporary rage for Rubik's Cube.

In Vonnegut, these references to what is current are more than general allusions or easy topical inclusions. Inevitably they are woven into the very fabric of the fiction and sometimes, as with Watergate in *Jailbird* or evolution in *Galápagos*, they appear to be its actual source. The degree of thought and detail in the development of these materials is remarkable. In *Jailbird*, for example, the Sacco and Vanzetti case, which in its punishment of proletarian-minded and probably innocent victims makes such an effective foil to the Watergate affair, is developed with considerable historical detail and with moral judgment. In *Galápagos* the equivalent might be his inclusion of Huntington's chorea, a rare disease which raises important questions about evolution. Huntington's is a hereditary disease which does not manifest itself until midlife but then proves fatal. One characteristic is that it produces an unusually strong sex drive in its carrier. This prompts the question of whether the urge to survive might not be gene driven rather than species driven. So again we see Vonnegut in his shaman role, questioning and teaching, and often preaching, pressing the moral imperatives that his scrutiny of events exposes.

In his 1976 interview with Robert Short, Vonnegut says, "People *can* be instructed. People can take *lessons*, and so they can go *beyond* what they must be. One of my complaints about this country is how little teaching goes on, particularly by the president" (306). Earlier in the same interview he makes a prediction about his fiction: "There'll be more and more to complain about in my fiction. People will say it's not fiction any more, it's editorializing. And, you know, the stories are getting sketchier and sketchier and sketchier" (300). Perhaps that is hyperbolic, but in terms of the relative balance between story and editorial in his work Vonnegut may have predicted accurately. About the complaints, his prediction seems to be less accurate. The reaction I have heard from audiences attending his "How to Get a Job Like Mine" evenings is one of pleasure in hearing someone who *was* prepared to instruct, to challenge, to take bold moral stands, in stark contrast to what was coming from most political candidates at the same time. As ever, Vonnegut's ability to amuse and delight with the humor and inventiveness of his stories and the charm of his personal style helps win and hold audiences. That, too, is important to Vonnegut, and he has spoken several times of his comedian-like role, helping to make life bearable. The shaman is also a comforter. Vonnegut's relationship to his audience, though, is not based on giving it comfortable half truths, and that is where Sale is so wrong about Vonnegut, his view of the contemporary human condition, his approach to his audience, and even about that audience. Vonnegut approaches us with a respect shown in his honesty, shows us the world we share, teaches, chides, understands, and comforts. He is the shaman who tries to teach us what he once described as the goal of his family's atheist tradition: how "to behave virtuously within the biological limits of being human beings" (Short, 289).

NOTES

1. "The Hocus Pocus Laundromat." *Swords and Ploughshares*. Nottingham, England: Bertrand Russell Peace Foundation, 1987.

2. *Slaughterhouse-Five*. New York: Delacorte/Seymour Lawrence, 1968.

WORKS CITED

Cornell Sun, Cornell University, Ithaca, New York. Cited issues, 1941–1942.

Fiedler, Leslie A. "The Divine Stupidity of Kurt Vonnegut." *Esquire* 24(3) (September 1970): 202–204.

Irving, John. "Kurt Vonnegut and His Critics." *New Republic* (22 September 22 1979): 41–49.

Lessing, Doris. "Vonnegut's Responsibility." *New York Times Book Review* (4 February 1973): 35.

Lundquist, James. *Kurt Vonnegut*. New York: Frederick Ungar, 1977.

Sale, Roger. Review of *Slapstick*. *New York Times Book Review* (3 October 1976): 3, 20–21.

Short, Robert. "Robert Short Interviews Kurt Vonnegut, Chicago—June 8, 1976." *Something to Believe In*. San Francisco: Harper and Row, 1978.

Shortridge Daily Echo, Shortridge High School, Indianapolis, Indiana. Cited issues, 1939–1940.

Vonnegut, Kurt. *Breakfast of Champions*. New York: Delacorte, 1973.

———. *Cat's Cradle*. New York: Dell, 1963.

———. *Fates Worse Than Death*. New York: G. P. Putnam's Sons, 1991.

———. *Galápagos*. New York: Delacorte, 1985.

———. *Jailbird*. New York: Delacorte, 1979.

———. "Kurt Vonnegut: A Self Portrait." 29 minute film, Films for the Humanities, Princeton, New Jersey, FFH 129, 1975.

———. *Mother Night*. New York: Harper and Row, 1961.

———. *Palm Sunday*. New York: Delacorte, 1987.

———. *Player Piano*. New York: Dell, 1952.

———. "Requiem: the Hocus Pocus Laundromat." *North American Review* 271 (December 1986): 29-35.

———. *Slapstick*. New York: Delacorte, 1976.

———. *Slaughterhouse-Five*. New York: Delacorte/Seymour Lawrence, 1968.

———."The Hocus Pocus Laundromat." *Swords and Ploughshares*. Nottingham, England: Bertrand Russell Peace Foundation, 1987.

———. *The Sirens of Titan*. New York: Dell, 1959.

———. "Thinking Unthinkable, Speaking Unspeakable." *New York Times* (13 January 1973): 31.

———. "War Preparers Anonymous." *Harpers* 268 (March 1987): 4.

Kurt Vonnegut: Public Spokesman

Jerome Klinkowitz

It was "as funny a lecture as I had ever listened to," reported Granville Hicks—no small praise from that old irascible advocate of social realism and political pertinence from the 1930s, who as the turbulent 1960s concluded was asked to introduce Kurt Vonnegut to his readers in the *Saturday Review*. Ostensibly reviewing *Slaughterhouse-Five* (1969), a nontraditional and defiantly anti-illusionistic novel worlds apart from the sociologically based fiction Hicks had been advocating for nearly half a century, he solved that oldest of journalistic problems by finding his lead not in the surely puzzling pages of this strange new book but rather in the warmly human and spectacularly funny impression the real Kurt Vonnegut had made on him at a literary festival the year before.

Seeing Vonnegut's name on the program, both Hicks and the student audience had assumed they were about to hear a science fiction author. This was 1968, after all, and the only Vonnegut novels then in print were dressed up as either space opera or spy thrillers. But after hearing him speak, no one could mistake Kurt Vonnegut for a Harlan Ellison, Isaac Asimov, or even for his own affectionately drawn portrait of the perennially misunderstood science fiction writer, Kilgore Trout. "What he really is," Hicks announced, "is a sardonic humorist and satirist in the vein of Mark Twain and Jonathan Swift." Twain and Swift, of course, are two of the English language's great public writers, addressing the major issues of their day in the most direct manner and in the most personably appropriate voice. There was much of that same quality in Vonnegut, Hicks learned in the audience that night, and he encountered it again in the pages of *Slaughterhouse-Five* (where the same real-life Kurt Vonnegut speaks directly in chapters 1 and 10).

Hicks' remarks were brought to Vonnegut's attention over twenty years later when I sent him a copy of my *Slaughterhouse-Five: Reinventing the Novel and the World*. They were what he singled out for attention in the letter he sent thanking me for the volume. He remembered that the *Saturday Review* was one of the first periodicals to praise his just-published novel, but had forgotten that Hicks had heard his speech the year before. "It really makes a difference, I find," he remarked, "if people hear me speak."

Abundant arguments have been made for the personally vocal qualities of Vonnegut's fiction: from the way he incorporates not just his own personality but also crucial elements from his autobiography into almost all of his mature works (beginning with the Iowa City preface to the 1966 edition of *Mother Night*) to his Twainian distrust of all language except the vernacular ("I myself find that I trust my own writing most, and others seem to trust it most, too, when I sound most like a person from Indianapolis, which is what I am," he admits on page 79 of *Palm Sunday*). What confirms the value of this strain in his work is the methodology it reveals within his style of composition. Because so much of what Vonnegut does results from the interaction of himself with his material, it is helpful to see the man himself in action. Like a jazz musician improvising a solo within the constructs of a familiar melody and set of chord changes, or an abstract expressionist painter using the canvas not as a surface upon which to represent but an arena within which to act, Vonnegut engages his subject but also the context in which it exists—which, in truly Heisenbergian fashion, involves himself as part of the experiment.

Were we privileged to see the author at work, hunched over his manual typewriter and improvising pages, one at a time, on his chosen themes, we might observe the process in his fiction. As it is, audiences at his speeches see and hear the same process at work virtually every time Vonnegut presents a lecture—few of which have ever restricted themselves to the prepared text. Indeed, his stump speech of the 1980s, "How to Get a Job Like Mine," was drawn from a loose-leaf binder of materials—editorials, protest letters, autobiographical musings, current news items, pages from his fiction in progress, and even a section from his rejected master's thesis from the late 1940s—which he would flip through and extract items as suited his mood and his listeners'. But from it Vonnegut would construct an hour's worth of wisdom and entertainment uniquely appropriate to the occasion at hand. Like a jazz musician's solo, it was different and familiar at the same time, just as any canvas by an action master painter bears the stamp of his or her style even though the specific work may be as distinctive as Jackson Pollock's "Blues Poles" and "Full Fathom Five."

In my own collection of Vonnegut materials are tapes of four speeches given over the broad range of his career, two of which I was lucky enough to attend myself. The first tape dates from a November 21, 1967, appearance at Ohio State University, where Vonnegut delivered a lecture titled "Address: To Celebrate the Accession of the Two Millionth Volume in the Collections of the Libraries of The Ohio State University." This is the only instance I know of where a yet-to-be-famous Kurt Vonnegut is captured on tape for posterity. After 1969 and the success of *Slaughterhouse-Five* he became one of the most interviewed, filmed, and televised authors in America, with a long list of speeches gaining national attention (such as his commencement speech at Bennington which was reported as the lead item in *Time* magazine's June 29, 1970, issue). But in 1967 Vonnegut had yet to be discovered and was in fact often misunderstood—in this case by the ceremony's organizer, Professor Matthew J. Bruccoli, who was following William F. Buckley's lead at *National Review* (where Vonnegut's short story "Harrison Bergeron" was reprinted on November 16, 1965) in assuming that Vonnegut was an outspoken political conservative.

Vonnegut, of course, is anything but a right-wing activist, and at Columbus he takes great delight in confounding expectations. He begins, as he would in speeches after he had become not just a recognized major author but an international celebrity as well, by disclaiming any merit for his speech. In this case, he explains, it will be impossible for him to simultaneously read his prepared text and maintain the sense of timing and audience interaction that good comedy demands. (His solution, it turns out, will be to use his speech as one of several texts to which he will refer in an offhand manner, much like comedian Mort Sahl's technique of improvising responses to a daily newspaper.) This introductory dichotomy leads to another, which becomes both the recurrent theme and organizing principle of his address: the irony of having Kurt Vonnegut, a college dropout, lecture at a university in celebration of its library's two millionth book.

That irony begins with some silly but exquisitely timed jokes and develops into a revealing portrait of both Vonnegut's beliefs in literature and the nature of his own literary art. Because he dropped out of so many universities (not revealing that it was the World War II draft that took him out of his first college and then transferred him in and out of two others during his training) and subsequently pursued life in the commercial rather than academic world, he admits that he has done a lot more browsing for reading materials in bus stations than in libraries—it would be more appropriate, he suggests, for him to be dedicating a new Greyhound Bus Terminal today. Here he encountered what the times considered tawdry fare: novels by D. H. Lawrence and Henry Miller, banned in respectable editions until the Supreme Court decisions of 1966, just a year before. This fascination with "dirty books" will pop up again and again, but first Vonnegut digresses to another point of irony: that without so much as an undergraduate degree he has just spent two years teaching M.F.A. students in the University of Iowa's postgraduate writing program.

How did he manage as a professor? By trying to follow a colleague's advice and not telling the class everything he knew in the first hour. Vonnegut's repertoire was actually used up in the first three minutes, he reveals to his audience at Ohio State. He sets down his microphone on the podium and walks over to a blackboard on which he performs a teacherly chalk-talk to the audience's great amusement. The topic itself is, we now know, drawn from the second of his rejected Master's theses in anthropology at the University of Chicago, "Fluctuations between Good and Evil in Simple Tales." In Columbus, Vonnegut uses it for a series of intertextual enfoldings, for as he scratches away between the vertical axis of "good fortune" and "bad fortune" and the horizontal axis of the hero or heroine's progress, he is simultaneously making fun of his teaching of literature and demonstrating how even the greatest of stories work (his examples range from a cartoon version of "Cinderella" to Kafka's "The Metamorphosis"). His conclusion comes as a casual disclaimer—"OK, that's what I taught at Iowa"—but the lesson has been an effective one, showing not just how the lowest forms of writing share elemental structures with the highest, but that such patterns can be elucidated by a dropout chemistry major who has used his GI Bill benefits to take advanced courses in anthropology.

With this reminder of the purportedly vulgar kinds of books that exist, Vonnegut makes another transition that one could call radical and even disorganized were it not for its idiosyncratic relation to his topic: the sex lives of writers. Do the men who write novels, dirty or otherwise, make good conjugal partners? Like Mort Sahl mocking the petty lunacies that we all encounter in the day's newspaper, Vonnegut pulls out a copy of *Cosmopolitan* magazine and starts quoting from its story on the Kinsey Report. Several citations are hilarious enough by themselves, but by virtue of illustrations from his own life Vonnegut makes them still funnier. But even here there is a lesson: Sex alone does not sell novels. Henry Miller's *The Rosy Crucifixion* has the most sex Vonnegut knows about in any book, and it is a poor seller. What stimulates sales is not sex per se but rather sex about somebody in show business, preferably based on rumors from the gossip columns. And even then such works are produced neither for titillation nor as reading material at all. Their purchasers are "lonely salesgirls" who are buying membership in a community that spends its off-duty time with books like these—the latest Jacqueline Susann, Jackie Collins, or Harold Robbins blockbuster, the owning of any one of which is simply "a cheap way of saying hello."

Nevertheless, everyone thrills at the notion of "dirty books." Considering the staggering number of volumes housed in the Ohio State University Library, Vonnegut asks a simple question that elicits gales of laughter: "Two million! I wonder how many of them are dirty?" Then even more laughter for his next question: "Which is the dirtiest?" Such a question is itself a joke, and its unanswerability is what prompts laughter—the laughter of relief at not having to come up with a serious answer, as Vonnegut has explained in *Palm Sunday* (1981) and elsewhere. But his question nevertheless prompts some others, for which there are indeed opinions, if not airtight judgments. All those books! Which is the greatest? *Ulysses*. The noblest? *The Brothers Karamazov*. The most effective? *The Catcher in the Rye*. The most humane? *The Tenants of Moonbloom*. The most important? As readers of *Slaughterhouse-Five* would be told again in less than a year and a half, *Death on the Installment Plan*, certainly an important book to Vonnegut just now since it was teaching him how to face the unspeakable nature of the Dresden firebombing that had kept his masterwork unwritten for over twenty years. All those books! Which leads to the story of another dropout, this time from Ohio State University itself: James Thurber, who stopped attending classes and just went to the library and read the books that interested him. Which book had been number two million? Wouldn't it be nice if it were one of Thurber's?

Like the other lists Vonnegut has been citing (colleges he dropped out of, statistics from the sex lives of authors, frequency of love scenes in paperback best-sellers), his catalogue of superlative titles is at once a parody and a serious lesson. That such lists can be reeled off is at once reductive and expansive, just like the library itself. And just as writing books is important (he digresses to tell how the story of Jesus Christ's crucifixion could be written more effectively, an episode later appearing in *Slaughterhouse-Five*), maintaining access to them is crucial for a free society. Although the typical English class turns the experience of literature into a version of hell week lasting all semester (here Vonnegut ticks off a syllabus assigning another 700 page classic every five days), there is always the library (for James Thurber) and the bus station paperback rack (for Kurt Vonnegut).

The irony, of course, is that at the present moment in 1967 the Columbus Greyhound Terminal probably had more Vonnegut titles available than did the university library with its massive collections. And on those paperback racks *The Sirens of Titan* (1959) was still being marketed as a dirty book, in print runs of hundreds of thousands, while any library searching for a copy had to unearth one of the just 2,500 hardcovers published years before. That is the subtext Vonnegut has been exploiting throughout his lecture as he has talked about himself, "dirty books," and a half dozen other apparent digressions. He starts displaying boredom (whether feigned or real), flips through his remaining notes, and comments on the egalitarian nature of book publishing, which can cost as little as $2,000 per title and be accomplished by as few as three people (the author, editor, and publisher), as opposed to the millions of dollars and hundreds of people needed to make a movie. That remark, in response to the newsworthiness of Marshall McLuhan's pronouncement that reading is dead, takes just a minute; and in just fifteen seconds more Vonnegut ticks off three other topical interests (marijuana, censorship, and astronauts reaching the moon) in a way that appears to reduce them to the trivia. What has mattered is his own engagement with literature and his audience's engagement with him, an experience that has filled the past hour and in no small way has helped create a readership for *Slaughterhouse-Five* and his other works that would be republished in its wake.

In my second tape, from almost ten years later, Vonnegut addresses an audience to whom he is not a stranger but a popular and even beloved figure. The occasion was his visit to the school where I and several of his former students and close friends teach, the University of Northern Iowa, on March 31, 1977. In the past decade he had gone from an unknown writer of bus station paperbacks and stories for the popular magazines to one of America's best-known and most eminent authors. He had had three novels top the best-seller charts, a play produced on Broadway, and *Slaughterhouse-Five* brought to even greater public attention as a major motion picture (directed by Arthur Penn). Several censorship cases had become celebrated causes. In the early 1970s he had been treated, much against his will, as a guru to disaffected youth of the Haight-Ashbury/Kent State era; now, in 1977, he had more willingly assumed the role of public spokesman on much larger issues concerning national and global conditions.

Yet even though his reputation has been transformed into something almost larger than life, it is the same Kurt Vonnegut who speaks in 1977 as 1967. Back at Ohio State, he had played his own reputedly vulgar status against the solemnly intellectual nature of the occasion and the audience's academic expectations. For Northern Iowa, he begins with the same technique, transposed to accommodate his change from anonymity to celebrity. His title, "Kurt Vonnegut: A Self-Interview," presumes just such fame and is built on what his audience expects it knows about him. To catalyze his relationship with this audience and generate the participatory attention a good speech needs to succeed, Vonnegut begins by confounding those expectations.

"How many of you," he asks his listeners, "believe in the value of meditation, of the inward contemplation recommended by the great Eastern religions?" Hands shoot up across the auditorium, as hundreds of eager students among the audience of nearly 2,000 seek to identify their case with his.

"Well, you're all full of crap," Vonnegut tells them, at once deflating their pretentions and correcting an erroneous expectation of his fame. The hand-raisers are shocked, while those who kept their hands in their laps are now both laughing and applauding this slightly cruel joke. Vonnegut joins the laughter, but in a warmly forgiving rather than critically sarcastic way, as if to remind us that for many years in the early seventies the joke had been on him (as it surely had been, from having to chase hippies off his suburban lawn in West Barnstable to warding off the endorsements of LSD cultists who presumed he was on their side). Yet even while he and the audience are laughing, there is a point to be made: that meditation and contemplation alone are too passive for much good to come from them alone, and that the more common practice of reading books (and reacting to them imaginatively) is a much better technique for growth and learning.

From here Vonnegut moves to another aspect of his fame: his status as a best-selling author whose works are filmed by Hollywood. Both practices rub against his fundamental belief in how a society should best operate. The ideal, he recalls from his anthropological training, is to have a folk society of about 2,000 people, in which there will be a role and meaningful work for everyone, including artists, musicians, and even a few storytellers. But now, in the mass-market culture America must produce, one musician performs on records and television for 200 million people. For writers it becomes a case of being a best-seller or going bust; there are just a few who can publish in such circumstances, he says, adding, "Thank God I'm one of them."

Most pernicious of all is the economic system that produces movies—a topic that had been part of Vonnegut's speech back in 1967 at Ohio State. Now, as a famous writer who has had his work transposed to the screen, he is even more aware of the dictatorial power of Hollywood economics. It is so expensive to make films, he has learned, that the medium excludes any possibility of individual expression. And the result, which is viewed passively by audiences being shown what to imagine, has given up the generative power than fuels great literature and rewards imaginatively active reading.

From here Vonnegut moves into the printed portion of his text, the "Self-Interview" soon to be published in the *Paris Review* (and eventually collected in *Palm Sunday*). The text itself is a transformation of several others, including fragments of four separate interviews done over the years by various people, none of whom had succeeded in getting a handle on Vonnegut and his art. So in intertextual fashion Vonnegut takes these unsuccessful bits and pieces and knits them together into a coherent narrative centered not just on himself but on the nature of his interviewing himself. For the audience at Northern Iowa, whose reaction is an integral part of this section of his speech, Vonnegut dramatizes the textual dilemma by saying he will use his "real voice" to speak his answers and a phony speaking voice to read the questions. The joke comes when he shifts into a comically squeaky timbre for the interview, asserting that is his true natural voice, and that for his previous remarks he has already been using the fake style which now signifies the interviewer. The physical difficulties in both employing and listening to such a voice soon allow Vonnegut to announce that he is giving it up, which brings the humor full circle.

As at Ohio State, Vonnegut works his audience by working himself. The "Self-Interview" especially shows him making art from his responses to life, then testing and adjusting that art by trying it out on the audience—a live audience here, and for his publications "the audience of strangers," which he has always told his students to face each time they write. In Columbus, Vonnegut had concluded his speech by testing out a section from *Slaughterhouse-Five*. Ten years later in Cedar Falls he is sufficiently eminent for his reading from a work-in-progress to be labeled as such, and the speech concludes with ten pages from "Unacceptable Air," a passage that later grew into Vonnegut's ninth novel, *Jailbird* (1979).

Another decade would be less kind to Kurt Vonnegut. In the 1980s his successive novels were best-sellers, but not always number one, as they had been in the 1970s. Reviewers, particularly in New York, became hostile toward his work and even toward him personally, reflecting the era's neoconservatism and revulsion toward attitudes presumed to be from the 1960s, (F. Scott Fitzgerald's fortunes suffered a similarly unmerited fall in the 1930s, as that decade viewed with scorn elements it considered reminiscent of the 1920s). Not surprisingly, Vonnegut chose this point in his career to write his requiem, something any number of reviewers from the *New York Times Book Review* and the *New York Review of Books* had tried to do themselves. Yet for Vonnegut writing the requiem was meant to be a happy occasion. Taking the traditional sixteenth century form of such works, which traumatize the nature of death with overabundant references to hellfire and damnation, he recasts the mode as one of peacefulness and beauty. To seal his artistic accomplishment into canonical history, he had it translated into Latin and set to symphonic music, the premier performance of which became the occasion for the third speech I wish to discuss.

Its title is the one Vonnegut used for most of his appearances in the 1980s: "How to Get a Job Like Mine." The videotape I have of it is from March 3, 1988, when in preparation for the first performance of his "Requiem, The Hocus Pocus Laundromat," by the Buffalo Symphony and the choir of that city's Unitarian Universalist Church, he delivered his current stump-speech as a fund-raiser to cover expenses for the event. Presented from the altar of the cathedral itself, where the Requiem would be premiered the next day, it is much the same lecture Vonnegut would give a year later at my own university.

Over a decade older and presumably even wiser, he now presents himself in an almost grandfatherly fashion, bringing snippets of wisdom to the audience in the hopes of making their lives more comfortable. He begins with what might be any speaker's local reference to the seasons. It was March in Buffalo and early April in Cedar Falls, but irritations with weather are a common enough topic to work anytime in anyplace, and it is to this factor that Vonnegut addresses himself. Why are we always so unhappy with the weather? Why does it seem to vex us so? Because we have been provided with the wrong information about it! How many seasons are there, he asks. Four? No—that's wrong, there are actually six. Summer, fall, winter, and spring fail to allow for those two in-between seasons: the "unlocking" of March and April, when the joy of spring is not yet here (even though we *expect* it to be), and the "locking" period of November and December when nature begins to shut down in preparation for the deep freeze of true winter. It is a piece of wisdom he himself picked up nearly forty years before from a friend when living in Schenectady, and which had made him happier about the weather ever since. As for his audience tonight, "I think that you'll be a lot more comfortable on this planet now that I've told you that."

From this introductory material (which sets the tone for his speech and indicates what its structure will be: that of wisely comforting advice), Vonnegut proceeds to an acknowledgment of his own somewhat fallen status as an author. To make this point, and also to comment wryly on its silliness, he apologizes. For what? For nothing in particular—just to make fun of the traditional rule for public speaking, which says that above all the speaker should "never apologize, never explain." Vonnegut reminds the audience of this supposedly sacred principle, and then violates it. "I'm terribly sorry," he says, and runs through a litany of apologies, saying he feels absolutely terrible about it, it will never happen again, and so forth, for almost a full minute. His tenor and demeanor are sincere; indeed, he projects the essence of apology, even as the audience notes that there is nothing whatsoever that he is apologizing *for*. Like his story about the weather, the item brought to the audience's attention is textual: a rule for public speaking, itself detached from any topic, is here turned inside out, again without reference to any subject. The audience is left with just Vonnegut himself, apologizing for being Kurt Vonnegut, who in breaking this tradition is setting the stage for other traditions his speech will question, and endearing himself to the audience in the process.

Both items have been generated by an interaction between Vonnegut and his listeners, and these points of interaction follow what he has described in *Palm Sunday* as the classic joke structure he favors for his fiction: asking a question, prompting a response, and then revealing that the response is off the mark because of either the humor or corrective information being supplied. The pages of Vonnegut's novels, written literally one at a time, are a series of just such settings and releasings of energy, kinetic in the sense that they incorporate the reader's movement as part of the text's larger progress. Just as the reader is asked to take a step and is then pushed a bit off balance and set in a different direction by Vonnegut's fictive texts, here in his lecture he cites a text, requests the audience's attitude toward it, and then comically deconstructs that attitude by showing how the simple facts of the matter lead elsewhere.

"How to Get a Job Like Mine" follows this practice with any number of other texts, some of which Vonnegut asks his audience to help him rewrite: the Requiem Mass of the sixteenth century, which his own version transforms from one of harsh judgment to one of beautitude and rest; the Bible, which he replaces with the Free Thought corrections from his grandfather Clemens Vonnegut's pamphlet, "An Instruction in Morals from the Standpoint of a Free Thinker"; and their own attempts at writing novels or short stories. Then there are the positive citations, from Nietzsche, Marx, and Eugene Debs, all of which indicate that true liberty is just now being born in America (which didn't free slaves or enfranchise women until the second century of its existence, with much progress yet to be made). Along the way there are rudely funny stories, such as Thomas Jefferson's being unable to free his slaves not because of any philosophical or moral reasons but because they were mortgaged.

The lecture ends with Vonnegut's storyline chalk–talk, an item in his repertoire since the 1960s (and drawing on late 1940s material from his studies in anthropology at the University of Chicago). But now, in the context of both Vonnegut's canon of works and his posture as a spokesman on public issues, it is used for a different purpose. Its first half reveals, as before, the common rise-and-fall structure to fabricated narratives that their readers' delight in. This time, however, he contrasts such patterns to the essentially flat nature of primitive tales, in which there are no perceptible highs or lows but simply level progress. Against what appears to be the flat-line boredom of Native American (and other primitive) narratives, Vonnegut displays with great panache the roller-coaster fortunes of Cinderella and other beloved protagonists. But can truly great literature be simplified along such structures, systematic enough to be generated by computers, which earlier in his talk Vonnegut has regretted as an evil of modern life? As a test, he subjects Shakespeare's *Hamlet* to such analysis, and finds out—to the audience's amazement—that its trajectory is just as flat as any primitive tale. There are no great rises or falls to Hamlet's fortune—no way of telling whether one incident or another is "good news" or "bad news."

Does this mean, as Vonnegut asks, "that Shakespeare couldn't write any better than an Indian?" Not exactly, for the genius of both the greatest writer in the English language and of the culturally central tales preserved by primitive societies is that each recognizes that the truth about life is that it does appear flat to us, because we really don't know what is the good news and what is the bad. Yet for our interest and entertainment we tell ourselves that we do, and such pretense yields such enjoyable tales as "Cinderella" and a million other narratives existing as novels, short stories, films, and television shows.

Is there a danger in such practice? Yes, because we become bored with our lives when they lack the delightful structural variances of entertaining stories, and we are therefore driven to great and petty mischief in order to liven things up. It is a fallibility that reaches from family life to national policy, including that of a recent administration that got the country into a little trouble (Grenada, Panama) and then got it out again, making for a manageable roller–coaster ride when in fact the role of government should be to keep things level.

Like his fiction, Vonnegut's public speaking exposes such pretenses behind our most commonly held truths, a style of deconstruction that characterizes the emerging philosophy of our age. From whence do Vonnegut's roots as a deconstructionist spring? According to his own testimony, from the fireboming of Dresden, where he saw every major "truth" of his education, from the improving quality of science and technology to the idealistic mission of American government, dismantled in an orgy of physical destruction and ethical contradiction. It is significant that his first major speech of the 1990s is on just this topic. Delivered on May 3, 1990, at the Smithsonian's Air and Space Museum as part of its year-long program of lectures and films on "The Legacy of Strategic Bombing," Vonnegut is featured as not only the author of *Slaughterhouse-Five* but, in contrast to the next month's speaker, bombing planner General Curtis E. LeMay, as a victim of aerial bombardment. *Slaughterhouse-Five* had been conceived as an act of witness, and the problematics of speaking about the unspeakable had determined its structure and generated its narrative force. The same thing will happen in this lecture.

Vonnegut's speech is noteworthy for several reasons. For the new decade, it shows him incorporating even more directly his position as a public spokesman with his mission as a public writer. Even more than at Buffalo, he addresses political and environmental concerns, much in the way that they contribute to the plot and thematics of *Hocus Pocus* (1990). He is also demonstrating how one of the central events in his life and arguably the organizing principle of his fictive canon, the firebombing of Dresden, remains absolutely pertinent to such present matters as the invasion of Panama and the catastrophe of global warming. But for the benefit of analysis, his speech is a perfect example for another, purely coincidental reason: As he approaches the podium he is handed a note that informs him that his old war buddy and colleague from his POW days in Dresden, Tom Jones, is present, sitting in the second row.

With the aid of the prepared text of Vonnegut's speech, titled "Tough Question, Tough Answer," as it appeared in the June 1990 issue of *Smart* magazine and a videotape of the actual presentation (courtesy of producer Robert Weide), I can indicate just how the surprising presence of Tom Jones allows Vonnegut to transform his lecture into something beyond his printed text. As always, his method has been to involve the audience (by asking them questions and challenging their assumptions), and since he is not now working from the loose-leaf binder of materials he used in previous speeches, there are plenty of chances for moving around and amplifying his text. But with an actual participant in the Dresden events present, Vonnegut is able not only to strengthen existing points but to improvise new ones, even discovering new truths in the process and sharing them with an audience uniquely situated to take part in the affair themselves. As a creative act, it is much like the structure of historical cross-references that generates the action of *Hocus Pocus*, a practice Vonnegut began emphasizing in *Slapstick* (1976) and perfected in *Jailbird* (for political history) and *Galápagos* (1985; for biological history).

"You're still alive!" Vonnegut exclaims, having read the note to his audience and identified Tom Jones down in front. "How nice!" As a spontaneous and necessarily offhand remark, it is a confirmation of Vonnegut's whole thesis before he even has a chance to elucidate it: that just as there is nothing intelligent to say about a massacre except the innocent bird chirpings that end *Slaughterhouse-Five*, so too is there no way to rationally and ethically explain the role of victims in the practice of strategic bombings. Such victims simply are wiped out, like germs being eradicated by a disinfectant, with any chance for individual consideration lost in the greater purpose. That Vonnegut himself survived was a meaningless accident, and now, meeting one of his few fellow survivors forty-five years later, he can only voice the same type of reflex that prompts a *"Poo-tee-weet?"* in *Slaughterhouse-Five*. Someone dies? "So it goes." Someone lives? "How nice!" Such is the most eloquent appraisal of strategic bombing that can be made.

Yet with Tom Jones present, there is a living, human bond between Vonnegut's material and the context in which it is being presented. After beginning his lecture with a familiar reference to the rule of public speaking that says one should never apologize (and adding the impromptu remark that never apologizing is probably the first rule of strategic bombing as well), Vonnegut explains that because he has criticized the Allied bombing he must establish how he was as unsympathetic to the Nazi war machine as any patriotic American. He fought against the Germans and was captured, he remarks—and at this point he looks up and adds that he's glad Tom is present to tell what a brave soldier he was, "how hard I fought before being subdued," and so forth, as he and Tom and then the audience break into laughter at this obvious ploy of old war buddies exaggerating the tales of their exploits. A few minutes later, after detailing the Dresden raid and his presence there, he breaks away once more to say, "So was Tom. See, this is all true! I could be snowing you. This is truth, isn't it, Tom?"

From here on Tom Jones becomes part of the speech, with every "I" turned into a "we," every "me" becoming an "us."

This corresponds to the prepared structure of Vonnegut's text, because the Dresden bombing is related in its victimization to bombings in Cambodia, Vietnam, and, more recently, Panama City. Also in the text is a question Vonnegut has prepared: "How many people in this very room here, in fact, have, in fact, while not in combat, been attacked from the air?" In addition to himself and Tom he finds that, from a show of hands, about six in the audience have been. Vonnegut's point is made easily: It is not a very exclusive club.

Yet it is a club of individual people, not just statistics, as Vonnegut demonstrates in another way, imprsovised most likely in response to finding Tom Jones present in the audience. To show how attacking civilian populations from the air has become not so much a military tactic as a symbol of national pride ("like the Liberty Bell"), Vonnegut cites the attack that killed Muammar Qaddafi's adopted daughter—"the same age and degree of innocence as my own adopted daughter"—and at this point departs from his text to say she's right here, pointing her out in the audience and advising, "There's another adopted daughter."

Yet condemning warfare itself is, as Vonnegut had to remind himself when writing *Slaughterhouse-Five*, about as practical as condemning a glacier. And so to avoid ambiguity and give his audience something specific, he ends this speech in the checklist manner that has concluded so many of his other lectures, asking which cities should have been bombed and which not. Dresden? "No" (for reasons that have been established). "Hamburg?" To the audience's anticipated "no," Vonnegut answers "yes"—momentarily surprising but, if one has been following his arguments, defensible because true tactics were involved. For the same reason Hiroshima merits a "yes" while Nagasaski a "no." And from there on it is all "no's," including Hanoi's civilian population, any part of Cambodia, Libya ("that was show biz"), and (added to the text) Panama City ("that was more show biz").

In public lectures from four decades, Kurt Vonnegut has shown the same manner in working with his materials as he has in his fiction. In 1967, while still an unknown and rather shabbily published author, he exploits that fact to make fun of his own predicament but also to deflate the presumptions of superior status. In 1977, he makes similar fun of a culture that has elevated him to star status (often for the wrong reasons), and again corrects misinformation as a way of showing how a better life is possible. By 1988 he is concluding another decade in which he has become that much more concerned with public issues and the need to deconstruct faulty assumptions. Finally, in 1990, as Vonnegut begins his sixth decade as a writer and fourth as a public speaker, he comes full circle to the matter of Dresden, using that experience as a model for critiquing behavior in any number of events that have happened since.

Like a jazz musician, Vonnegut boasts a familiar yet steadily expanding repertoire of materials, on which he improvises as befits the occasion. His mark characterizes all those occasions, just as the action painting of an abstract expressionist can be characteristic and innovative at the same time, given that its purpose is to bring the act of one's work in contact with the materials of its expression in order to capture creation itself. With an audience present, one can witness Vonnegut's proposing and responding, acting and reacting, drawing on his own experience to meld it with the experiences of his listeners in order to produce a work that succeeds as performance. It is an analog to what he accomplishes on the printed page, where the same living presence engages a subject matter that is part historical and part fabrication, but which in combination becomes an action painting with words.

BIBLIOGRAPHY

Hicks, Granville. "Literary Horizons." *Saturday Review* 52, xiii (29 March 1969): 25.

Klinkowitz, Jerome. *Slaughterhouse-Five: Reinventing the Novel and the World.* Boston: Twayne, 1990.

Vonnegut, Kurt. "Address: To Celebrate the Accession of the Two Millionth Volume in the Collections of the Ohio State University Libraries." Columbus, Ohio, November 21, 1967. Private audiotape.

——. "The Art of Fiction LXIV." *Paris Review* No. 69 (Spring 1977): pp. 56–103. Reprinted as "Self-Interview" in Palm Sunday, pp. 82-117.

——. *Galápagos.* New York: Delacorte Press/Seymour Lawrence.1985

——. *Hocus Pocus.* New York: G. P. Putnam's Sons, 1990.

——. "How to Get a Job Like Mine." Buffalo, New York, March 3, 1988. Private videotape from film in progress by Robert Weide.

——. *Jailbird.* New York: Dell, 1980.

——. "Kurt Vonnegut: A Self Interview." National Public Radio Options Series audio cassette OP-770726.001, Ol-C. 1981. A partial transcription of Vonnegut's lecture of the same title at the University of Northern Iowa, Cedar Falls, Iowa, on March 31, 1977 (a full copy of which exists on private tape).

——. Letter to Jerome Klinkowitz, January 3, 1990.

——. *Palm Sunday.* New York: Delacorte Press, 1981.

——. "Requiem: The Hocus Pocus Laundromat." *North American Review* 271, Dec. 1986: 29-35.

——. *Sirens of Titan.* New York: Dell, 1959.

——. *Slaughterhouse-Five.* New York: Seymour Lawrence/Delacorte Press, 1969.

——. "Tough Question, Tough Answer." *Smart*, June 1990, pp. 73-79. Private videotape of this May 3, 1990 lecture at the Smithsonian Institution's Air and Space Museum provided by Kurt Vonnegut and Robert Weide.

Unsigned. "Vonnegut's Gospel." *Time* 95 (29 June 1970): 8.

Kurt Vonnegut as a German American

Robert Merrill

> No matter where I am and how old I become, I still speak of almost nothing but my youth in Indianapolis, Indiana.
>
> Kurt Vonnegut[1]

> This is how you get to be a writer, incidentally: you feel somehow marginal, somehow slightly off-balance all the time.
>
> Kurt Vonnegut, *PS,* 65

I

The above quotes point to Vonnegut's obsession with the scene of his youth and his continuing sense of marginality. Both are keys to Vonnegut's art, its typical themes and ambience, and both suggest that we should review Vonnegut's curious status as a German American. I say "curious" because, crucial as his heritage is to his childhood in Indianapolis and his subsequent sense of alienation, Vonnegut has only come to address his roots directly in the 1980s, and his earlier statements (or silences) often pointed even his best critics in odd directions. Peter J. Reed once spoke of Vonnegut "revering" his father, for example (Reed, 159), and Jerome Klinkowitz has referred many times to Vonnegut's "solid, middle-class heritage" and his "happy childhood in a large family in the Midwest" (Klinkowitz, "Vonnegut in America," 7). We now know that Vonnegut most definitely did *not* revere his father and that it is inadequate to characterize his childhood as "happy." Indeed, Vonnegut's relationship to his middle-class background seems to me extremely complex. To understand this relationship we must remind ourselves that Vonnegut is a German American, for his Indianapolis childhood and his sense of marginality begin (if not end) with his Germanic heritage.

When Klinkowitz refers to Vonnegut's happy childhood, he is thinking primarily of the "ideals" Vonnegut derived from his parents and his family (Klinkowitz, "Vonnegut in America," 9). Vonnegut has said again and again that his atheism, pacifism, and general tendencies toward free thought were homegrown: "I learned my outrageous opinions about organized religion at my mother's knee" (*W*, 240). In *Palm Sunday* (1981) he reprints much of John Rauch's history of the Indianapolis Vonneguts and takes obvious pride in the family lore. He notes that the entire history from 1848 forward reveals "no war lovers" (*PS*, 18), and his fondness for his great-grandfather Clemens Vonnegut, a lover of Voltaire, is especially obvious. His family history reminds Vonnegut of the "idealistic, pacifistic nation" (*W*, 274) America used to be before World War II, a theme that recurs throughout Vonnegut's writings. This history in particular and Vonnegut's familial memories in general seem to be happy indeed.

Moreover, Vonnegut's happier memories seem to account for his nostalgic celebrations of "a permanent community of relatives" (*W*, 242), his oft-repeated prescription for contemporary loneliness. Vonnegut's true ideal would be something like Robert Redfield's folk societies, in which everyone thinks and feels like a relative (see especially *W*, 176–79), but as a response to our "jerry-built society" (*PS*, 147) we would do well to settle for what Vonnegut calls "artificial extended families" (*W*, xxiv) of whatever sort. Such "families" offer precisely what we need most: "stable communities in which the terrible disease of loneliness can be cured" (*PS*, 198). If the folk societies of the past are gone forever and we simply do not have enough friends and relatives (*PS*, 180), we must seek out ample associations that will recall the "large family" Vonnegut enjoyed in Indianapolis.

The problem with this reading of Vonnegut's early life and late philosophy is that neither the life nor the philosophy is quite so simple. Vonnegut does seem to admire the earliest American Vonneguts, and especially Clemens Vonnegut, but this admiration definitely has its limits and in any case does not carry over to his own immediate family. Even in his admiring review of John Rauch's history, Vonnegut notes the growing family tendency to distrust art and to emphasize commerce. Indeed, the Vonnegut family history is one of almost uninterrupted commercial success (up to but definitely not including the Great Depression), and money is the principal value embodied throughout its many episodes. At one point Vonnegut notes that his ancestors had prepared many "comforts" and "privileges" for him, all based ultimately on the money now taken away by the depression (*PS*, 61). Everything Vonnegut has written, but especially *God Bless You, Mr. Rosewater* (1965), should alert us to the unpleasant irony, for Vonnegut, in receiving these comforts and privileges along with his free-thinking proclivities. Similarly, his family's great trust in technology—the source of its money, after all—must seem to Vonnegut deeply ironic. He remarks at one point that their only religion was technology, but that the bombing of Hiroshima compelled him to see "how vile that religion of mine could be" (*PS*, 69). Vonnegut comments on Germany's "amazing rockets in World War II" as a similar effort to dominate others by means of technology (*W*, 79), and of course a general distrust of technology pervades his novels.

Vonnegut's reservations about his parents are even more direct and broadly based. John Rauch notes that German Americans almost uniformly supported the United States in World War I and World War II (*PS*, 20-21), but Vonnegut explains that his own parents were so "shamed and dismayed" by anti-German sentiment during World War I they resolved not to acquaint their son with German language, literature, music, or oral family histories: "They volunteered to make me ignorant and rootless as proof of their patriotism" (*PS*, 21). When captured at the Battle of the Bulge, Vonnegut was asked by the Germans why he was making war on his "brothers." He found the question "ignorant and comical," for, as he says, "My parents had separated me so thoroughly from my Germanic past that my captors might as well have been Bolivians or Tibetans, for all they meant to me" (*PS*, 88). Thus his parents are credited with fashioning that sense of rootlessness Vonnegut's artificial extended families are supposed to overcome.

Vonnegut's parents are subjected to even more personal attacks. Vonnegut speaks with disdain of his father's weltschmerz ("a sort of skeptical and fatalistic contempt for life"—*PS*, 56), dismisses "the empty graces and aggressively useless possessions which [his] parents, and especially [his] mother, meant to regain someday" (*PS*, 59) (a charge combining Vonnegut's contempt for their nostalgic formalism and their materialism), and tells with some relish the story of how they were duped into investing in a legally dubious (and mythical) coal monopoly during the depression (*PS*, 223-24). He says bluntly that his parents were "so woozy with weltschmerz that they weren't passing anything on—not the German language, not their love for German music, not the family history, nothing" (*PS*, 195). Vonnegut's "admiration for large families, whether real or artificial" (*PS*, 66), hardly seems to derive from nostalgic recollections of his own family.

Here we come up against Vonnegut's oft-remarked double vision, inspired, I am suggesting, by the nature of his experience (or lack thereof) as a German American in the 1930s. The rootlessness he experiences in an all too assimilated German American family eventually gives rise to numerous celebrations of large families, real or artificial; yet Vonnegut knows perfectly well that large groups can be "the worst possible describer[s] of mental health" (*PS*, 243). The false nature of such groups is exposed in virtually every one of his novels, perhaps most memorably in *Cat's Cradle* (1963), the novel in which he first defines a *granfalloon* ("a proud and meaningless association of human beings" as later refined in *W*, xv), then illustrates the term by reference to people from his home state, "Hoosiers." Vonnegut's novels testify to an almost universal search for the meaningful association he calls a *karass*, but repeatedly—or is it always?—they dramatize the ultimate failure of such quests. No doubt a Bokononesque paradox, our unquenchable need for a sustaining culture is perhaps Vonnegut's principal theme and certainly his recurring dramatic subject.

If Vonnegut knows that human communities usually fall apart because "their members aren't really relatives, don't have enough in common" (*W*, 243), he also knows that he has no real ties with Indianapolis, Indiana, if indeed he ever had such ties. The youth he is always speaking of (sometimes fondly, sometimes not) has given way to a more cosmopolitan (and rootless) maturity. Vonnegut has not lived in Indianapolis since 1940, when he was eighteen, and by the 1970s he had only one surviving friend there (*PS*, 115). By 1980 he was saying, "I scarcely know any of the few Vonneguts still living in Indianapolis, and my own children will know and care about them as much as I know or care about my German relatives" (*PS*, 238). Vonnegut's Indianapolis relatives are not enthusiastic about his works, as he laconically puts it (*PS*, 185), and the city's respect for language in general is like its attitude toward art: "Common speech sounds like a band saw cutting galvanized tin, and employs a vocabulary as unornamental as a monkey wrench" (*PS*, 79). An interviewer once interrupted one of Vonnegut's hymns to "ancestral homes" by remarking that Vonnegut now lived in a New York apartment. Vonnegut's reply was either very honest or very evasive (or perhaps both): "Well, I'm used to the rootlessness that goes with my profession" (*W*, 242). Indeed he is.

I am suggesting that Vonnegut's childhood roots are known primarily by their absence. Only once, to my knowledge, has Vonnegut directly identified himself as a German American. (Speaking of Irwin Shaw's *The Young Lions*, Vonnegut once said, "As a German-American, of course, I was sorry to see him make the Nazis the bad guys"—*PS*, 138.) One might more aptly think of Vonnegut as "a planetary citizen," as he once identified himself (*PS*, 122). But of course Vonnegut's vision of a stable community, or an artificial extended family, is just as real as his recognition that "there were some vile and lively native American Fascists in my home town of Indianapolis during the thirties" (*MN*, v). The "intolerable sentimentality" (*W*, xxv) he identifies in his own works is just as real as the cultural intolerance he is able to sense in American young people because of his own experience (and lack of experience) as a German American in Indianapolis, Indiana (*W*, 196). In his best works Vonnegut dramatizes this double vision as embodied in characters like himself—indeed, in *Slaughterhouse-Five* (1969) and *Breakfast of Champions* (1973) the character *is* himself—who must strive for the communion they have never experienced but know they must have to be fully human. We may suspect, however, that to be fully human in one of Vonnegut's books is to experience this double vision without being able to escape from it by closing one's eyes, either literally or figuratively.

II

In a somewhat speculative spirit, I would like to glance at several of Vonnegut's novels to see what difference it makes that their author is German American. In at least one sense all the novels might be adduced, for Vonnegut's campaign against loneliness informs even his earliest novel, *Player Piano* (1952). (The key work on this theme would of course be *Slapstick* [1976].) Among the relatively earlier novels, however, *Mother Night* (1962) and *Slaughterhouse-Five* are the most relevant texts, while *Deadeye Dick* (1982) and *Bluebeard* (1987) are the crucial later works.

These four novels reflect Vonnegut's German American background in various ways. One is Vonnegut's apparent concern to avoid Irwin Shaw's error in *The Young Lions*. When German characters appear in these novels, and most notably when they are minor characters, Vonnegut works very hard to avoid trafficking in the more obvious stereotypes. *Mother Night* and *Slaughterhouse-Five* are especially relevant here, whereas the later novels employ Vonnegut's background by transmuting his personal history. It is perhaps ironic that the most autobiographical of Vonnegut's novels, *Slaughterhouse-Five*, makes virtually nothing of its author's German heritage (nothing overt, that is).

To begin with a general and rather negative observation, I would suggest that Vonnegut's German American background issues in nothing remotely profound about the larger themes of modern German history. Indeed, the novels hardly engage such matters: Even *Slaughterhouse-Five* is concerned with the behavior of the Allies far more than with that of the Germans. Vonnegut's nonfiction tends toward historical commonplaces. Vonnegut consistently refers to World War II as a "just war" on America's part, and once he even says that it was just to torture Germany during World War II (*W*, 170). Indeed, Vonnegut refers to World War II as "a war against pure evil" (*W*, 99), an evil embodied not in the German people but in Hitler, who is credited with producing "a generation of warriors and police" (*PS*, 214), who is said to have "resurrected Germany, a beaten, bankrupt, half-starved nation, with hatred and nothing more" (*PS*, 181), and who is seen as thriving because he claimed to know everything "about divine and natural law" (*PS*, 10). For Vonnegut, then, Hitler provided reassuring answers about his people's place in the scheme of things and offered up scapegoats—hardly a profound or original analysis. Whereas Vonnegut is often credited—and credits himself —with never portraying a full-fledged villain in his fiction (an exaggeration, I think), his Hitler serves this function throughout the nonfiction.

Vonnegut's most interesting observation about these historical matters is profoundly relevant to *Mother Night*, the first novel with German characters and themes. Vonnegut suggests that it was very bad for the Americans to fight such a "just war" in World War II, for the experience created the illusion that "we" are good only if "they" are bad. Thus we get such disasters as the firebombing of Dresden and the later massacre at My Lai (*W*, 212-14). In *Mother Night* what we get are a collection of American Nazis to match their German counterparts. Vonnegut's concern for balancing his fictional ledgers is obvious enough in his 1966 introduction:

There were some vile and lively native American Fascists in my home town of Indianapolis during the thirties. . . . And I remember some laughs about my aunt, too, who married a *German* German, and who had to write to Indianapolis for proofs that she had no Jewish blood. (*MN*, v)

The novel provides numerous examples on both sides to support Howard W. Campbell's definition of evil as "that large part of every man that wants to hate with God on its side" (*MN*, 181). Unreliable as Campbell is on some matters, he speaks for Vonnegut and indeed the novel as a whole on this point. As we will see in *Slaughterhouse-Five* as well, Vonnegut's German American heritage seems to have pushed him toward an unusually nonparochial reading of the antagonists in World War II.

Vonnegut's background may also have tilted him toward this novel's version of the intellectual/philosophical conflict or contradiction that informs all of his books. On the one hand, men and women appear to be "so sick and so much the listless playthings of enormous forces" (*S-5*, 164), determined by these forces to do precisely what they do. On the other hand, men and women are to be admired—and emulated—when they act like real and humane "characters," people who assert their wills for the general good. These apparently irreconcilable points of view collide in Campbell's debate with himself, but they also emerge at many other points in the novel. In his introduction Vonnegut says, "If I'd been born in Germany, I suppose I would have *been* a Nazi, bopping Jews and gypsies and Poles around, leaving boots sticking out of snowbanks, warming myself with my secretly virtuous insides" (*MN*, vii). Yet Vonnegut has one of his characters congratulate Campbell for his bad conscience about what he did in the war: "Everybody else, no matter what side he was on, no matter what he did, is sure a good man could not have acted in any other way" (*MN*, 24). Campbell's decision to judge and hang himself at the end might seem to validate this view that a good man *can* act otherwise, but the forces working against him (or her) are such that Vonnegut imagines he would have fallen prey like *almost* everyone else ("There are *almost* no characters in this story," as Vonnegut puts it in *Slaughterhouse-Five* [164] [emphasis added]). Like *Slaughterhouse-Five* and many of Vonnegut's other novels, *Mother Night* is enriched by Vonnegut's painfully direct engagement of this philosophical and moral issue as illustrated most vividly in time of war but also during its aftermath.

Elsewhere I have argued that Vonnegut debates this issue most compellingly in *Slaughterhouse-Five* and somewhat less successfully in *Breakfast of Champions*.[2] In *Slaughterhouse-Five* Vonnegut means to warn us against what he now calls "a brand-new method for committing suicide": "To say nothing and to do nothing about what some of our businessmen and military men are doing with the unstable substances and the most persistent poisons to be found anywhere in the universe" (*PS*, 71). Vonnegut's profound sense of cultural relativism, at least reinforced by his status as a German American, leads him to a relatively optimistic conclusion: "[Cultural relativism] is also a source of hope. It means we don't have to continue this way if we don't like it" (*PS*, 276). In terms relevant to *Slaughterhouse-Five*, we do not *have* to bomb Dresden, as General Rumfoord claims (*S-5*, 198); we do not *have* to keep fighting in Vietnam until we achieve victory, as a Marine major insists (*S-5*, 59); we do not *have* to believe "that every creature and plant in the Universe is a machine," as the Tralfamadorians teach Billy Pilgrim (*S-5*, 154). Whether or not I am right about all this, I am sure that Vonnegut's background contributed fundamentally to his humane treatment of the Germans in *Slaughterhouse-Five*.

The range and number of German characters in *Slaughterhouse-Five* far surpass what Vonnegut presents in other novels. The range is not complete, however, for Vonnegut includes no higher ranking officials or officers (recall that Eichmann is a speaking character in *Mother Night*). Presumably he wished to exclude the sources of "pure evil" and to concentrate instead on a cross section of normal Germans. At the less noble end of the spectrum we have whoever hangs a Pole for having sex with a German woman (*S-5*, 156), an episode meant to balance the Germans' execution of Edgar Derby for "stealing" a teacup in the aftermath of the Dresden firebombing; the guard at the concentration camp who beats up an American for virtually no reason and "explains" his act in straight Tralfamadorese: "Vy you? Vy anybody?" (*S-5*, 91); and the sophisticated major (of suspicious rank to begin with) who considers the English prisoners of war his "friends" and shares their contempt for bedraggled Americans such as Billy Pilgrim (*S-5*, 128). Less objectionable but still implicated in the nastiness of war are the guards on the boxcars who retire to their well-furnished quarters while their charges are smashed together without food or toilets for three days (*S-5*, 68) and the corporal who admonishes Roland Weary for his "cruel" trench knife but then effectively kills him by taking away his combat boots (*S-5*, 55) (Weary will die of gangrene). In the middle of the spectrum Vonnegut offers "eight ridiculous Dresdeners" who have been charged with overseeing the American prisoners of war at Dresden. Once the Dresdeners encounter the "hundred ridiculous creatures" who are simply "more crippled human beings, more fools like themselves," they first smile and then laugh as their terror "evaporates" (*S-5*, 150). Similarly, Vonnegut depicts Werner Gluck, a young and innocent guard who shares with Billy Pilgrim the experience of first seeing naked women in a shower at Dresden (*S-5*, 158-59). With the fated Edgar Derby, Werner and Billy constitute "the three fools" (*S-5*, 159) who then go about their business. The ridiculous Dresdeners and the foolish Werner are part of a human comedy they share with Billy Pilgrim and the other American prisoners, but also with the German majors and corporals and guards who do not *intend* to do evil of any kind, let alone "pure evil."

More admirable are the Germans at the other end of the spectrum. The surgeon who castigates Billy for his absurd clothes wrongly supposes that Billy means to make light of war (something Billy will only do later, once he learns the

good news from Tralfamadore), but his mistake is understandable and in any case
he is naturally irritable after operating all day (*S-5*, 151); if it is "a lovely thing"
for Mary O'Hare to be a trained nurse (*S-5*, 12), it must be especially admirable
to operate on the wounded throughout the day. No less helpful in his own way is
the blind innkeeper who feeds and houses the American survivors of the Dresden
firebombing (*S-5* , 181). And most admirable of all, perhaps, are the two doctors,
man and woman, who deliver babies until the hospitals burn down and who call
Billy's attention to the intense suffering of the Americans' horses (*S-5*, 196).
These doctors are said to have nine languages between them and surely represent
the humane sense of justice all those with sufficient education and a modicum of
authority should pursue.

The Germans in *Slaughterhouse-Five* appear briefly, but collectively they
constitute a very sympathetic human community—realistically diverse but marked
by several genuine "characters" and no villains. Rather obviously these are
anything but the Huns of popular lore. They are, of course, the very *people* the
Allies are bombing at Dresden, just as Billy Pilgrim, Edgar Derby, and the other
"ridiculous" Americans are the targets of those "amazing" German rockets
Vonnegut has deplored. *Slaughterhouse-Five* is as humanely sensitive to all sides
of the war as any war novel, including many far more realistic in form and
technique, and I cannot believe it is an accident that Vonnegut is German
American (though the Tralfamadorians would laugh at me for saying so).

Vonnegut's later novels are in many ways as personal as *Slaughterhouse-Five*,
though often in rather playful ways.[3] In his preface to *Deadeye Dick* Vonnegut
acknowledges this reading—and holds it at arm's length—by "explaining" the
main symbols in his book:

There is an unappreciated, empty arts center in the shape of a sphere. This is my head as
my sixtieth birthday beckons to me.

There is a neutron bomb explosion in a populated area. This is the disappearance of so
many people I cared about in Indianapolis when I was starting out to be a writer.
Indianapolis is there, but the people are gone.

Haiti is New York City, where I live now.

The neutered pharmacist who tells the tale is my declining sexuality. The crime he
committed in childhood is all the bad things I have done. (*DD* xii–xiii)

I suspect this reading is far from frivolous, but it does not do justice to the
intricate transformations Vonnegut achieves on materials drawn from his sixty
years on planet Earth. The narrator, Rudy Waltz, is ordered by his father to
become a pharmacist rather than an artist (Vonnegut's father recommended the
sciences in general); the father, Otto Waltz, collects guns, is "proudly agnostic"
(*DD*, 22), cherishes his German heritage (especially German music) before
turning his back on it in the face of American political reaction, derives his
fortune from a drug company (the Vonnegut family business was a hardware
store), and loves to paint; the mother, Emma Waltz, resembles Vonnegut's
mother Edith. But of course Emma does not kill herself, as Vonnegut's mother
did, and the shifts in the father's history are almost as important. A crucial

example is Otto's active Nazi sympathies (based on friendship with Hitler himself!), which must be publicly rejected once war becomes inevitable; by contrast, Vonnegut's father (and mother) simply declined to instruct Kurt in things Germanic because of American attitudes during World War I. Otto's infatuation with the Nazis is an active if fatal preference, whereas the Vonneguts seem to have simply resigned their German heritage. Interestingly, however, Otto and Emma practice a similar retirement both before and especially after the twelve-year-old Rudy kills a pregnant woman by firing a shot aimlessly from the top floor of their house. The Waltzes seem to undergo the same disengagement from life Vonnegut perceives in his own parents. So perhaps Rudy Waltz and his strange failure(s) of will do represent the bad things Vonnegut has done. Vonnegut's presence in this novel is such that we should not be surprised by his Hitchcockian appearance near the end, his first since *Breakfast of Champions* (and wearing the same large sunglasses with mirrored lenses! [*DD*, 198]).

By means of such personal transformations and sleights of hand (or perversities, as some would say), Vonnegut tells the story of the asexual Rudy Waltz's search for his personal Shangri-La. This quest is as much a failure as Rabo Karabekian's is a success in Vonnegut's most recent novel, *Bluebeard* (1987). Perhaps this is because Rabo is burdened with a Vonnegutian past rather more of his own making than Vonnegut usually permits his protagonists. What *he* has wrought, Rabo is able to break apart and remake. (Though only for a year. Rabo's dates are included at the beginning of his "autobiography": 1916–1988. The novel ends in 1987.)

I do not have space to explore this wonderful novel in any detail, but it is important to note that Rabo is the first of Vonnegut's protagonists to overcome first the problems he inherits from his parents, then the mistakes he commits in compensating for his childhood. What the ineffectual Rudy Waltz could not do, the more capable (and talented) Rabo achieves with a good deal of help from Circe Berman. For years Vonnegut has been telling us that love is nothing when set against respect; *Bluebeard* seems to suggest that love and respect may occasionally coexist.

In *Bluebeard* Vonnegut's Germanic heritage is so transformed it becomes Armenian! The pattern is familiar, however, as the protagonist's parents struggle unsuccessfully to adapt to American ways (some of them downright treacherous) and the protagonist tries to escape from their unhappy influence in pursuit of his goals as an artist. Many, many years later (Rabo is 71 in 1987), the protagonist achieves both personal and artistic syntheses after just as many false starts and failures, among them divorce from his first wife and the loss of two children who won't speak to him (the former reflecting Vonnegut's 1970 divorce from Jane Cox Vonnegut, the latter the "loss" of two daughters to born-again Christianity), the loss of all contact with his relatives (a familiar Vonnegut plight), and a prolonged but flawed career as an abstract expressionist (both as painter and collector)—an artistic failure that *may* parallel Vonnegut's career as he now sees it, but we should remember the very high grades Vonnegut gives his books in

Palm Sunday: A's for *The Sirens of Titan* (1959), *Mother Night, God Bless You, Mr. Rosewater*, and *Jailbird* (1979), A+'s for *Cat's Cradle* and *Slaughterhouse-Five* (Vonnegut may not have been kidding when he praised Arthur C. Clarke's *Childhood's End* as "one of the few masterpieces in the field of science fiction," then added, "All of the others were written by me"—*PS*, 174.) In any case, Rabo's list of failures at the end recalls his creator's: as commercial artist (Vonnegut's early short stories, or the early books published first in paperback), as serious artist (the judgments of Vonnegut's critics, especially recent ones), as husband and father (Vonnegut's own verdict). And the source of Rabo's redemption (in addition to his interplay with Circe Berman) also recalls Vonnegut's life, for like Vonnegut Rabo was captured near the end of World War II, sent to a camp near Dresden, and then abandoned by his captors at war's end along with many other prisoners of war representing many nationalities. Rabo's huge painting of this event (eight feet by sixty-four feet!) is a fantastic synthesis of realistic detail and symbolic, fabulistic design (including perhaps the kind of "moral" to which the Tralfamadorians objected in earthling novels). Rabo's ability to conceive *and* execute this painting signals his improbable reconciliation with his past as it is represented in the picture itself.

One hopes, perhaps fondly, that Vonnegut is as contented as Rabo seems to be in the last lines of *Bluebeard*. But this is quite unlikely. As I remarked earlier, Vonnegut's recurring subject has been a man like himself (now defeated, now sustained) who must try to reconcile his seemingly contradictory personal experiences and philosophical insights. The convincing depiction of this inner struggle distinguishes Vonnegut's better works, whether comic like *Bluebeard* or somber like *Slaughterhouse-Five*. To be marginal seems to have been crucial to this art, as Vonnegut has said himself; to be German American has therefore played its role, large or small, in this self-reflexive artistic process.

NOTES

1. *Palm Sunday* (New York: Delacorte Press, 1981), 327. Hereafter abbreviated as *PS*. Other abbreviations for Vonnegut's works are as follows: *Deadeye Dick* (New York: Delacorte Press, 1982) as *DD*; *Mother Night* (1962; New York: Avon Books, 1966) as *MN*; *Slaughterhouse-Five* (1969; New York: Dell, 1971) as *S-5*; *Wampeters, Foma & Granfalloons* (New York: Delta, 1974) as *W*.

2. See Robert Merrill and Peter A. Scholl, "Vonnegut's *Slaughterhouse-Five*: The Requirements of Chaos," 142–51; and Robert Merrill, "Vonnegut's *Breakfast of Champions*: The Conversion of Heliogabalus," in *Critical Essays on Kurt Vonnegut*, ed. Robert Merrill (Boston: G. K. Hall, 1989), 153-61.

3. As I remark above, *Slaughterhouse-Five* is the most autobiographical of Vonnegut's novels. This is confirmed by materials recently reprinted in Jerome Klinkowitz's *Slaughterhouse-Five: Reforming the Novel and the World* (Boston: Twayne, 1990), 86–106. The materials in question—the memoir of a British officer who was in the same concentration camp as Vonnegut and letters written by Vonnegut and his uncle Alex in 1945—confirm the remarkable accuracy of Vonnegut's account. Nonetheless, the later novels seem to me more personal insofar as they are *about* Vonnegut's life in a way *Slaughterhouse-Five* is not.

WORKS CITED

Klinkowitz, Jerome. *Slaughterhouse-Five: Reforming the Novel and the World*. Boston: Twayne, 1990.

———. "Vonnegut in America." In *Vonnegut in America*, ed. Jerome Klinkowitz and Donald L. Lawler, 7–36. New York: Delta, 1977.

Merrill, Robert, ed. *Critical Essays on Kurt Vonnegut*. Boston: G. K. Hall, 1989.

Reed, Peter J. "The Later Vonnegut." In *Vonnegut in America*, ed. Jerome Klinkowitz and Donald L. Lawler, 150–86. New York: Delta, 1977. 150-86.

Vonnegut, Kurt. *Bluebeard*. New York: Delacorte Press, 1987.

———. *Cat's Cradle*. New York: Dell, 1963.

———. *Deadeye Dick*. New York: Delacorte Press, 1982.

———. *God Bless You, Mr. Rosewater*. Dell, 1965.

———. *Jailbird*. New York: Delacorte, 1979.

———. *Mother Night*. New York: Avon Books, 1966.

———. *Palm Sunday*. New York: Delacorte Press, 1981.

———. *Player Piano*. New York: Dell, 1952.

———. *Slapstick*. New York: Delacorte, 1976.

———. *Slaughterhouse-Five*. New York: Dell, 1971.

———. *The Sirens of Titan*. New York: Dell, 1959.

———. *Wampeters, Foma & Granfalloons*. New York: Delta, 1974.

Bokononism as a Structure of Ironies

Zoltán Abádi-Nagy

An unmistakable feature of Kurt Vonnegut's creative genius is a refreshing originality in devising new ways in which to examine American culture and society. His originality is exercised in multitudinous new fashions in a highly complex satiric art. Among other things, he invented and fully elaborated two ideologies that are central and all-pervasive in two novels. One is the ironic gospel preached by what he calls "The Church of God the Utterly Indifferent" in *The Sirens of Titan*, and the other is the Bokononism of *Cat's Cradle*. The two ironic religions are constructive and destructive; they mean salvation and damnation to the ironic worlds that choose to be pivoted upon them. Both are satiric syntheses with multiple ironies condensed in them and with multiple satirical functions to perform. This is what the term "ironic religion" is intended to describe in this paper. Parallels with conventional religions *are* part of the game, but instead of ironically treated historical religions, we are dealing with *fictitious* religions, whose manifold ironic functions reflect and project the American past, present, and future. They are Vonnegut's original looks at "origins" in diagnostic and prognostic senses. The former is the retrospective look tracing the origins of the social and cultural present in the past; the latter is the prophetic warning pointing to some aspects of the present that can be origins of an apocalyptic future.

Bokonon's is the more elaborate ironic religion of the two with a comic cosmogony and admirably systematic ironic teachings related to man, society, and transcendence. Vonnegut markets the whole thing with the bargain gift of his original terminology. The cult founder's secret pact with the dictator of San Lorenzo, the Caribbean locale of the novel, makes Bokononism an outlawed religion, reckoning that anything outlawed and persecuted attracts more followers. It is a tragicomic social game made much more intricate by Bokonon's gospel. A tough nut to crack, his new religion is rendered even tougher for the critic to interpret when the founder himself seems to crush that nut by the deceptively self-discrediting statement on the title page of *The First Book of Bokonon:* "Don't be a fool! Close this book at once! It is nothing but *Foma!*" "*Foma*, of course, are lies," the narrator explains.[1] According to a more accurate definition, *foma* are "harmless untruths" (p. 4). For those to whom this doubly ironic negation is still beautifully simple—some aspects of reality negated in Bokononism, then Bokononism negated by its founder—there is Vonnegut's own ironic disclaimer at the head of the novel turning it into a book of triply ironic negation: "Nothing in this book is true" (p. 4). And this time not just the religion of lies is meant, but Vonnegut's whole novel with the implication that Bokonon's warning about his religious truths being untruths is itself an untruth.

Cat's Cradle's Bokononism unfolds parallel with the plot so the obvious way to interpret it is to confront it with the plot. After all, it is on the one hand a reaction against San Lorenzan social conditions, but on the other hand its social relevance undergoes the crucial test of the apocalyptic annihilation of the same society. When correlated with San Lorenzan social developments, Bokononism appears to be a subtle interpenetration of five ironic layers each representing a cardinal constituent of Vonnegut's satire:

1. the ironic layer of belied truths;
2. the ironic layer of true lies;
3. the layer of ironic fatalism;
4. the ironic layer burlesquing conventional religions;
5. the ironic layer of self-invalidating Bokononist contradictions.

The first layer is the bedrock of Vonnegut's innermost historically and sorely tried but basically unshaken belief in the sanctity of man. Inviolable convictions violated by history, time-honored truths slighted in our time. San Lorenzan history *is* an insult to humanitarian principles, something that causes Vonnegut to introduce them in bitter irony as *foma*. Bokononist beliefs in the sanctity of man are not allowed to shape San Lorenzan history which slights and belies these truths thus indirectly requalifying them as untruths. So let them be untruths—*foma*—Vonnegut suggests ironically. Central to the layer of belied truths is the Bokononist conviction that only man is sacred, "not even God" (p. 143). And as man is sacred, the *sin-wat* "who wants all of somebody's love" is a wicked person since "Bokonon tells us it is very wrong not to love everyone exactly the same" (p. 141). The true Bokononist vision is "of the unity in every second of all time and all wandering mankind, all wandering womankind, all wandering children" (pp. 55–56). In other words, we are urged to think in terms of all time and all mankind. The comic Bokononist foot ceremony, *boko-maru*, is an exercise in this; it is a ritual of "the mingling of awarenesses" (p. 109). Besides being based on the sanctity of man, Bokononism is also tailored to less imposing realities of human existence. Disappointment and pain (pp. 134, 176) are taken into consideration as part and parcel of human life, as are "the shortness of life and the longness of eternity." The founder of Bokononism reports his "avocation" as "being alive" and his "principal occupation" as "being dead" (p. 95).

The ironic layer of true lies differs from that of belied truths in the function it performs in the ironic structure called Bokononism. In a sense, when the novel is viewed from outside (when viewed as authorial messages), both types of "untruths" are truths, of course. The layer of what we called belied truths—some of Bokonon's *foma*—are Vonnegut's set of human norms applied to a dehumanized world and found to be violated, dead, and absent. On another level, Vonnegut is exploring the very essence of that dehumanized reality, providing the reader with a sarcastic anatomy of what *is* present in that world. So some of Bokonon's *foma* are Vonnegut's diagnoses concerning the negativity of San Lorenzo. While in the realm of belied truths Vonnegut's irony aims at absent positivity, in the true "lies" of Bokononism prevailing negativity is rebuked. The very existence of Bokononism is a scornful judgment passed on a bloodsucking, ridiculously corrupt dictatorship. "Well, when it became evident that no governmental or economic reform was going to make the people much less miserable, religion became the one real instrument of hope. Truth was the enemy of the people, because the truth was so terrible, so Bokonon made it his business to provide the people with better and better lies" (p. 118).

But some of those lies are too good to be lies. Some of them *are harmful* if not subversive social *truths* ironically masked as harmless untruths. We must put it out of our mind that Bokonon deceptively calls them "lies" since it is easy to see them as sheer, sober social criticism. That is why this layer of irony is called that of "true 'lies.'" Bokonon's strategy in presenting appalling social truths is the old ironic one that says, "Don't listen to me! I'm a liar." By using this simple device, by disguising truths as untruths, he can be as outspoken as he wants to. Some examples: "Pay no attention to Caesar. Caesar doesn't have the slightest idea what's *really* going on" (p. 173); "good societies could be built only by pitting good against evil" (p. 74). This makes it possible for Vonnegut to rage at twentieth-century madnesses of all kinds. Here is Bokonon's utopia: "Let us start our Republic with a chain of drug stores, a chain of grocery stores, a chain of gas chambers, and a national game. After that, we can write our Constitution" (p. 190).

The third layer of irony is that of ironic fatalism. A recurring idea in *Cat's Cradle* is that there was no other course for events to take. "Bokononists believe that humanity is organized into teams, teams that do God's will without ever discovering what they are doing. Such a team is called a *karass*" (p. 11). A *karass* has nothing to do with national, institutional, occupational, familial, and class communities. In a *karass*, lives are "tangled up" with each other "for no very logical reasons" (p. 12). The pivot of a *karass* is a *wampeter*: "Whatever it is, the members of its *karass* revolve about it in the majestic chaos of a spiral nebula." The orbits are "spiritual orbits, naturally" (p. 42). The *wampeter* of the novel's *karass*, the novel's hub about which the characters revolve, is *ice-nine*. Actually, there is a term in Bokononist vocabulary, *Zah-mah-ki-bo*, meaning "fate—inevitable destiny" (p. 126).

As for the whys of Bokonon's fatalism, Vonnegut interspersed the novel with answers. The most comprehensive one is expressed in Bokonon's closing remark implying that the history of San Lorenzo is that of "human stupidity" (p. 191). Vonnegut's Bokononist fatalism is an ironic pose condemnatory of man who instead of drawing a lesson from history, is stupid enough to repeat the same dreadful mistakes that invite devastation. This hopelessness is to a great extent occasioned by science. *Cat's Cradle* lashes out at human stupidity and brazen dictatorships, but the irresponsibility of science is also one of the main targets. What San Lorenzo rates from progress is the electric guitar and world-freezing *ice-nine*.

The fourth fold of Bokonon's fivefold ironic religion is itself twofold: a direct satirical attack launched against Christian dogma and an indirect parody of the origin of religions in general. The former is the philosophical; the latter is the social side to the same coin. The Bokononism of *Cat's Cradle* is, in a way, a descendant of the Church of God the Utterly Indifferent, Vonnegut's other ironic religion in *The Sirens of Titan*, in that he allows for the existence of a God almighty only to cast God's indifference, even cynicism into God's teeth. When the apocalypse comes and "the moist green earth" is frozen into a "blue white pearl" in no time, Bokonon paints this on the arch of the palace gate, "the only man-made form untouched":

And if, on that sad day, you want to scold our God,
Why Go right ahead and scold Him.
He'll just smile and nod. (p. 174)

It is exactly this sentiment that solidifies in the most fundamental doctrine enunciated by Bokonon,

. . . a really good religion
Is a form of treason. (p. 118)

Since Bokononism is declared to be an "untruth" by its own inventor, it is no exaggeration to infer that the novel extends the doctrine symbolically to all religions. And this *is* the Bokononist idea, no mistake. As one of the followers, Dr. von Koenigswald puts it, "all religions, including Bokononism, are nothing but lies" (p. 148). But we propose that the new religion itself is more than a lie, it is treason, too.

The irony afforded by Bokononism as a parody of the rise of religions is indirect but richer and more refined than in *The Sirens of Titan* and enhances Vonnegut's social satire. Religions are generally considered to have originated as primitive man's attempt to codify his dependence on transcendental powers believed to be determinative of his fate and also as an attempt to influence those powers. Opposed to all this is Bokonon's attitude that transcendental forces are disinterested in man; there is no way to communicate with them and no way to influence them. A predominant feature of religions is that they use *fantasy* to minister to needs unappeasable in the world of reality. Bokononism also rests on the recognition that certain needs are not answered but these are needs that traditional religions do expect social reality to appease and where Bokonon has no answers—fantastic or otherwise.

The narrator of the novel has a clear vision of what really good news would be for the island in contrast to all the political and religious histrionics: "There would have to be plenty of good things for all to eat . . . nice places for all to live, and good schools and good health and good times for all, and work for all who wanted it." These, he adds helplessly, were things "Bokonon and I were in no position to provide" (p. 152). So Bokonon's ironic religion glosses the truth rather than reveals it, but the emphasis on the necessity of untruths to gloss over truths implies a highly revealing irony burlesquing the function that traditional religions performed in human history when state and religion became entwined. Bokononism is an opiate, its persecution is a secret arrangement between its inventor and the dictator of the island to divert San Lorenzans' attention from a sordid reality.

Bokononism is invalidated not only by its founder who defined it as *foma* and warns that "he would never take his own advice, because he knew it was worthless" (p. 182), but also by those contradictions that Vonnegut builds into the new faith. It is built-in vulnerability, the fifth fold of the fivefold irony, something that undermines Bokononism. When all is said and done, or to put it more appropriately, when all Bokononist teachings are said and the apocalyptic deed with *ice-nine* is done, and the earth is frozen up into an iceball, Bokonon's "harmless untruths" prove to be not so harmless after all. The intentional and refined deception of San Lorenzans has been devised and executed too well: the religious game has distracted the people's attention from the most essential social developments too well. The general social teaching, "pay no attention to Caesar" (p. 73), is subversive and socially activizing on one level, but it is vague and worse, it is ambiguous in that it can be read as an encouragement to turn away from social problems and not pay attention to what is going on; it may be just another Bokononist distraction. Besides human stupidity and irresponsible science, the social passivity of depoliticized San Lorenzans is one of the factors culminating in global catastrophe. By depoliticizing San Lorenzo, Bokonon commits treason. He is a traitor to San Lorenzans because he delivers them as helpless prey to uncontrolled irresponsibility. Bokononist fatalism is not only justified but also undercut by events since Vonnegut's counterpointing plot demonstrates that nothing happened because it *had to*. The tragic conclusion to the island's history was shaped under the San Lorenzans' nose by irresponsible people, who could just as easily have done the very opposite of what they did. The gospel of Bokononist "harmless untruths" *is* inclusive of noble ideas and sane social criticism, but their ironic Messiah discredits himself with his method of distraction, thereby becoming a *wrang-wrang*, a person "who steers people away from a line of speculation by reducing that line, with the example of the *wrang-wrang*'s own life, to an absurdity" (p. 59). Bokonon steers San Lorenzo away from a grim social reality by reducing it, with the example of his own life, to an absurdity. While he believed this act to be harmless, he inflicted irreparable harm, a cataclysm that reduces Bokononism to an absurdity on this level of the fivefold irony. Bokononism cancels itself.

The self-discrediting fivefold irony of Vonnegut's Bokononism illustrates the structure of his ironies: "the cruel paradox of Bokononist thought, the heartbreaking necessity of lying about reality, and the heartbreaking impossibility of lying about it" (p. 189).

NOTE

1. Kurt Vonnegut, *Cat's Cradle* (New York: Dell, 1972), p. 177. Originally published in 1963. All ensuing references to the 1972 edition are given parenthetically.

WORKS CITED

Vonnegut, Kurt. *Cat's Cradle*. New York: Dell, 1963.
——. *Sirens of Titan*. New York: Dell, 1959.

Beyond the Slaughterhouse: Tralfamadorian Reading Theory in the Novels of Kurt Vonnegut

Marc Leeds

In order to understand Tralfamadorian reading theory it is essential to understand their unique sense of time as laid out in *Slaughterhouse-Five*. As Billy Pilgrim explains it,

All moments, past, present, and future, always have existed, always will exist. The Tralfamadorians can look at all the different moments just the way we can look at a stretch of the Rocky Mountains, for instance. They can see how permanent all the moments are, and they can look at any moment that interests them. It is just an illusion we have here on Earth that one moment follows another one, like beads on a string, and that once a moment is gone it is gone forever. When a Tralfamadorian sees a corpse, all he thinks is that the dead person is in a bad condition in that particular moment, but that same person is just fine in plenty of other moments. (23)

To illustrate the recurrence of all time, the Tralfamadorians explain to Billy that they blow up the universe when one of their pilots, experimenting with a new and unstable fuel for flying saucers, presses the starter button. Billy protests, asking why they don't stop him. And they respond, "He has always pressed it, and he always will. We always let him and we always will let him. The moment is structured that way" (101).

Tralfamadorian literary structures are also based on their fourth dimensional, nonlinear sense of time. For them, time is actually circular and closed, recursive, recognizing "no beginning, no middle, no end, no suspense, no moral, no causes, no effects. What (they) love in their books are the depths of many marvelous moments seen all at one time" (87). Implicit in this theory and as illustrated by the narrative structure and events of *Slaughterhouse-Five*, all history awaits repetition in the future: All existence is-as-it-was-and-is-supposed-to become; all moments exist simultaneously. Whereas Santayana's axiom concerning the lessons of history is conditional upon one's knowledge of other lives and histories, Vonnegut's fiction presents a time–looped fatalism that demands all his protagonists relive the central moment of his life: the entombment within the slaughterhouse meatlocker during the firebombing of Dresden, Vonnegut's structured moment.

As the subtitle of *Slaughterhouse-Five* indicates, his is "A Duty Dance with Death." Dresden has clearly been his life's torment. While the structured moment concept explains the time-looped fatalism of Tralfamadorian time-tripping, Vonnegut's Dresden moment becomes the informing structure of all his novels. Displaying an Ancient Mariner's tenacity, Vonnegut clearly and deliberately foreshadows the entombment and resurrection of nearly all his main characters. The absolute recurrence of entombment and/or resurrection, the defining arch of the novels, establishes it as the preeminent foundation of Vonnegut's work. Against this backdrop of narrative and structural determinism, Vonnegut displays a consistent concern for some of the more threatened values in our society.

Vonnegut's values are middle-class virtues: purposeful employment, decent living accommodations, neighborliness, security, and a modicum of respect for one's effort at living. These were the values developed from his awareness of the terrible human toll taken on middle America during the Great Depression, when one's seeming uselessness and consequent despondency particularly affected his father. His ancestors emigrated from Germany prior to the Civil War and their descendants proudly upheld their heritage until the shame of World War I and the eventual rise of Nazism forced them to abandon their traditions. The family business, Vonnegut Hardware of Indianapolis, fell into ruin as the depression put a hold on the dreams of so many.

After Pearl Harbor, Vonnegut enlisted in the army. In 1944 he received a three-day pass, arriving home in the early hours of Mother's Day. He was persuaded into going upstairs to wake his mother only to discover that she committed suicide just a few hours earlier. Shortly after returning to his post as a battalion scout in the European theater, Vonnegut was taken prisoner at the Battle of the Bulge when he was caught behind the German lines. A few months later, on February 13, 1945, while a POW in Dresden and employed in a vitamin factory specializing in elixirs for pregnant women, Vonnegut was herded into an underground slaughterhouse meatlocker doubling as an air-raid shelter while the allies firebombed Dresden for nearly an entire day. The method of its destruction was intensive, laborious, and effective. At first high explosives were dropped in waves on the city, then incendiary bombs were dropped on all the kindling. Next more waves of high explosives were dropped, driving the firemen away for cover. Then more incendiaries. When the firestorm subsided and he rose from the meatlocker, Vonnegut was put to work digging out the bodies. What has always stood out for Vonnegut was the sheer meticulousness of the attack. That an open city would be targeted and the method of its destruction be so calculated by the "good guys" went against all for which he thought the Allied forces stood.[1]

Then again, the irony of his being a German American at war with his ancestral past and taken prisoner behind enemy lines—only to become witness to the largest massacre in European history—forever raised his doubts about the concept of identity. And once Hiroshima economized the forces of the rude sciences he witnessed in Germany, he knew science would provide no useful alternative to our religious and nationalistic myths. Concerning the establishment of identity, Vonnegut muses to himself in the preface to *Mother Night*, "If I'd been born in Germany, I suppose I would have been a Nazi, bopping Jews and gypsies and Poles around, leaving boots sticking out of snowbanks, warming myself with my secretly virtuous insides. So it goes" (vii). Contrasting with Vonnegut's own queasy speculations about how life might have been were he raised in Germany is the example of *Mother Night*'s Arnold Marx, the eighteen-year-old Jewish prison guard watching over Campbell in his Old Jerusalem basement cell. The grandson of a World War I Iron Cross medal winner, Marx knows nothing about the war criminals of World War II. Practicing as a partisan archaeologist, Arnold overlooks the ancient Jews' slaughter of 40,000 Assyrians, instead concentrating on the atrocities of their Arab avengers twelve centuries later, failing to grasp the cycles of attempted genocide. His acculturated schizophrenia prevents him from understanding that Israel's present occupation of land once held by the Palestinians would be viewed as cultural oppression and could only encourage more war.

The slaughterhouse meatlocker becomes the sepulchre from which Vonnegut rises questioning the myths engendered in the presentation of the American experience. But how does he go about this business of demythologizing our culture? How does he dovetail myth and history in order to seek a more appealing—if not truthful—explanation of life? An answer may be found in José Ortega y Gasset's *Meditations on Quixote*, in which he discusses "The Myth, Leaven of History." Ortega explains that "the Greek novel is only corrupted history, divinely corrupted by the myth, or rather, like the voyage to the country of the Arimaspi, fantastic geography, *memories of voyages which the myth has distorted and later put together again freely*" (Ortega, 129-30, my emphasis added). Vonnegut's demythologizing process inverts this formula: Vonnegut has *memories of myths which his various voyages have distorted and later put together again freely*.

The result is a sort of Copernican shift, removing man from God's divine focus or from any endowed external power including governmental or scientific authority. Vonnegut's voyages deny some of America's mythic birthrights such as the freedom to labor with purpose and profitability under the benevolent guardianship of the government (*Player Piano*; *God Bless You, Mr. Rosewater*; *Breakfast of Champions*; *Jailbird*; *Deadeye Dick; Hocus Pocus*). However, he also denies science the ability to replace our myths—both religious and nationalistic—by showing how our mythic righteousness at once controls and is controlled by science (*Player Piano*; *The Sirens of Titan*; *Mother Night; Cat's Cradle; Slaughterhouse-Five*; *Deadeye Dick; Galápagos; Hocus Pocus*). As Ortega notes, "When the vision of the world which the myth supplies is deprived of its command over human souls by its hostile sister, *science*, the epic loses its religious gravity and dashes forth in search of adventures" (130). Vonnegut's novels are a series of adventures that dissolve man's anthropocentrism.

By consistently recasting his own resurrection, which in the hands of almost any other author would simply be borrowing a biblical motif carrying the consequent baggage of revelation and epiphany, Vonnegut dovetails autobiography and myth to establish a subgenre characterized by resurrection sans epiphany. Ortega's sublime discussion on form and theme in constituting genre holds significant implications for reading Vonnegut:

> The form is the organ and the content the function which creates it. Literary genres are, then, the poetic functions, the directions, in which esthetic creation moves . . . the difference is the same as that which exists between a direction and a road. To take a road is not the same thing as to have gone all the way to our destination. The stone which is thrown carries within it already the curve of its flight. This curve becomes, so to speak, the explanation, development and fulfillment of the original impulse. . . . The form therefore contains the same thing that was in the content, but it presents in a clear, articulated, developed way what in the content was only a tendency or mere intention. Hence the inseparability of content and form as the two distinct moments in the creation of the same thing. (112–113)

Vonnegut's stone is Dresden, and the recurrence of resurrection permits the reader to view the curve of its flight from many different perspectives.

Player Piano's Paul Proteus is twice taken captive in underground jail cells. Through the haze of a drug-induced twilight consciousness in the underground bunker of an old Ilium air-raid shelter, Paul's ambivalence and indecision are stripped bare by drugs. A moment of serenity overcomes him before his initial underground entrapment is complete. He sees that he was part of a recurrent play of events having little to do with anything other than the clashing of historical forces: "Paul knew that he was alone again, and that *History*, somewhere on the other side of the door, would let him out only when it was good and ready to" (276). Paul already knew these forces were at work on his life; he just never gave into their fatefulness. Rather than revelatory, this episode is self-affirming.

In *The Sirens of Titan*, Malachi Constant is exiled for three years in the caves of Mercury, and the finale of the text is closely allied to the revival of the messianic Ghost Shirt Society in the previous novel, affirming Vonnegut's belief in the recurrence of simple tales of good and evil. Invoking the American Indians permits Vonnegut the anthropologist to re-present the record. The close of *Sirens* recasts the Indian presence from defeat to honor. Malachi Constant's last wish is to return to Earth at the point known as Indianapolis because it was the first city to execute the murderer of an Indian, thereby granting Indians equal status with the white race (314–315). As always, Vonnegut's tales seek to allow individuals to be the purposeful center of their existence.

The close of *Sirens* eliminates any possibility for a universal sense of what reality is all about when it is revealed to Malachi after his entombment in the caves of Mercury that he was mechanistically manipulated by Tralfamadore. Vonnegut opens *Mother Night* editorially detached from the dynamic tensions impacting our lives by stating, "We are what we pretend to be, so we must be careful about what we pretend to be" (v). Ultimately, Howard Campbell commits suicide in the basement cell of an Old Jerusalem prison while awaiting trial for his war time persona as a Nazi agent, since evaluating his own record leads him to surmise that his crime was in serving evil too openly and good too secretly. This is after he was rescued by the FBI in the basement of a Greenwich Village brownstone. Campbell had been simultaneously targeted by the Soviet Union seeking to kidnap him for a war crimes trial and by the Iron Guard of the White Sons of the American Constitution, a neo-Nazi youth group seeking the same spiritual infusion he grudgingly afforded Hitler's Ministry of Propaganda and Enlightenment. The FBI rescued him because of his significant contributions as an American spy using his propaganda broadcasts to transmit coded messages.

While *Mother Night* chronicles schizophrenia as the sole method for one's personal survival, *Cat's Cradle* begins along the same lines with John/Jonah attempting to write *The Day the World Ended*, a search for dissociative symptoms among those scientists who shaped the great physical—therefore political—forces which brought World War II to a close. John was looking for the ironical backyard barbecue on the day Hiroshima was roasted. Though relinquishing his original research into the men behind the Bomb, John discovers the roots of community as well as conflict on the island of San Lorenzo. It was there he came to understand the artificial dynamic tensions created by Bokonon and McCabe to promote a new communal order. For John, the discomforting truths and lies of Bokononism reveal schizophrenia as the engine of activity (at once creative and destructive). The revelation that the nature of power itself is schizophrenic and that schizophrenia is the revealed state of powerful forces comes to John/Jonah as he sits in a cave beneath a waterfall and again when he is later forced to retreat to an oubliette doubling as an air-raid shelter during the icy destruction of the Earth.

God Bless You, Mr. Rosewater's, Eliot Rosewater reads Kilgore Trout's science fiction tale *Pan-Galactic Three Day Pass* in which an earthling space traveler learns the Milky Way has exploded, and this pushes Eliot over the brink of his own tenuous sanity. He falls into a catatonic trance in which he sees Indianapolis consumed in a firestorm. Sergeant Boyle's loss of his universe followed by Eliot's hallucination represents an expansion and inversion of Vonnegut's experiences in 1944 and 1945. Vonnegut's loss of his mother is analogous to Boyle's lost Milky Way, and the immolation of Indianapolis is the flip side of Dresden in the very tenuous balance of hyphenated lineage. Eliot's experience is the only instance in which Vonnegut's main protagonist remains above ground. However, Eliot's reading experience brings on a catatonic collapse and a one year gap in the narrative during which time he is ministered to in an insane asylum by his father and Kilgore Trout.

Slaughterhouse-Five's Billy Pilgrim lives through Dresden's bombing as did Vonnegut—in the slaughterhouse meatlocker—and in this version Howard Campbell takes refuge with him. Vonnegut rises from *Slaughterhouse* and enters the text of *Breakfast of Champions* to "be born again." *Breakfast of Champions* presents a showdown of artistic impressions concerning the true nature of human experience. On one side is the mechanistic philosophy of Kilgore Trout. His novel *Now It Can Be Told*, which presents all of one's actions as prearranged and whose "only purpose is to stir you up in every conceivable way, so the Creator of the Universe can watch your reactions," is largely unsatisfying and triggers Dwayne Hoover's violent episode (254–255). On the other side is Rabo Karabekian's philosophy of art which disregards any consideration of the eternal collisions benefiting only the awareness of a Creator. Instead, one's awareness of his own circumstances is all that can be appreciated. Karabekian's $50,000 painting of Saint Anthony, nothing more than a single vertical band of luminescent color, "is the immaterial core of every animal—the 'I am' to which all messages are sent. . . . Our awareness is all that is alive and maybe sacred in any of us" (221). Karabekian's message is clear: whatever the state of one's existence, accepting those circumstances is easier if unencumbered by wishes for divine intervention.

Vonnegut joins Trout and Karabekian in the text because he is suddenly transformed by what he has done. He had gone to Midland City to be born again. The apple he extends to Trout is a symbol of knowledge which simultaneously satisfies our demands for intellectual freedom, yet implies the liability and consequence of discovery. Trout understands this symbol and shrinks from the offering by shouting "Make me young, make me young, make me young!" as though youth were somehow protected from the mythical archetypes man creates for himself (295). Indeed, it is during childhood that myths are presented and perpetuated.

Slapstick's Wilbur Swain is forced to enter a mausoleum from an underground passage to retrieve a scientific treatise stored in an urn. China uses the information for experiments which result in disrupting Earth's gravity, rendering superpower politics ineffective. *Jailbird*'s Walter Starbuck is imprisoned as an unwitting coconspirator in the Watergate case because the safe in his White House subbasement office was used to store hush money. He is later imprisoned in a New York City police department basement cell and subsequently witnesses Mary Kathleen O'Looney's final moments in the catacombs beneath Grand Central Station. As Mary lies dying she absolves him for his lack of conviction in life. She tells him, "You couldn't help it that you were born without a heart. At least you tried to believe what the people with hearts believed—so you were a good man just the same" (220). Her words cut deep. Walter understands the full dimension of his problem and the implications it holds for society in general. Before returning to jail for concealing Mary's will, he tells a group of dinner guests:

You know what is finally going to kill this planet? . . . A total lack of seriousness. Nobody gives a damn anymore about what's really going on, what's going to happen next, or how we ever got into such a mess in the first place. (238)

(This harkens back to Eliot Rosewater's address to the science fiction writers' convention during which he asks them to consider the silly ways money gets passed around and to think up more plausible uses.) Walter Starbuck decries having to operate with only a limited understanding of the forces at work on life; moreover, he argues that neglecting history makes the foundations of the future that much more frightening. (*Mother Night*'s Arnold Marx is a prime example of such an outcome.) This loss of history is further punctuated by Vonnegut's reference to Sacco and Vanzetti. The irony of their conviction and execution along with the confessed murderer is not lost in Vanzetti's last words as he is strapped into the electric chair.

Never in our full life could we hope to do such work for tolerance, for justice, for man's understanding of man, as now we do by accident. (197)

And Judge Thayer's response:

This man, although he may not have actually committed the crime attributed to him, is nevertheless morally culpable, because he is the enemy of our existing institutions. (177–178)

Perhaps this, along with the opening chapters of *Breakfast of Champions*, is meant to mock the false history taught in the mythmaking days of our earliest education/indoctrination. Our willful ignorance of historical truth consigns us to continued victimization. Ignoring objective truth in the name of institutional salvation opens the way for *establishment schizophrenia*. As a result, people live by the designs of conspirators (the Judge Thayers) and participate in the conspiracy of design (by clinging to and perpetuating the myths presented in youth).

    Jailbird's implication of institutionalized schizophrenia becomes the central concern in *Deadeye Dick*. The genesis of the story is a series of four murder plots, two of which are accidental, the other two not so accidental. The neutered pharmacist Rudy Waltz is known as "Deadeye Dick" for his accidental murder of Mrs. Eloise Metzger and her unborn child. Her death date is the same as Vonnegut's mother's suicide, Mother's Day 1944. As Rudy recalls, "So this was Mother's Day to most people, but to me it was the day during which, ready or not, I had been initiated into manhood" (61). The second murder involves Police Chief Morrissey, who accidentally blew the head off August Gunther while on a hunting trip, and Rudy's father helped coverup the crime.

    The other two murders appear accidental but with more calculation behind their circumstances. Rudy's mother was the victim of bureaucrats at the Nuclear Regulatory Commission who believed selling off contaminated cement would make the Manhattan Project more cost effective than just the mere avoidance of invading the Japanese mainland. Consequently, the fireplace in her home was severely contaminated and eventually caused her death.

    Finally, there is the neutron bombing of Midland City. There are two theories about how it occurred. The government claims the bomb accidentally exploded when it fell off a transport truck heading out west. After studying the blast configuration, however, a university professor hired by the local community determines that the blast occurred sixty feet above the pavement. Rudy's own guess is that it was the only way the government could determine if the aftereffects of a neutron bomb were as harmless as advertised without starting an international incident.

Rudy's world is cruel and duplicitous. He assumes the guilt for wrecking his brother's marriage in a manner that describes his continuous failures. "It was an accident-prone time in my life, just as it was an accident-prone time in my life when I shot Mrs. Metzger. That's all I can say" (*Deadeye Dick*, 147). Everything seemed rigged to fail. "I wasn't to touch anything on this planet, man, woman, child, artifact, animal, vegetable, or mineral since it was very likely to be connected to a push-pull detonator and an explosive charge" (*Deadeye Dick*, 113).

Prior to the neutron bombing, Rudy Waltz is forced to visit his mother, still alive, in the basement morgue of a hospital after a terrific snowstorm hit the town. Years after Midland City's destruction, Vonnegut manages to supply a voodoo resurrection with hope as its message despite Rudy's awareness of the inconceivability of innocent personal activity and the ominous speculations about the actual reasons for the neutron bombing. Hippoloyte Paul De Mille, the Haitian chef from Rudy's hotel, is capable of resurrecting the dead. Together they stand in Midland City's Calvary Cemetery as Hippolyte Paul raises the spirit of Will Fairchild, a stunt flyer who died in an air show because he failed to wear his parachute. Rudy invents the explanation that Fairchild will forever roam Midland City searching for his parachute. In the midst of all he has concocted, Vonnegut is still looking to undo irrational and fatal impulses in a search for survival.

Galápagos' narrator is the decapitated spirit of Leon Trout, a Vietnam era deserter who lost his head in a sheet metal accident in the lowest part of the cruise ship *Bahía de Darwin* during its construction. His story tells of the end of humanity as we know it, but the race continues through the offspring of a genetically mutated Hiroshima victim cunningly impregnated with the sperm of a German American sea captain.

Throughout all of Vonnegut's novels is the implication that due to our loss of history man has forgotten—or refuses to believe because of our egocentric mythmaking—that our biological uniqueness is due to the practical applications of biochemistry and genetics, as well as dumb luck. In *Galápagos* our sense of becoming is reliant upon the same appreciation. And who is to say his vision is wrong? After all, current debates over the extent of a nuclear-winter have at its core concern over genetic survivability. *Galápagos* is unsettling and dark if we reject any intimation that man could fall from his present position atop the great chain. It is certainly unsettling and dark to portray man so alone, without divinity, or at least without the awareness of community. And yet, there is the promise of regeneration. Having once risen from the primordial ooze, why not again?

Galápagos seeks to relieve the pressures from the dynamic tensions by pointing out the puzzle palaces in our brains. Vonnegut is eternally hopeful that we may learn and grow from our experiences, which is, in part, why all of his novels end in resurrection and begin with a new näif. For the moment, *Galápagos* drops our eternal schizophrenia from the cycle by providing the future of humanity with a restful pause from the anxieties of the present (humans evolve into small-brained animals similar to sea lions). The evolutionary leap into the water is made possible by the product of man's destructive will. The sperm of the nearly sexless German American Captain Adolf von Kleist is used to artificially inseminate Akiko Hiroguchi, the daughter of an Hiroshima bombing victim whose genes had been mutated due to radiation exposure. Vonnegut seems to be saying that within the seeds of our destruction resides the promise of our salvation—regardless of the eventual life form—and that is hopeful.

Bluebeard's Rabo Karabekian, the fictional cofounder of the abstract expressionist school of art, enjoys an artistic rebirth in part because a sixty-four foot, eight-panel painting of his, which is stored in the third subbasement of a Manhattan office building, sheds its defective paint, providing a tabula rasa for Karabekian to make new sense of his life's most significant moment: the day of his release from a POW camp into a vast meadow outside Dresden, together with over five thousand homeless, stateless survivors.

The new eight panel painting is composed of the more than the 5,200 souls Rabo (Vonnegut) saw in the meadows outside Dresden upon the close of the war. With his back to the viewer and looking down upon the newly liberated souls below, Rabo's self-portrait spreads across two panels, the blank space running up his spine representing his own immaterial core. The text's constant references to entombment, resurrection, and Lazarus are brought into focus when Rabo says he has twice been a Lazarus: once revived by his wife Edith (also the name of Vonnegut's mother) and again by Circe. Painting his masterpiece brought Rabo in touch with what had eluded him for so long, "soul, soul, soul" (247). The "vision quest" Joseph Campbell speaks about is brought to a peaceful reconciliation within Karabekian. His immaterial core is forever poised before the relics of his past, the essential awareness of what brought him to the present. Like the Maori in the painting who is studying an old newspaper, Karabekian's image will forever gaze out on the meadow "in the hope of learning what we would all like to know about ourselves: where he is, what is going on, and what is likely to happen next" (296).

Hocus Pocus' Eugene Debs Hartke wins his often-mentioned silver star for personally going down a North Vietnamese tunnel and using a hand grenade to kill five enemy soldiers. He later learns three of the five were a mother, grandmother, and baby. His unjust imprisonment for aiding the prison break in Athena permits him the opportunity to collect his memoirs which include considerations of parental fraud (his father), the legacy of genetic disabilities (the Tarkingtons), and the loss of a traditionally dynamic communal bond held by the wealthy in common with the working classes (harkening back to themes in *God Bless You, Mr. Rosewater*).

It would seem we have two choices when reading *Slaughterhouse-Five*: accept (our cosmic optometrist) Billy Pilgrim's enlightened vision of the structured moment as a science fiction trope permitting Vonnegut to avoid confronting his history in the first person or accept the structured moment not as a contrivance but as a given property of the universe—of Vonnegut's vision of the mechanics of the universe. Why should we have to face an option about the supposed reality of a fictive device? What comfort is there within a rigidly structured universe? Ultimately, at stake is Vonnegut's own philosophical (religious?) determinism about the structures in which we find ourselves. The choice of options determines our ability to read Vonnegut's works individually or to see the whole of his work operating within a single dimension.

Billy the optometrist and other narrators construct memoirs, thereby enabling their tales to be cast as structured moments. That is, they tend to see an event's genesis and outcome as its total and immediate perception. They seek a more enlightened vision of the occurrences in their lives. Joseph Campbell calls this a vision quest. Campbell notes that within these myths,

> You leave the world that you're in and go into a depth or into a distance or up to a height. There you come to what was missing in your consciousness in the world you formerly inhabited. Then comes the problem either of staying with that, and letting the world drop off, or returning with that boon and trying to hold on to it as you move back into your social world again. That's not an easy thing to do. (129)

Indeed not. The various choices made by Vonnegut's characters upon their return is what distinguishes the works, though their forms are analogous.

Slaughterhouse-Five is born from death. In some sense, Vonnegut's life as a novelist was conceived in the death of Dresden. Just as the life of the biblical Adam is described in sensory terms, "And the Lord God formed man of the dust of the ground, and breathed into his nostrils the breath of life; and man became a living soul," Vonnegut, too, is infused through the olfactory senses: "There were hundreds of corpse mines operating by and by. They didn't smell bad at first, were wax museums. But then the bodies rotted and liquefied, and the stink was like mustard gas and roses" (185). To paraphrase Rudy Waltz in *Deadeye Dick*, Vonnegut had caught life; he had come down with life. To "have come down with life," much as one would describe the onset of a disease, is precisely the effect the corpse mines had on Vonnegut.

> I have this disease late at night sometimes, involving alcohol and the telephone. I get drunk, and I drive away my wife with a breath like mustard gas and roses. And then, speaking gravely and elegantly into the telephone, I ask the operator to connect me with this friend or that one, from whom I have not heard in years. (*Slaughterhouse-Five,* 4–5)

Having risen from the meatlocker sepulchre inhaling the death stench of Dresden, Vonnegut continually struggles with the disease of life, not so much pondering the meaning of life as tracing the inertial forces which describe life. The Tralfamadorian message to Billy Pilgrim is not that there is no death, but that death is only a moment within the life cycle. *Slaughterhouse-Five* is nothing if not a chronicle of deaths wrought by greed, bigotry, and sheer maliciousness—to say nothing of plain old craziness. As Vonnegut writes the final chapter of *Slaughterhouse-Five*, Martin Luther King has been recently buried and Bobby Kennedy has died the night before. Billy's own earthly death date is the thirty-first anniversary of Dresden's bombing which just happens to fall in the year commemorating the 200th anniversary of American independence. Though Billy survives the bombing, his sixteen-year-old distant cousin, Werner Gluck, becomes one of the innocent victims. Within the throes of our national despair are indications that pieces of Vonnegut the American and Vonnegut the German die as well.

The Tralfamadorians teach Billy that on the other side of death is an understanding of the eternal inertia of competing and compelling forces, a solemn resignation about one's ability to enact change, and a sacrosanct sense of compassion for those who haven't the benefit of knowledge of the structured moment (similar to the Alcoholic's Anonymous prayer inscribed on Montana Wildhack's locket).[2] Despite Kurt's/Billy's knowledge of the forces at work in the future-past, neither capitulates to destiny/history. Breathing mustard gas and roses, they look at the times and hold out for compassion, and as Lot's wife looked back and turned to a pillar of salt, so too did Vonnegut's concern take permanent shape.

As each plot inexorably moves toward the resurrection, we find the main characters forced underground (only Eliot Rosewater is kept above ground—though confined to a sanitarium for a year). And what is the revelation of all these resurrected spirits? The revelation is that there are no polarities of good and evil; one's sense of these values depends on one's culture and upbringing. Revelation comes in understanding man's artificial construction of these values. It is ultimately explained as man's thirst for power (to facilitate reordering the community) which is the creative force behind the contrived dynamic tensions, enabling schizophrenia to prevail. In Vonnegut's world, people live by the designs of conspirators and participate in the conspiracy of design. All are culpable. His demythologizing efforts attempt to free the mind of superstition though his process relies upon resurrection—and he accomplishes his task by simultaneously voiding and validating each group's egocentric world view. Institutionalized, or establishment, schizophrenia is creative; it is the state during which all things prosper and go broke all at once. Resurrection/revelation is Vonnegut's poised state of insight and impotence—and the structured moment of his autobiographical fictions.

NOTES

1. There is some dispute concerning Dresden's classification as an "open city." In *Mother Night* and *Slaughterhouse-Five*, Vonnegut refers to Dresden as an open city. Vonnegut's use of the term derived from what his captors told him. They called it an open city because they chose not to defend it (phone conversation with the author, April 27, 1993). Dresden was first bombed in a short raid (as a secondary target) in October 1944, and the destroyed areas became tourist traps (Irving, 1963, p. 69). However, there is no such modern military designation.

2. Montana Wildhack is the porn queen taken captive by the Tralfamadorians to be Billy's mate and later gives birth to their child.

WORKS CITED

Campbell, Joseph. *The Power of Myth with Bill Moyers*. New York, N.Y.: Doubleday, 1988.

Irving, David. *The Destruction of Dresden*. New York, N.Y.: Holt, Rinehart and Winston, 1963.

Ortega y Gasset, José. *Meditations on Ouixote*. New York, N.Y.: W. W. Norton, 1961.

Schatt, Stanley. *Kurt Vonnegut, Jr*. Boston, Mass.: Twayne, 1976.

Vonnegut, Kurt. *Bluebeard*. New York: Delacorte Press, 1987.

——. *Breakfast of Champions*. New York: Delacorte, 1973.

——. *Cat's Cradle*. New York: Dell, 1963.

——. *Deadeye Dick*. New York: Dell, 1982.

——. *Fates Worse Than Death*. New York: G. P. Putnam's Sons, 1991.

——. *Galápagos*. New York: Delacorte, 1985.

——. *Hocus Pocus*. New York, N.Y.: G.P. Putnam's Sons, 1990.

——. *Jailbird*. New York: Delacorte, 1979.

——. *Mother Night*. New York: Harper and Row, 1961.

——. *Palm Sunday*. New York: Delacorte, 1987.

——. *Player Piano*. New York: Dell, 1952.

——. *Slapstick*. New York: Delacorte, 1976.

——. *Slaughterhouse-Five*. New York: Delacorte/Seymour Lawrence, 1968.

——. *The Sirens of Titan*. New York: Dell, 1959.

Jailbird: A Postmodern Fairy Tale

Kay Hoyle Nelson

Walter Starbuck's witness to the nation's near loss of its democratic process during Watergate develops by virtue of a kaleidoscope of stories, legends, and fairy tales. The title ostensibly refers to the narrator of the main story, a man who presents himself as another, a yet unknown coconspirator, here to tell one more tale of imprisonment and release. His story, which stands between a prologue by Vonnegut and an epilogue, clarifies central dilemmas for American culture. Fact and fiction shift with reference to World War II, the McCarthy era, the Sacco and Vanzetti case, Einstein's theory of relativity, the Sermon on the Mount, Sleeping Beauty, and the legacy of labor relations along the Cuyahoga River. Thriving on duplicity, the era recalls the beloved Cinderella story while reestablishing the less popular success parody. A mosaic of clock and clothing images unite male and female Cinderellas in a most arresting angle on gender imprisonment.[1] The female rags-to-riches motif, now not for women only, slips into the riches-to-rags pattern of a Hans in Luck, as images of hands repeatedly point up the failure of the American Dream.[2]

After a lengthy prologue establishes a "storytelling" stage, the narrative picks up themes of magical transformation as protagonist Walter F. Starbuck discounts control by logic or reasoning in a world of wish fulfillment. His own fairy story began early with a name change from Stankiewicz to Starbuck, the act designed to transform an ill-smelling son of Russian-Lithuanian cook and Russian-Polish bodyguard/chauffeur into an Anglo-Saxon, Harvard-educated product of the American Dream. This lucky boy was rescued from the arms of immigrant parents and transported to the backseat of big-car respectability, there to play chess with Alexander Hamilton McCone, stammering heir to a Cuyahoga legacy. However, the promise of a happy ending from this lucky beginning fades as this storyteller introduces himself as an unwitting, inadvertent and misguided Watergate coconspirator harboring a trunk of campaign funds in the White House subbasement. This offense prefigures the one later when three years after his release, the jailbird returns due to "withholding the will of a woman."

Fairy tale and "anti-fairy tale" examine the 1970s questions of political and sexual power in an attracting counterpoint.[3] The oldest, if not the best known, of Nixon's cronies, briefly establishes his position as the president's special advisor on youth affairs of a political (rather than sexual) nature, then proceeds, in quasi-classic fashion, with the story of his female helpers and handmaidens. He allies himself with the reader with an early confession. A Cinderella moment surfaced as he waited for a supply clerk to outfit him for a new life (the old). With hands dutifully clasped, as if in prayer or in hope like any believer in the promises of the Sermon on the Mount, he began what might have looked like a mysterious, religious ritual. Periodically, he clapped. Three times. But he clapped not in applause anticipating the upcoming release, but in mechanical response to the ditty that had broken into the mind he wished to keep vacant. This annoying and repeated intrusion into his solitary confinement elicited a spell-breaking routine which the present telling prompts him to disclose, thereby breaking a bond of male secrecy entrusted years earlier when he was a college student. His claps completed "a song to be kept secret from women" (53):

Sally in the garden,
Sifting cinders,
Lifted up her leg
And farted like a man,
The bursting of her bloomers
Broke sixteen winders,
The cheeks of her ass went—

Here the singers, in order to complete the stanza, were required to clap three times (55).

Attempts at isolation (necessary for the hero) bring the obscene song which, in turn, demands participation. Other twists ensue. Hand clapping, a conventional sign of approbation, becomes the mechanistic signal to banish the banal and unwanted ditty. The poetic parody, a modern variant of the girl of cinders, patently chauvinistic when power accrues to the female who acts like a man, delights and entertains in rude imitation of the fairy tale by playing off power (strength always positive) against its source (unseen and unexplained) and its nature (detected by its odious effect). Further pleasures await the attentive listening reader, for when Vonnegut uses the adolescent word play that ties upper and lower bodily reaches, air through the lower cheeks a mimicry of sounds of air through the upper, the magical power of language produces a joke at its own expense.

Compelled to rationalize the ritual, Starbuck explains the charm needed by school boys "mocked by their own virginity . . . petrified by all the things women of that time would expect of them" (53). In fairy tale fashion, he names three central expectations, three types of confinement, to be warded off by three claps. Women expect men "to earn good money," "to be brave soldiers" and "to be perfect lovers" (53–54). Logically women become the feared enemy, and imaginatively they take the shape of their own expectations. Thus, the three female partners—take up the roles they would ascribe to him. First in appearance, though second in importance, is the wife Ruth, the dedicated fighter who, by virtue of her linguistic skills, masterfully guides him out of the political dangers of post–World War II Germany and into apparently more hospitable Washington suburbs. Second is the virtuous college sweetheart nurse Sarah, the lover who can press a gentle hand to a dying patient or whisper an obscene joke through telephone handset into the ear of a scandalized recipient. The third, former college mistress Mary Kathleen O'Looney, also known as Mrs. Jack Graham, widow and majority stockholder in the largest company in America, provides financially.

Only at the conclusion does Starbuck find protector, healer, supporter. In the beginning, he appears hero and helper. He succeeds in transforming his strange, foreign World War II "Gypsy boy" (64) into a wife. He recalls their meeting in the concentration camp near Munich—that earliest, least discussed imprisonment where death gives rise to love. In good princely fashion, he rescues the young Jewish prisoner of war, transforms her by dress and by marriage. With international "woolens from Scotland, the cottons from Egypt—the silks from China . . . the shoes . . . French" (67), he turns her from an "asexual stick" (64) into a plump partner. Nevertheless, fairy tale appearances deceive. His wife controls. As a personal interpreter during the war, she enables his understanding of the foreign land; as a wife giving him a son, she extends his life; as an interior decorator, she maintains financial stability. Willingly, he confesses that while he won the manly medals, she "worked the miracles" (68). Many talents make her his superior: a keen ear gives her special access to life and facility with the arts. She could have been a professional interpreter, photographer, or pianist. Her work never moves from the domestic realm, so that the fighter is better suited to be his personal interpreter, a wedding photographer, or a nightclub pianist. A handmaiden to him, as her name testifies, her sensibilities reinforce his. His craft, his handiwork, executed the sculpted version of the Dürer picture *Praying Hands*, centers their life. Their home, their castle, their sacred domain, is chosen by virtue of its possessing a proper fireplace, altar place, to display this prized wedding gift. Her "whither thou goest" posture plays into the promise of the women's movement, the end of which we see in the labors of her hand which turn forbidden fruit from the backyard flowering crabapple tree into apple jelly—Eden commercialized.

The old stories persist. Sarah Wyatt, from an early New England family with its fortunes in decline, represents the Anglo-Saxon ideal, powerful, arresting beauty established in all such tales—tall, slender, golden-haired, blue-eyed, teeth of pearls, skin of satin. Yet a simple contrast following the glowing pictures makes the dream of real fulfillment impossible, for "She *radiated* [emphasis added] about as much sexuality as her grandmother's card table" (141). She would be a perfect mate if not for the fact that Cinderella evinces no eroticism:

She "believed that sex was a sort of pratfall that was easily avoided" (141). The point is underscored on the night of courting, scripted and underwritten by the rich fairy godfather McCone. It follows the pattern of young prince coming to take the young woman who has fallen on hard times into a better and brighter world. The Hotel Arapahoe's fantastic dining room contributes its thousand candles with silver, crystal, and china aglimmer in mirrored walls, with violin playing. But at every turn, the circumstances of a real world break the illusion. Sarah must cut through the confusing accents of the hotel's French waiter, and Starbuck inadvertently slips a twenty-dollar tip into the palm of the gypsy violin player. Minor twists of gypsy hand and mishandled money corrupt the simple pleasure to keep in view the failing dream.

The history of the couple dramatically indicts the capitalist system with a simple word, a *detail*. Sarah's family-owned Wyatt Clock Company accepted a navy contract to hand paint on black dials clock hands in a *radiant* radium white, giving employment on the one hand, death on the other. In a stunning counterbalance to this oblique reference, Starbuck mentions that during his college years as student activist/newspaper editor he slept with a woman whose mother's voice died as she wet the brushes that produced those clock hands that could glow magically white in the night. While in love and courting the daughter of the death clocks, he mated with the daughter of the untimely deaths.

Using the chain pattern common to the tale of Hans in Luck or Lucky Hans, Vonnegut envisions the human condition. With the third expectation, the modern corporate world joins the traditional fields of war and romance. Contemporary women expect great lovers and fighters, but money makers head their list. The prince, released to the streets of New York, stands free; his college mistress Mary Kathleen O'Looney appears magically, suddenly, out of nowhere, to drop down (he feels her like a bat) to his wrist. As he meets and talks with his old friend Leland Clewes, husband of Sarah Wyatt and the man who was sent to jail by Starbuck's testimony during an earlier McCarthy era, Mary Kathleen's hand clasp seems a handcuff. She closes a circle. Again transformation comes in details. Stepping forth a stinking, ugly bag hag of big city streets, she changes, on closer observation, into a "shopping bag" lady with a taste for the finest—Bergdorf Goodman, Bloomingdale's, Abercrombie and Fitch. To ensure that listeners do not miss the riches under wrap or the role reversals to come, Vonnegut's narrator explains how onlookers assume that the man in the suit will rescue the woman of the streets. Later, however, this former college activist/lover, now widow/shareholder, rescues and rewards Starbuck's magical troupe of seven. Those who have been kind to the woman's long-lost, now-found lover are picked up in a modern carriage, a limousine reminiscent of the earlier McCone's, escorted to the top of the towering American business world, rewarded with high offices of "vice" presidencies.

Once more, language facility, the chief asset of women, enables the move into another discourse community. Starbuck's college sexual, political, and linguistic "circulation" manager, who once helped the Harvard-educated communist speak to American workers, takes him to the Babel of big business where linguistic talents do not protect. This woman who rules a vast corporate empire is as isolated as a young Cinderella confined to the hearthside. Others would seize control, cut off the hands that direct the empire and their destiny, remove the fingerprints that secure identity, and allow free reign. As images of hands drive the dream undercover and this corporate female takes up the hooded garb of Little Red Riding Hood, a saving prince is needed. Preparing to meet his mistress/mentor Mrs. Jack Graham after elevation to a vice presidency with RAMJAC, Starbuck would literally play the prince to her Cinderella. Vonnegut tracks this notion in the steps of the male Cinderella looking for shoes. Having erred by leaving behind his shoes in an escape from a cell where he had been held briefly for theft of clarinet parts, Starbuck too needs a fairy godperson. Little Dexter, son of Mrs. Graham's chief administrator, produces a pair of "black patent leather evening slippers with little bows at the instep" (254). Questions of sexual identity lie unexplored as Starbuck accepts: "I might have been a kindly elf in a fairy tale, and he might have been a princeling, making a gift of magic dancing shoes" (254). These magic dancing shoes offer an unlikely counter to Mrs. Graham's ungainly basketball shoes, both posit the gratuitous nature of change in political and sexual power as their underground meeting clarifies the transaction of giving and taking of her "will."

All the embedded motifs complicate the simple tale, and often the show of power converts the apparent receiver into a doer. Conversion in this novel, whether political, sexual, or religious, insinuates a power that works through the images of hands. The range has implications for the novelist. When the clapping Walter F. Starbuck claims credit for inventing the *Praying Hands* statuary, a relic of which graces his mantelpiece, only to show chagrin with its devaluation, the uplifting symbol turned souvenir art, Vonnegut motions.[4] A by-play can be seen in the fate of the restaurant owner who, to save an expensive time piece inadvertently dropped in the fat fryer, thrust his hand in the deep fat and came up with a french-fried hand. A fairy tale warns those who try to keep a hand on time. To ensure time as a conspirator in his tale, the narrator recall years past with names rather than numbers to make them characters rather than figures.

Change for the contemporary writer means a reckoning with the telling/listening process, altered by virtue of the pervasive visual media. The storyteller must create a vision as powerful as that overwhelming, omnipresent technological visual medium it must stand against; the writer must engage in a little spellbinding. Even the simplest message requires active reception, with activity not unlike that of the artist who will uncover, discover, and recover. The listener/reader must meet and match the speaker/writer's telling and retelling. In an early interview with author John Casey, Vonnegut offered his version of the reader's imaginative part: "He has to restage your show in his head, costume and light it. His job is not easy" (Irving, 41). In a much later "Self-Interview," he ties the notion of the joke and the reader's part to the central act of storytelling, the plotting. He argues that "all the great stories are great practical jokes that people fall for over and over again," then contends that "no modern story scheme, even plotnessness will give a reader genuine satisfaction unless one of those old fashioned plots is smuggled in somewhere." These familiar elements do not function as any "accurate representation of life" but simply "keep readers reading" (*Palm Sunday*, 109–110). Thus, artistic creations become, for Vonnegut, re-creations.

With *Jailbird* recycling curious fragments of old plots, its "smuggling in" makes the past more visible, more insistent, more instructive. With the electronic media insinuating itself into the fabric of postmodern life, Vonnegut tests the strength of that cloth. His would capture the fleeting moments of contemporary culture and leave, as his legacy, a record of that experience, not unlike the cultural anthropologist abandoned after his graduate student years. Not an anthropologist but a storyteller, as he insists, Vonnegut finds company with writers and scholars like the dedicated Brothers Grimm who collected, edited, and published the representative tales of their nineteenth-century German culture.[5] Vonnegut, too, devotes himself to preserving the twentieth-century American experience, producing, as he goes, a comparable catalog of tales with its mix of themes and motifs of American cultural, historical, political, literary, religious, and social heritage.

As a storyteller, he is kin to the *Marchenfrau,* female source and teller of tales. With stories easily read and readily understood, like those a child might hear at its mother's knee, he delights in his own version of the happy ending, the "comforting lies" (*Wampeters*, 240). But as he collects and sorts, arranges and edits, the picture of the human condition, the comfort zone narrows; he insists on drawing together the imagination of the speaker and listener to re-establish, reassert, and revitalize communication.

The novel's prologue examines the dynamics of storytelling. The very first few lines lay out the interrelationship of the writer, reader and situation. Kilgore Trout enacts the plight of the author: "He could not make it on the outside" (9). First and foremost, the storyteller is a prisoner, its form clear in the statement of a clever young man who claims to have captured the meaning of this writer's entire artistic output in the seven-word message: "Love may fail, but courtesy will prevail" (10). To ensure the notion of confinement will not escape the reader, Vonnegut develops his picture with customary verve. In a seeming digression, triggered by this fan's association with Crown Point, Indiana, he launches into a reflection on the legendary John Dillinger who was once incarcerated there and gained special recognition, notoriety and freedom through an ingenious fictive device—"a pistol made of soap and shoe polish" (9). Should any nodding, careless, and casual attendant to this story not marvel at this clever ploy, Vonnegut inserts what dare not be construed as a throw-away quip, "His jailor was a woman" (9).

A tiny stretch of imagination makes this a comically obscene Cinderella story with explicit rendering of imprisonment and release in a graphic deception with device of purely pleasurable foreplay. Although this wonderful "pointing" to the superiority of manmade designs and the insinuation of the weakness of female perception sounds the opening shots in *Jailbird* and undeniably asserts that man has the upper hand in craft as well as craftiness, later prologue stories shoot holes through this point. Additional legends, myths and fairy tales add contrasting and contradictory perspectives on gender identification and behavior. In the variant forms inescapable crossing, recrossing, and double-crossing messages confirm the differences between men and women as cultural constructs, ever subject to transformations and divergent interpretations.[6]

Pairing Cinderella with Hans in Luck allows Vonnegut to highlight the fairy tale quality of the Watergate "story." He understands well how art can disclose or conceal differing aesthetic and political ends. In various essays he has addressed the hazards of the mixing. Trained as an anthropologist, he monitors the customs and codes, and has warned: "This is a national tragedy, of course—that we've changed from a society to an audience" (*Wampeters*, 273). For Vonnegut, the challenge is obvious. When politicians usurp the role of fiction-makers, then fiction-makers must take up the political stance. The artist may offer the only source or an alternate vision. Acutely attuned to the cultural context, Vonnegut positions himself to serve as an agent of change (*Wampeters*, 237), a man of messages. He must be clear and straightforward.

The Prologue's long legend of the Cuyahoga uprising, an invented history that speaker Vonnegut describes as a "mosaic composed of bits taken from tales of such riots in not such olden times" (21–22), addresses the merger of fiction and fact in the annals of history and culture.[7] The story, which persists into the narrative proper as a formative story for the adolescent Starbuck, begins with a straightforward action. Men strike because of wage cuts. The event becomes complex and confused with the arrival and involvement of the wives. A riot develops when the women, who had assembled in order to accede to management demands, make an offhand comment about an eventual return. The factory owners had at first refused to listen to what the women wanted say, do not understand the women later stand at their gate because they have nowhere else to turn. Mismatched communications turn a Christmas gathering into a bloody battle without point, plot or plan. Neither men nor women ever get the upper hand; all parties turn witless when pressed to control their own actions, much less try to understand them. Disaster ensues when groups try to communicate.

Vonnegut's new fairy tale might be tested by criteria set by those who study the form. William Bascom has offered widely accepted criteria for the fairy tale—that which protects, validates, justifies, and teaches the culture they represent. Vonnegut's patchwork commentary in this legacy mirrors the culture and confirms many of its rituals while resisting principles that prove mean-spirited and/or support conforming behavior. His postmodern tale would open up possibilities. Tales concocted by Starbuck's mentor Dr. Fender, also known as Kilgore Trout, counterbalance with an emphasis on listening. This recognition of the receiver fits neatly with other reception themes in the prologue, and indirect allusions to the religious teaching of the Sermon on the Mount lead to a science fiction story. A disembodied judge from Vicuna who, having left the planet after it used up all its fossil fuel and food, flies through the universe looking for a body to inhabit since life without form (so to speak) offers no pleasure to the flesh. In so searching, the judge cannot judge; he cannot tell that turkey buzzards are not the rulers of earth, cannot see prisoners are not free. The story ends later as the judge enters into the body of the narrator, his ear the point of entry. For all its sexual suggestiveness receiving only familiar and fatuous argument or foreign mysteries of magical incantations, this science fiction version of Starbuck's immigrant story parallels the brief inserts that highlight real and more famous Sacco and Vanzetti, immigrant shoemaker and his helper, who, unlike the narrator's more physically attractive parents, were lucky enough to receive employment and protection from McCone. Like the luckless judge, these men met a hapless fate.

Another Fender fairy tale variant entitled "Asleep at the Switch" does not pursue the transforming power of electric technology or the American Dream/Cinderella but instead features the unwittingness of transformations. Albert Einstein, the master converter, the father of $E=MC^2$, arrives in heaven to question the rationality of the "auditing stories" by which an individual is held responsible for missed opportunities. The powers offer a choice: he may persist with logic, or he may keep his favorite fiddle. He loves his fiddle. This absence of logic and control in daily events appears in most stories. The father's story of an early morning adventure told to son and brother gathered round a restaurant table—the place of some significance since the wife/mother did not cook and eventually declined to go on living—relies on this approximation of a cultural context to forward its meaning and can be construed as a tale about women even though "the story was a sort of fairy tale, with a moral for everyone" (16). The story is short. On his way to this meeting, his father had found a long plank of wood which had an intriguing grain. Thinking it would provide special boards, he removed the nails and took it to a sawmill for ripping. He gave his word that all nails had been removed; however, one nail that had lost its head remained. It brought down the mill. This story immediately follows another that Vonnegut had once tried to write. He attempted to create a myth of reconciliation, bringing all unruly characters of his family to heaven, giving them the power to choose an age for a life happily ever after. His mother chose to leave at the age of sixteen, before meeting her husband and having her child. She brought down the dream—and the story.

The fairy tale unites what Vonnegut maps out as the domain of the human species: our desire for control, community, and compassion. The insidious transformation of society by unremarked transfers of powers produce subtle changes in values, the fading of the human voice behind the growing din of an electronic media, the increasing difficulty of waking the sleeping audience. He fears the loss of language in the pervasiveness and invasiveness of the electronic media. The cultural artifacts that Vonnegut finds, dusts off, and pieces together to a show a world of duplicity present a simple message that may offset the small comfort in the storyteller's art. Not surprisingly these issues develop in the Cinderella story. Given Vonnegut's tendency to absorb and reflect the primary contemporary impulses, this step into women's shoes seems appropriate since women have been and are, after all—or should we say *before all*—the primary models for transmission of cultural messages. As spinners of yarns at the hearthside, as first tellers of stories, they belong at the center of this period piece. No one should be terribly shocked or disconcerted at the "feminine" bias of style of *Jailbird*, an autobiography personal, familiar, idiosyncratic, anecdotal—all features frequently ascribed to writings by women. Even in the prologue, which purports to be Vonnegut's voice, a familiarity and closeness develops in the shared information about daily affairs, making the introductory notes autobiographical in appearance if not in fact. Though primarily a document that examines the making of stories and the artist's very tenuous control over his material, the postmodern fairy tale offers a version of the author who slips into and out of roles much like Cinderella transformed into a Hans in Luck.

The reworking of 1970s issues and problems lays out the rise and fall of the Nixon era, the emergence and the stalling of the women's movement; the promise and failure of Christianity kept in view by allusions to the Sermon on the Mount create a background of patched, historical foils for those immigrants who came with visions of freedom only to find themselves sometimes isolated or segregated or executed—but always transformed by the experience.

NOTES

1. Vonnegut's interest in Cinderella and his understanding of the theory and criticism of the field of fairy tales is documented in his essay "The Sexual Revolution" (*Palm Sunday* 312-315).

2. In a narrative where images work overtime, the hand of this writer may just be pulling our leg or whispering jokes in our ear. The word *hand* which "sounds like" Hans hands us a hand-y way to trace the handwriting on this mosaic. Many lines in *Jailbird* seem to be simple recounting of this word's dictionary listings. A terminal part, a specialized function, but it can grasp, hold, control, retain, and thereby suggest possession, custody, authority, power. It can indicate direction or position; it refers to actions of agency, service or assistance. It can be used for an oath, pledge or vow. *Hand* can refer to work with the hands, especially manual labor, but also brings us reminders of skill with things done by hand. Identity resides in the handwriting as well as in fingerprints. We show approbation with applause. We signal by pointing, take measures of time and space with the hand. It has long been a symbol of source, shape, charm, execution, especially that performance of the artist. It signals a way to behave, to manage, manipulate, seize, deal with, guide, conduct, transmit. Word combinations preview this mosaic, for Vonnegut gives us fiction that seems offhand even as he worries that it gets out of hand. *Jailbird*, as we shall see, explores many images at hand—with its hands off, hands on, hand over, or hand down; it develops with handmaidens in hand or hand-in-hand with imitation handbags and

handstamps; actions become symbolic with a handshake or a handset; meaning resides in the allusions to a handicraft, handiwork, or handicap.

3. Max Luthi defines the "farce fairy tale" or "anti-fairy tale": "The hero fails in the face of every difficulty, avoids everything requiring any effort, and always takes the easiest way out; he moves backward, not forward; he regresses" (137). This hero, totally dependent on helpers is *"the receiver (der Begabte) par excellence"* (138).

4. Vonnegut does not claim to compete with television even though he recognizes that television has, in effect, taken over the short story as a vehicle (Palm Sunday, 2). Yet his works do resemble popular media productions. Making entertaining, informative and simple messages to draw an audience away from the mesmerizing electronic screen is no easy task, and may require creating fiction that, in some ways, replicates the form it challenges with the danger that it will be no different.

5. Drawing a parallel between Vonnegut's role and the Brothers Grimm makes sense if we consider Vonnegut's continuing examination of his heritage. In *Wampeters, Foma and Granfalloons* and *Palm Sunday*, Vonnegut's autobiographical archives, we find an overwhelming fascination with his German ancestry, his family's personal and professional history, as well as a record of his own thoughts and writings on this country's traditions.

6. Luthi opens his introduction to the form and content of fairy tale art with the a comment that describes Vonnegut's art in *Jailbird*: "Anyone who speaks of the special artistic character of the fairy tale—of its style and construction—and of the portrait of man it projects cannot fail to have noted that various tellers show a certain uniformity in the way they construct their stories, that orally transmitted narratives tend to be similar to one another.
They are similar in they way they are told, and they are also similar in the way their plots unfold. And while each story appears to offers its own version of the portrait of man, one is still left with the impression that the fairy tale as a genre offers its hearers a representation of man which transcends the individual story, one which reappears time and again in countless narratives" (ix).

7. Gestures toward blurring of fact and fiction can be seen in the novel's structure which contains a prologue, quotation for Sacco, novel proper, epilogue, and index.

WORKS CITED

Bascom, William R. "Four Functions of Folklore." In *The Study of Folklore*, ed. Alan Dundes, 279–298. Englewood Cliffs, NJ: Prentice-Hall, 1965.

Irving, John. "Kurt Vonnegut and His Critics." *New Republic* (September 22, 1979): 41–48.

Luthi, Max. *The Fairytale as Art Form and Portrait of Man*. Jon Erickson, trans. Bloomington: Indiana University Press, 1985.

Vonnegut, Kurt. *Jailbird*. New York: Dell, 1979.

——. *Palm Sunday*. New York: Dell, 1984.

——. *Wampeters, Foma & Granfalloons*. New York: Dell, 1976.

Lonesome Once More: The Family Theme in Kurt Vonnegut's *Slapstick*

Peter J. Reed

In several respects, *Slapstick* marks a return to characteristics prevalent in those novels that preceded *Slaughterhouse-Five* in Vonnegut's canon.[1] While it would hardly pass for an earlier novel, bearing as it does such conspicuous trademarks of the later Vonnegut as the catchphrase refrain, a brusk rapidity of style, an integrated autobiographical introduction and departures from a simple chronological ordering of plot, in theme and method it reaches backward. *Slapstick* returns to a first-person narration similar to that used in *Cat's Cradle* and *Mother Night*; it constructs a future world projected from the characteristics of our own and makes use of science fiction elements as do *Player Piano* and *The Sirens of Titan*; it presents major characters of odd physical proportions, as does *Cat's Cradle*; and perhaps most important, though less easy to define, it is pervaded by the sense of longing, or nostalgia, that haunts the earlier works. Moreover, like those earlier novels, *Slapstick* builds around one theme, and in this case that theme is the family.

To say "the family" necessarily limits that theme too narrowly. Family is affirmed in the novel, as the subtitle *Lonesome No More* may suggest, yet that subtitle, for all its enthusiastic denunciation, points to loneliness and should instruct us that what this novel really speaks to is the demise of and need for family in contemporary American society. The family theme in *Slapstick* becomes yet another expression of the question that David Daiches claims the modern novel has repeatedly probed: "Loneliness is the great reality, and love the great necessity: how can the two be brought together?"[2] That Vonnegut's answer to this question—family—retains some ambivalence is obvious. The absurd and the serious frequently stand side by side. The concept of artificial extended families that the novel offers is undercut by the ludicrous Swains around whom it is built. Clearly *Slapstick* is serious more in the needs it speaks to than in what it proposes. And here, perhaps, that undercutting absurdity of the monstrous twins may actually enhance the serious purpose in that it emphasizes the pathos of the human dilemma addressed. As in the slapstick of Laurel and Hardy or of Charlie

Chaplin and others, the ludicrousness that encourages dispelling laughter coexists with a poignancy that makes the serious import the more acutely felt. Vonnegut has used such a technique before, perhaps most sharply in the characterization of Diana Moon Glampers in *God Bless You, Mr. Rosewater*. Such grotesquely unlovable figures as Glampers and the Swains surely serve as hyperbolic demonstrations of the need for love and the burden of loneliness that are so much a part of the modern, and perhaps especially the American, experience.

Slapstick's family theme, with its correlative opposites of loneliness and lovelessness, presumably has the same sources—be they the author's own emotional needs or his observation of his society's malaise—which lead to the recurrent nostalgia expressed in the earlier novels. Its genesis may be glimpsed in Paul Proteus' yearning after the camaraderie and sense of place he believes flourished in a past era or in the search for friend, mate, and "home" in *The Sirens of Titan*, among other backward strivings for identity, relationship, and security in the early works. Likewise, the family theme might be seen as answering the deficiencies evident in Vonnegut's much earlier portrayals of unsatisfactory parent-child relationships; inadequate marriages; flawed sexual unions; and the recurrent appearances of isolated, lonely individuals. These pointers toward *Slapstick*'s theme in earlier works, again, may be both psychological and sociological in origin, and the period immediately preceding this novel might serve to intensify Vonnegut's impulse to develop the topic. The precise impact on Vonnegut of his passing his fiftieth year, his separation from his wife, or his son's experience with schizophrenia remains hard to define but difficult to dismiss. Similarly, the more frequent public commentary on the decline of the family (as earlier in the Moynihan Report), the division of the nation during the Vietnam War, and the effects of the McGovern-Shriver campaign and the Nixon impeachment might all be seen as contributing. Certainly one senses a coalescing of the public and the private in Vonnegut's rendition of theme in *Slapstick*.

In the earlier works, Vonnegut has already shown concern with the seeming demise of the family as what sociologists have called the "nuclear unit" of American society. He has also appeared disturbed by the implications of this demise: the separation of the generations, the severance from roots, the added burdens imposed on the conjugal relationship, and the continuing resultant growth of feelings of loneliness and rootlessness in individuals. These concerns, which are so explicitly expressed in *Slapstick*, appear to have preoccupied him more insistently in recent years. In an interview with *Playboy*, reprinted in *Wampeters, Foma and Granfalloons*, Vonnegut speaks of writing "a Kilgore Trout story" about an American president who visits Nigeria and is impressed by the huge families there which take care of any relative in trouble.[3] This allusion to an apparent forerunner of *Slapstick* also points us to another essay in the same collection, "Biafra: A People Betrayed." There Vonnegut suggests that Biafrans were "able to endure so much so long without bitterness" because they had "the

emotional and spiritual strength that an enormous family can give" (*WFG*, 147).
General Ojukwu's own family numbered 3,000.

A more typical Biafran family might consist of a few hundred souls. And there were no
orphanages, no old people's homes, no public charities—and, early in the war, there
weren't even schemes for taking care of refugees. The families took care of their own-
perfectly naturally. (*WFG*, 147–148)

Without pursuing more that Vonnegut says about Biafran families, we can see the
connection with the Kilgore Trout story in which *Slapstick* apparently finds its
genesis.

The *Playboy* interview shows Vonnegut applying his Biafran experience to
the American scene. He advances the idea of "artificial extended families" in
which the Social Security Administration would assign everyone thousands of
relations. Middle names would be changed, with newly assigned family
names—like Daffodil—replacing them. There could be family directories and
magazines. Relatives would help each other, and there would be defenses against
exploiters.

If they asked for too much, he could tell them to go screw, just the way he would a blood
relative. And there would be ads and articles in the family monthly about crooks or
deadbeats in the family. The joy of it would be that nobody would feel alone and anybody
who needed seven dollars until next Tuesday or a babysitter for an hour or a trip to the
hospital could get it. (*WFG*, 248)

Vonnegut obviously sees the potential drawbacks to the scheme, and may not
seriously give the idea more than a Kilgore Trout rating, but he seems serious
enough about the human needs that extended families might alleviate, which are
at present being neglected. It is in much the same vein that he presents his
essentially similar family plan in *Slapstick*.

In the novel, as its title would predict and as is characteristic of Vonnegut,
the idea comes wrapped in undercutting irony and farce. In the first place its
inventors are the two monstrous Swains, who hit upon the idea after discovering
that an eccentric ancestor had changed his middle name. Some of the invented
middle names become subject to Vonnegut's characteristic name-play, giving the
scheme overtones of one of his favorite games. Wilbur Swain's wife, Sophie,
feels outraged at being transformed from a Rothschild to a Peanut, and when
Swain suggests that she may discover that she has distinguished relatives she
responds, "I already *am* related to many distinguished women and men"
(*Slapstick*, 165). Others reject the whole idea and wear buttons reading,
"Lonesome Thank God!" (*Slapstick*, 160). Swain finds himself claimed in
brotherhood by a White House dishwasher, and hoards of social misfits besiege
the gates seeking to declare their kinship to the president and first lady. The
continuing feud of Hatfields and McCoys, who have no time for the new names,
demonstrates another aspect of extended families, real or artificial. And so,
Vonnegut might say, it goes.

Much of what the family plan stands for, nevertheless, appears to be affirmed. Even the odd assemblage outside the White House, Swain says—and Vonnegut might well speak through him here—has gained something. They are the misfits who never have had friends or relatives, have never been welcomed nor given purpose, and who must indeed have felt that "they were perhaps sent to the wrong Universe" (*Slapstick*, 163). (There are distinct echoes of *God Bless You, Mr. Rosewater*, in this section.) Some serious indications of the potential of the scheme emerge in the Daffodil family meeting in Indianapolis, too. Those anxious to kill are not sent to war, and there are reminders that enemies are human, too. Those with social responsibilities are held to them, and the recklessly altruistic are discouraged. But the strongest endorsement is held back for the conclusion and explains why Vonnegut chooses to dismiss his first-person narrator early and shift focus at the end. The story of how Swain's granddaughter Melody made her way to New York, alone and at great peril, puts the ultimate claim for the value of family. "She would encounter relatives everywhere—if not *Orioles*, then at least birds and living things of some kind" (*Slapstick*, 277). The phrase "birds and living things" remains ambiguous, referring doubtless to other artificial families with bird or beast names but almost as surely to all living things as relatives. Certainly the notion of a human family is underlined in the recitation of the aids and comforts rendered to Melody as she treks eastward.

If there remains in this conclusion a repetition of Vonnegut's familiar appeal for human fellowship in the broadest sense, it seems apparent that the novel points toward the most particular needs of contemporary American society and, as suggested by the prologue especially, the author's personal yearnings, too. Once again, the *Playboy* interview in which Vonnegut speaks at length about extended families paves the way for *Slapstick*. Addressing the problem of "what's happening to America," he argues that "the answer is perfectly simple. We're lonesome. We don't have enough friends or relatives anymore. And we would if we lived in real communities" (*WFG*, 242-243). He also argues for roots as well as relatives: "I would like there to be ancestral homes for all Americans somewhere" (*WFG*, 242). Later in the interview he discusses ideas for a speech to be delivered by vice-presidential candidate Shriver that hinge on bestowing to Americans a spirit of unity with the war cry, "Lonesome no more!" *Slapstick* returns to such ideas, but the prologue intensifies the personal note, as Vonnegut discusses his own family and its home territory, Indianapolis.

When we were children in Indianapolis, Indiana, it appeared that we would always have an extended family of genuine relatives there. Our parents and grandparents, after all, had grown up there with shoals of siblings and cousins and uncles and aunts. Yes, and their relatives were all cultivated and gentle and prosperous, and spoke German and English gracefully. (*Slapstick*, 5)

That changes in the aftermath of World War I and its residual anti-German feeling and of the Great Depression. By the end of World War II, the ties had eroded: "We didn't belong anywhere in particular anymore. We were inter-changeable parts in the American machine" (*Slapstick*, 6). Even Indianapolis itself became such a part. "It was just another someplace where automobiles lived, with a symphony orchestra and all. And a race track" (*Slapstick*, 7).

The personal note becomes even stronger as Vonnegut speaks of his immediate family. His older brother, Bernard, is discussed at length. Their bond remains close, obviously, though Vonnegut notes that they have "hugged each other maybe three or four times—on birthdays, very likely, and clumsily . . ." and that Bernard apparently "respects but is baffled by" his writing. Together, Bernard and Kurt Vonnegut visit their dying sister Alice and attend the funeral of their Uncle Alex. Alice was the middle child, and Vonnegut's closeness to her becomes obvious when he speaks of her as the secret audience to whom he wrote his fiction. After the nearly simultaneous deaths of Alice and her husband, Vonnegut took in three of her children. Uncle Alex was one of the last of the old Indianapolis Vonneguts, and the author muses about his having belonged to Alcoholics Anonymous probably as much from loneliness as from addiction to drink. Going to the uncle's funeral with his brother, thinking of the dead sister who might have occupied the empty seat between himself and Bernard gives rise, he says, to the novel. There are other family notes in the prologue—his mother's and son's mental problems, his grandmother's dying of cancer, his adopted son's departure for the Amazon with the Peace Corps, and his brother-in-law's death in a train crash. Through all of these episodes Vonnegut demonstrates that life is, as his dying sister called it, "slapstick"—often bizarre and painful—but that relatives treating one another with compassion and respect go far toward making it tolerable.

Nostalgia for what once was, or might have been, pervades the prologue. The warm recollections of family bonds are touched with poignancy and loneliness. Vonnegut writes of being turtle-like, "able to live simply anywhere . . . with my house on my back . . ." (*Slapstick*, 9), which in the *Playboy* interview he describes as "the rootlessness that goes with my profession" (*WFG*, 242). Nevertheless, one might sense a yearning for the comforts of love in this prologue, especially if predisposed by the epigraph, "Call me but love, and I'll be new baptiz'd." Yet it is not Eros that Vonnegut espouses so much as what he calls "common human decency." In typical fashion, he says he finds his love for people and his love for the dogs he has romped with indistinguishable. More pointedly, he adds this:

Love is where you find it. I think it is foolish to go looking for it, and I think it can often be poisonous. (*Slapstick*, 3)

Eros, then, has limitations which "common decency" largely escapes. Common decency can hardly turn poisonous, after all.

I wish that people who are conventionally supposed to love each other would say to each other, when they fight, "Please—a little less love, and a little more common decency." (*Slapstick*, 3)

Within *Slapstick*, Swain's sister Eliza voices the objections to love. When the brother declares his love, Eliza is far from pleased.

"It's as though you were pointing a gun at my head," she said. "It's just a way of getting somebody to say something they probably don't mean. What else can I say, or *anybody* say, but, 'I love you, too?'" (*Slapstick*, 101)

The scene echoes those in *Player Piano* where Paul and Anita Proteus recite,

"I love you, Paul."
"And I love *you*, Anita."

While obviously bearing upon the subject of individual isolation and loneliness in modern society, the limitations of "love" as compared with "common human decency" bear directly on Vonnegut's family theme. The novel reveals failures of love, in the family context, which common decency would transcend. For example, Swain's father is horrified when the twins reveal themselves as more than the drooling idiots they have pretended to be. Previously, the father has been freed from having to love "since there was nothing about us, objectively, that anyone in his right mind *could* love. But now it was his *duty* to love us, and he did not think he could do it" (*Slapstick*, 67). Soon after this, when the mother springs to the defense of her children, her actions are not ascribed to love but to chemistry, to something subhuman (though "in the finest sense"). Parents and brother fail in decency in the treatment of Eliza that follows, whatever their protestations of love, and fall short of taking care of their own in the way relatives at their best might.

Among the virtues that Vonnegut apparently sees in the ideal extended family are its perpetuation of decency, its offering of an "uncritical affection" free of the coercive potentialities in love, and its simply being there without having to be sought. The conjugal relationship, or even the immediate parent-child relationship, appears more dependent on love and therefore more vulnerable. The contrast becomes apparent when Vonnegut comments on extended families.

Until recent times, you know, human beings usually had a permanent community of relatives. They had dozens of homes to go to. So when a married couple had a fight, one or the other could go to the house three doors down and stay with a close relative until he was feeling tender again. Or if a kid got so fed up with his parents that he couldn't stand it, he could march over to his uncle's for a while. And this is no longer possible. Each family is locked into its little box. (*WFG*, 242)

The immediate family is in a "box," a confining set of relationships that seems to separate the individual from the larger society rather than provide a bridge to it, and support within it, as does the extended family. That conception immediately calls to mind the "nation of two" of *Mother Night* or the *duprass* of *Cat's Cradle*. And in general there are few good marriages in Vonnegut's fiction, and there is very little conjugal love. Frequently the novels set up a contrast between such romantic love between individuals and a broader human love, synonymous perhaps with *agape* or *caritas*. *Cat's Cradle* makes this distinction, with its Bokononists approving *boko-maru* as a gesture of love between any and all humans but disapproving *sin-wats* or persons who want all of someone else's love to themselves. The dichotomy reappears in *God Bless You, Mr. Rosewater*, in the opposed quotations from William Blake, one espousing a Christian love and the other decrying a selfish romantic love.[4] *Slapstick* continues this line of contrast, again making an approximate connection between love and the immediate family on the one hand, and the broader compassion and respect that result in treating others with common decency, associated with the extended family, on the other.[5] Conjugal love apparently flourishes between Melody and Isadore, but even this is supported by the family context provided by grandfather Swain and Vera Chipmunk-5 Zappa and her slave family. But Melody's treatment by artificial relatives and other decent beings on her long trek east remains unreservedly the novel's high point.[6]

While the social justifications for Vonnegut's views are conspicuous—the evidence of loneliness, lovelessness and rootlessness, of the absence of compassion and decency in daily relationships, is all around—some part of his vision is certainly intensely personal. He begins this novel, after all, by calling it, "the closest I will ever come to writing an autobiography" (*Slapstick*, 1). He explains that statement by saying that the novel is "about what life *feels* like to me" (*Slapstick*, 1). It could be argued that in these terms most of his novels might be seen as autobiographical, and certainly in several of them situations are created that draw on Vonnegut's experiences or that reflect his declared state of mind at the time.[7] In fact, the autobiographical element in the novels appears to have increased perceptibly. Since the addition of an author's introduction to *Mother Night* in 1966, the importance of the authorial prologue to the work itself has grown. *Slaughterhouse-Five*, besides being heavily autobiographical in content by drawing on Vonnegut's wartime experiences, uses an enclosing frame of authorial narration and introduces the author periodically as a minor character. *Breakfast of Champions* takes author as character many steps forward and is intensely personal as Vonnegut speaks about his art, his family and his own state of mind throughout the novel. In *Slapstick*, Vonnegut announces that autobiographical intention, declares that he and his sister appear as monsters (the Swains), and recounts personal history in the prologue which connects with episodes in the novel itself. Yet *Slapstick* may be a less specifically autobiographical book than the previous two. It is "close" to autobiography in the sense that its first-person narrator writes *his* autobiography, one that contains features that might be adaptations from Vonnegut's life. These features include the parent-child relationships, the pill-popping, the sister relationship, the presidential campaign with a "Lonesome No More" slogan, and perhaps even the marriages. But to seek narrow factual correspondencies and precise autobiographically based psychological implications in a work of this kind would be both difficult and, perhaps, dangerous. Suffice it to say that this novel retains the personal quality typical of Vonnegut, without being exclusively private, and says a good deal about "how life feels" to him. It can also be said that the sadness and loneliness suggested elsewhere in his writing reemerge here, although in comparison with *Breakfast of Champions* in particular this novel conveys, by tone as much as content, the impression of a less strained state of mind. Without turning the novel into a psychological allegory or biographical cryptogram, it remains clear that the extended family thesis serves to express very personal anxieties and to posit potential means of relief from them.

To argue, even tentatively, to such a conclusion about the autobiographical component of the novel is not to imply a limitation. Earlier Vonnegut novels, at least in part, have been intensely personal, and possibly therapeutic, attempting to come to terms with or even to dispel the more worrisome aspects of his own psyche or of the daily business of life. But these personal anxieties become the shared fears of the society, and from that meeting stems much of Vonnegut's success as a contemporary novelist. Taken in isolation and lifted from context, personal musings can appear self-indulgent and social generalizations can become clichéd. In Vonnegut, the blending of the two provides a happy balance, at its best adding conviction and insight on the one hand, recognition and universality on the other. In this regard, his work perhaps resembles that of the comics to whom the novel is dedicated: Laurel and Hardy. Their comedies frequently involved clichéd formulae—the shrewish wife, the confining sleeping berth, the contrary automobile—yet remained peculiarly Laurel and Hardy. Their plights were in essence universal, but that universality gains in relevance through the unique style of its presentation. In Vonnegut's fiction the distinctive manner includes the closeness of the author to his material and the intimacy he achieves with his reader through his personalized style. Even where the authorial voice is not heard, the author's presence is felt and his attitudes are frequently conspicuous. This is not simply a matter of prologues, of interjections like "hi ho" or "so it goes," of repeated appearances of familiar characters and situations, or of the introduction of self into the fictional world. These things contribute, no doubt, but are ultimately only the more superficial manifestations of an authorial stance which inevitably makes itself felt through the usual modes of diction, attitude, theme, structure, and the total texture of the novel. And, to repeat, that characteristic stance in Vonnegut is an intensely personal one, where the author, far from being refined out of existence like Stephen Dedalus' aloof artist, remains a constantly felt presence. In *Slapstick* this presence never becomes intrusive, being shielded by first-person narrator and later omniscient narration, and it adds a rather poignant note of personal involvement to the presentation of the extended families theme.[8]

To speak of Vonnegut's "authorial stance" and then to consider his methods with such solemnity may seem anomalous, especially given a novel called *Slapstick*. That title fairly describes the type of humor so abundant in Vonnegut and that he in this prologue calls "grotesque, situational poetry." One of Vonnegut's favorite means for portraying that "grotesque, situational poetry" has been science fiction. But one reason he should never have been classified simply as a science fiction writer is that his exploitation of that genre has been so frequently comic. For Vonnegut, science fiction remains largely a means to demonstrate the ludicrous, the incongruous, the absurd aspects of life. These are often painful, too. So is the situation of Vonnegut's sister Alice when she describes life as "soap opera!" and "slapstick." The science fiction—or *near* science fiction—elements in this novel partake of the same tragicomic mix. Variable gravity and mysterious fatal epidemics are the two principle subjects. The fluctuations of gravity are certainly hideous in the death and destruction they cause as are the "Green Death" and "Albanian influenza," yet they are as comic in some of their side effects as are the two diseases in their causes and antidotes. Wilbur Swain's artificial extended families also come under the same kind of science fiction mantle. This places his program in the same undercutting context as such incongruous inventions as miniaturized Chinese and the "Hooligan." Nor is it the first idea with some serious merit that Vonnegut has chosen to present through the medium of comic science fiction. If, then, the concept of artificial extended families is presented as slapstick, so, too, are loneliness, lovelessness, and other painful realities of life.

NOTES

1. Kurt Vonnegut, *Slapstick, or Lonesome No More!* (New York: Delacorte Press/Seymour Lawrence, 1976). Hereafter cited parenthetically in text following quotations.

2. David Daiches, *The Novel and the Modern World* (Chicago: Phoenix Books, 1965), 10.

3. Kurt Vonnegut, *Wampeters Foma & Granfalloons* (New York: Dell, 1975), 247. Hereafter cited parenthetically in text following quotations, using the abbreviation *WFG*.

4. Kurt Vonnegut, *God Bless You, Mr. Rosewater* (New York: Dell, 1965), 51–52.

5. This correspondence is suggested, for example, in the prologue, where Vonnegut says, "human beings need all the relatives they can get--as possible donors or receivers not necessarily of love, but of common decency" (*Slapstick*, 5).

6. The contrasting "nadir" comes with the intrusion of the ironically named Cordelia Swain Cordiner, leading to the separation of the twins from each other and their parents. Her basic rule of life—"Paddle your own canoe" (*Slapstick*, 86)—expresses her antifamily feelings and is the opposite of the morality upheld in the aiding of Melody on her journey.

7. *Deadeye Dick* (New York: Dell, 1982) is conspicuous for its correspondencies between the lives of the author and the narrator, Rudy Waltz. Rudy is made ten years younger than Vonnegut, so that he goes through some experiences that might be the metaphorical equivalents of Vonnegut's own a decade later. For example, Rudy's play runs in New York in 1960, Vonnegut's *Happy Birthday, Wanda June* (New York: Dell, 1970). Rudy's great shock, the shooting, comes when he is 12; the suicide of Vonnegut's mother

when he is 22. (Vonnegut even contrives to have these events occur on the same date: the second Sunday, the 14th, of May 1944.) Rudy's play *bombs* catastrophically on February 14; Dresden, as Vonnegut records in *Slaughterhouse-Five* (New York: Delacorte/Seymour Lawrence, 1968), was bombed from the night of February 13 through 14.

8. It is perhaps indicative of this connectedness that in the two most recent novels. *Galápagos* (New York: Delacorte, 1985) and *Bluebeard* (New York: Delacorte Press, 1987), there is less overt reference to either the autobiographical or the family theme.

WORKS CITED

——. *Cat's Cradle*. New York: Dell, 1963.
——. *Deadeye Dick*. New York: Dell, 1982.
——. *Galápagos*. New York: Delacorte, 1985.
——. *Mother Night*. New York: Harper and Row, 1961.
——. *Player Piano*. New York: Dell, 1952.
——. *Slaughterhouse-Five*. New York: Delacorte/Seymour Lawrence, 1968.

Dancing with the Muse in Vonnegut's Later Novels

Loree Rackstraw

In *Breakfast of Champions*, the novel he called his "fiftieth birthday present" to himself, Kurt Vonnegut imaged himself as "crossing the spine of a roof—having ascended one slope." This twenty-year ascent in a novel-writing career that began in 1952 with *Player Piano* and peaked with *Breakfast of Champions* did seem to mark a pivotal point in both his personal and his professional life.

By his fiftieth birthday, he had left his Cape Cod home and family and was living in Manhattan with Jill Krementz, who would later become his second wife. His six children, like their parents, had survived some painful crises and were now on their own. He had enjoyed the New York premiere of his first successful play, *Happy Birthday, Wanda June*. His masterwork, *Slaughterhouse-Five*, was generating worldwide acclaim, as was its author. In a letter written four days after his birthday, Vonnegut said: "I am fine at fifty. New York jazzes me up. . . . People speak to me on the street. I glow. I feel like a useful citizen. . . . I've finished another book, which will be out in April. I never thought I'd finish another book."[1]

As a significant turning point, this novel is complementary to *Slaughterhouse-Five*, in part because it offers an affirmation of life despite its paradox and pain. In *Breakfast of Champions* the image of the Dresden column of flame which is central to *Slaughterhouse-Five* and pivotal in *God Bless You, Mr. Rosewater* (201), is transformed into the abstract painting by Rabo Karabekian as an image of "awareness," that which is sacred in all life (*Breakfast*, 221).

An appraisal of Vonnegut's more mature work has been noted in the past decade or so by several careful readers. In 1982, Kathryn Hume published three major articles that identify *Slaughterhouse-Five* and *Breakfast of Champions* as turning points that signal Vonnegut's resolution of "large segments of his past, especially Dresden, his mother's suicide, long obscurity, and wild and sometimes insane recognition" ("Heraclitean Cosmos," 213–214).

Lawrence R. Broer's *Sanity Plea: Schizophrenia in the Novels of Kurt Vonnegut*, published in 1989, is a comprehensive Freudian study of Vonnegut's fiction which posits his opus as "an autobiographical psychodrama—a career-long process of cleansing and renewal" (152). Broer emphasizes Vonnegut's gradual resolution of the destructive Oedipal relationships between fathers and sons in his work, and likewise sees a major shift occurring with *Breakfast of Champions*. Both critics recognize the entrance of stronger female characters into Vonnegut's fictional world beginning with his next novel, *Slapstick*, published in 1976.

Forever Seeking Eden is Leonard Mustazza's 1990 study of Vonnegut's consistent use of the mythic themes of creation, retreat to innocence, and the Fall in his first twelve novels. He believes Vonnegut moves away from his "darker visions" after what he calls the "crossroads novel" of *Breakfast of Champions*.

I agree that one can rightly choose this novel as the starting point of a search for maturing literary wisdom. Here we find Vonnegut's explicit determination as a writer to transform the often violent turmoil of reality into an art form that is life enhancing. It is here that he identifies his writing experience as therapeutic catharsis, and announces his serious literary intent to create a new aesthetic: a culture shaped by "humane harmony" (Mustazza, 5). In so doing, he confronts a problem that has long concerned him as a writer: the paradox that language—the specifically human device invented to order and control—often results in the exact opposite it intends. As critic Robert Scholes puts it in his lucid *Textual Power*, language "acquisition alienates humans from all those things that language names. The name is a substitute for the thing; it displaces the thing in the very act of naming it, so that language finally stands even between one human being and another" (112). This act of differentiation makes every linguistic statement incomplete, requiring, as Scholes notes, "a perpetual supplementary activity, a de-constructing of language by means of more language" (113).

This paradoxical nature of language is at the heart of what has come to be called the deconstructionist school of criticism and thought shaped by philosophers like Jacques Derrida and Paul de Man. Their philosophy calls into question the very nature of reality, interrelated as it is with the ubiquity of language.

One of the ways writers have tried to cope with this problem is by signaling a difference between "the real" and the literary artifact by making their fictions self-critical, by making stories function to reflect the story-making process itself. *Breakfast of Champions* is the most candidly self-reflexive of Vonnegut's novels, since the author explicitly appears in the text as a character inventing the narrative. Literary theorist Linda Hutcheon may have had this text in mind when she extolled the vitality of metafiction in its capacity to express the nature of "human imagination instead of telling a secondhand tale about what might be real in quite another world." Such novels, she says, are "not really about 'reality' but about the imaginative processes of coming to grips with it in formal aesthetic terms" (*Narcissistic Narrative*, 45).

One of the realities Vonnegut begins to come to grips with in this metafictional novel is the importance of feminine aspects of consciousness to the generative imagination in its aesthetic function. He has his authorial persona disagree with the traditional view that a unifying idea in fiction should be a hero's search for a father. Rather, he says, "It seems to me that really truthful American novels would have the heroes and heroines alike looking for *mothers* instead. This needn't be embarrassing. It's simply true. A mother is much more useful" (*Breakfast*, 268).

If his characters in successive novels never actually find mothers, they at least seem to celebrate the strengths and values traditionally associated with the eternal feminine. They value transformation over static essence, adaptability over principled inflexibility, and compassion over righteousness. They tend to see life as interdependent flux rather than as a rational hierarchy. They may very well reflect the upturns in Vonnegut's personal and psychological life and his sympathy with the social concerns of the 1970s: feminism and civil rights and the antiwar and environmental movements.

Most importantly his metafictional novels attempt to examine how language ironically conceals, rather than illuminates reality, and how it shapes cultural perception by its inherent function of differentiation. The most pervasive and destructive differentiation he finds is what structuralists like Claude Lévi-Strauss call "binary opposition." All Vonnegut's novels seek to illuminate the problem of this fundamental way humans seek to control chaos: the perception of reality as sets of opposed units is a practice that "in reality" often creates more chaotic violence rather than order. In this, his work reflects Hutcheon's view that the postmodern aesthetic holds contradictions in ironic tension so as to problematize binary certainty (*Poetics* 47). Vonnegut does this by inventing new fictional cultures that defamiliarize the one we live in, so as to expose its actual contradictions and imbalance. After *Breakfast of Champions*, these new cultures show a feminine aspect to be their animating force, with female protagonists who grow in complexity and power. They present a distinct difference from his earlier novels in which women played minor roles and were often stereotyped as silly and unsuccessful wives or mothers. They also seem linked to a tempering of the dark pessimism that informed his first six novels.

Hence, I agree with Kathryn Hume that Vonnegut's later novels take on a more affirmative stance in his struggle to work out a value system compatible with the reality of our times. I believe he begins this effort by introducing two major aesthetic changes in *Slapstick* (the novel that follows *Breakfast*) that he will continue to develop with growing realization in successive novels: (1) for the first time he shapes a strong female character who functions as a complement and anima to a male protagonist; and (2) he uses parody as a thematic and structural basis for the novel. These changes make it possible for him to directly address the dilemma he expressed in *Breakfast of Champions*: "The things other people have put into my head . . . are out of proportion with one another, are out of proportion with life as it really is outside my head. I have no culture, no humane harmony in my brains. I can't live without a culture any more" (5).

Vonnegut's new use of the female in *Slapstick* is the origin of his recognition that gender differentiation is fundamental in shaping cultural perception. As Scholes puts it, "The categorical opposition of male/female is built into our language, and therefore into our thought, at the very deepest level. . . . The linguistic categories male and female are not only more absolute than any natural differences and more pervasive, they are also loaded with cultural baggage, much of which is highly invidious" (115). All of Vonnegut's remaining novels are primarily concerned with the invidiousness that ironically issues from stories or other inventions created by human imagination to make sense out of the chaos and paradox of life.

Slapstick is the story of how a civilization struggles to adapt to the disastrous effects of its own achievements. Wilbur and Eliza Swain, the "neanderthaloid" twin protagonists, are the parodies of Adam and Eve, but they also symbolize both the double-lobed nature of the human brain and the relationship of Vonnegut and his beloved sister who died when he was thirty-six.[2]

The story of the twin's relationship can be read as the author's metaphorical effort to restore "proportion" in his own psyche when one sees the twins as a personification of the dynamic of the intuitive and rational aspects of the mind. But their duality functions most importantly, I think, as a parody of Friedrich Nietzsche's classic study of the interplay of opposites in the origin of Greek drama, *The Birth of Tragedy*.[3] Eliza is the Dionysian energy that combines with the Apollonian form represented by Wilbur. Nietzsche believed this was the synthesis that generated the empowering tragic worldview of Greek culture. In Vonnegut's parody, however, their effort to maintain androgynous synthesis results in an adaptive, comic struggle. Their slapstick life story becomes an allegory—Vonnegut's revision of Western history—that allows us to look more critically at the polarities and values shaping our tradition.

In the prologue, Vonnegut says the novel grew out of a daydream he had on a flight with his brother to an uncle's funeral. The empty seat between them seems symbolic of his dead sister, Alice—the person he had always written for, a woman whose cancer death in 1959 followed by two days her husband's accidental death in a railroad accident.[4]

With the explanation that this novel is the closest he will ever come to writing an autobiography, he says, "It is about what life *feels* like to me . . . grotesque, situational poetry—like the slapstick film comedies, especially those of Laurel and Hardy." (1). He links this feeling to his sister ("the secret of whatever artistic unity I had ever achieved") when he says that despite the painful deterioration of her illness and the stunning shock of her husband's tragic death, she managed enough cheer to refer to her situation as "soap opera" and "slapstick" (*Slapstick*, 10-11).

I think it is useful to focus on how the psychological internalization of his sister's energizing spirit is expressed fictionally in the relationship of Eliza and Wilbur. Their interplay becomes Vonnegut's self-reflexive exploration of the nature of creative imagination in its search for a more androgynous integrity. *Slapstick* suggests that an integration of the polarities shaping human perception is fundamental in the effort to understand the cause of human destructiveness and transform it into a new aesthetic—the therapeutic art of comedy, a genre that has traditionally conveyed the view that society can be transformed and renewed.

Thus, Vonnegut as healing "doctor," offers the levity of *Slapstick* to lighten the gravity of the flight we are all taking with him to a funeral, our own, of course. Dr. Mott (whom Eliza and Wilbur call "Flocka-butt"—instead of Vonnegut?) attends to the twins through their lonely childhood and eventual separation in the Eden-like setting of their orchard estate near Galen. Likewise, Vonnegut attends to his readers and signals that *Slapstick* is to be read as a new myth from a reinvented garden—a myth whose defamiliarization of history might encourage us to look carefully as how his-story and human values are interdependent.

History is not a new concern for Vonnegut. Painful chronicles of Western civilization have functioned as a contextual forge for the often pessimistic social criticism in all his novels. But here he apparently uses an insight made explicit in *Breakfast of Champions*. In that novel he says he has discovered why Americans are so cruel and dangerous: "They were doing their best to live like people invented in story books. This was the reason Americans shot each other so often: It was a convenient literary device for ending short stories and books" (209–210). Thus he resolves to "write about life" as it really is. "If all writers would do that, then perhaps citizens not in the literary trades will understand that there is no order in the world around us, that we must adapt ourselves to the requirements of chaos instead" (210). This is precisely his goal in *Slapstick*.

Of course the biblical myth of Eden is not the only story that informs our culture's sense of historical order and purpose. As any student of the liberal arts will argue, the literature of the Greeks is a powerful force informing the worldview and perceptions of Western civilzation. Surely the values of principled behavior and individual heroism in an ethically structured cosmos stem from figures like Odysseus and Oedipus, models for some of the most noble—as well as disastrous—goals and achievements in the West.[5]

In *Slapstick* those achievements have helped bring on disaster. Technological progress has exhausted the energy supply. Life in America has deteriorated into a feudal state of civil strife and plague. The land ruled by President Wilbur Swain is not unlike the Thebes of Oedipus.

It was the inspiration of the great Theban tragedies like *Oedipus* that Nietzsche sought to understand in his nineteenth century work, *The Birth of Tragedy out of the Spirit of Music*. In exploring the Greek fascination with the creative interplay of opposites, he postulated that the glory of the Greek tragic view derived from the ancient feminine spirit of primal unity in dance and music as it empowered later Greek arts with their masculine spirit of order, discrimination, and ideal beauty.

This is the same creative interplay explored in the parody of Vonnegut's novel: Eliza, symbolizing Vonnegut's sister and the brain's right lobe, is a personification of the intuitive, primal vision of the Bronze Age which celebrated the wine god Dionysus in group rites of rapture-inducing music and dance.

Wilbur, as a stand-in for Vonnegut and the dominant left lobe, is symbolic of the rational Classical art of sculpture and architecture that Nietzsche saw as a celebration of the "individuated" form and image associated with the sun god Apollo. Nietzsche said the Greeks' recognition of the interplay of these two orders of spirituality led to a "metaphysical miracle of Hellenic 'will'" that generated Attic tragedy (33).

It is this context of Nietzsche's treatise on tragedy that signals the reader to read *Slapstick* as its parody and puts a different light on that "metaphysical miracle." In *Slapstick* the balanced interplay of these two orders generates creative genius when it occurs for its own sake as in the protected experience of innocent children. But put to the test of adult accountability and competitive problem-solving required by the chaotic realities of life, it loses its balanced integrity, a condition that limits the ability to respond creatively to life's actual absurdity. Given this limitation, Vonnegut seems to say, people might live more adaptively and less destructively by recognizing that earnest comics do less damage than righteous heroes.

While clownishness may seem demeaning when compared with the transcendent nobility modeled by the tragic hero, the novel suggests it is more in keeping with how one might survive the chaotic nature of our post-Classical and post-Nietzschean age. But Vonnegut does not use parody as satire merely to subvert an outdated philosophy. Instead, he uses it to help illuminate our own dilemma and to draw attention to how important stories are to what we believe to be valuable and real. It is linked to his worry in *Breakfast of Champions* about the disasters that can occur when people and societies unconsciously imitate characters and structures in imaginative literature.

Theorist Hutcheon says this kind of parody is peculiar to contemporary metafiction in that it self-consciously and self-critically calls attention to its own nature while pointing out its differences from the older context on which it ironically depends. It is what she defines as "imitation with critical ironic distance, whose irony can cut both ways" (*Parody*, 37). That irony signals the reader's active recognition of differences between the backgrounded text and the new incorporating one. But at the same time, it requires the reader to reconstruct a second meaning out of these differences. Thus new meaning and form ironically arise out of the old without destroying it, in what Hutcheon identifies "as the inscription of continuity and change" (*Parody*, 36).

It is with this use of parody, I believe, that Vonnegut has managed to express the duplicitous nature of our culture and the paradox of traditional values which have sustained our civilization "despite the Medusa-face our era has worn," as Kathryn Hume has observed ("Myths and Symbols," 445). With parody he seems to have found a form to contain what Hume rightly sees as the "tension in his work between the pessimism born of experience and the optimism stemming from background and values" ("Myths and Symbols," 429).

I would agree with Vonnegut himself that he was not entirely successful in his *Slapstick* effort. He gave the novel a D grade when he evaluated his own works in *Palm Sunday* (312). In fact, he felt rushed in getting the book into print. On April 25, 1976, he wrote me that the completed manuscript was immediately computer-set and distributed for book club consideration after he turned it in. He expressed concern because anything he wrote by then would sell, "and my publishers won't tell me honestly what they think of my work, since their opinion doesn't mean a damn thing commercially. Nobody's opinion matters commercially. We just publish, and off we go."

Nonetheless, I believe this novel was an important aesthetic turning point, and that understanding his use of parody in *Slapstick* can be a key to the richness and intent of his more successful later works.

Like Nietzsche who said, "The existence of the world is *justified* only as an aesthetic phenomenon" (22), the twins in *Slapstick* attempt to make some kind of graciousness and beauty out of their strange dilemma of being born neanderthaloid mutants and hidden away by unloving parents who find them disgusting. Allegorically, they represent humanity, accidentally evolved and trying awkwardly to survive and invent a humane civilization. Publicly they behave like the idiots they are believed to be. But they discover that when they secretly put their heads together, they become one genius capable of creative brilliance. Thus they evolve toward more mature vision, even as the primitive Greek culture emerged into the later Classical tradition.

Together they comprise the dynamic psychic harmony that enables them to read all the books in their late grandfather's library by hiding away in his mausoleum, a metaphor of the larger historical literary and scientific context. Their androgynous genius allows them to gain new insights about the planet which they record and hide away in a funerary urn for later use, one of which Wilbur introduces when he eventually becomes president: a humane reform to combat loneliness. It is not a mythic Theban monarchy or an idealized Platonic *Republic*. Instead, it is "a utopian scheme for creating artificial extended families in America by issuing everyone a new middle name. All persons with the same middle name would be relatives" (*Slapstick*, 107). (Vonnegut uses one of their insights later, too. Their "critique of Darwin's Theory of Evolution" would become a parody central to his 1985 novel, *Galápagos*.)

As parody, the separation of the twins has parallels to what Nietzsche saw as the failure of Greek culture when rational philosophy separated from and subverted the value of poetic vision. When Eliza and Wilbur are separated, they become boring and dull "Betty and Bobby Brown;" Wilbur goes to Harvard to study medicine and Eliza is confined to an institution.

This kind of parody also calls attention to its own metafictional nature. Vonnegut turns the metaphor of Eliza and Wilbur's creative interplay into an incestuous orgy to reflect the writer's frustrations and painfully won craft. (He has often described the completion of a manuscript as an orgiastic experience followed by a kind of postpartum depression.) As adults, Eliza and Wilbur put their heads together to invent a book on child-rearing called *The Cry of the Nocturnal Goatsucker*. By then Eliza is a chain smoker who is coughing her head off (a habit Vonnegut is known to suffer), and she threatens to bite Wilbur and cause him to die of rabies. The book that issues from this five-day orgy could symbolize Vonnegut's driven effort to make "humane sense" of his own life trauma. His Dresden experience transformed into *Slaughterhouse-Five*, for example, is a novel whose subtitle is *The Children's Crusade*.

Nietzsche also played with the metaphor of orgiastic experience when he said that "some enormously unnatural event—such as incest—must have occurred" in order for "nature to surrender her secrets" and reveal her "Dionysian wisdom" (68). In *Slapstick*, this Dionysian wisdom is signaled by the rapturous but ominous song of the whippoorwill, whose scientific name is the "Nocturnal Goatsucker," Its cry, "Whip poor Will?" is heard the evening before Eliza and Wilbur are banished from their childhood paradise. Vonnegut readers will recognize his use of birdsongs as an epiphanic response to life's paradox, such as the *"Poo-tee-weet?"* at the end of *Slaughterhouse-Five*. The cry seems to echo Nietzsche's view that "contradiction, the bliss born of pain, spoke out from the very heart of nature" (47). Wilbur and Eliza's loss of innocence is the painful existential paradox of all humanity, one the Greeks sought to ameliorate with tragic drama. In a general resonance with Nietzsche, Vonnegut's many birds and music are often associated with the female as the creative animating energies that dance through this and other of his novels to generate renewal or transformation.

In *Slapstick*, after the death of Eliza in an accidental avalanche of fool's gold, Wilbur suffers through a life burdened by "heavy gravity" and the presidential tasks of running a country brought to a standstill by civil strife and economic collapse. Like Vonnegut, who says his own psychic imbalance can be assuaged by writing (pursuit of the muse), Wilbur keeps searching for the eternal feminine in his struggle to restore harmony to himself and his country. He unknowingly fathers a son in Illinois during a minor orgy with a woman who has helped him communicate with Eliza again in her boring afterlife at a heavenly "Turkey Farm." He finally retreats to Manhattan to practice the healing art of medicine in a dangerous and deteriorating world. This is the world that "ends" with his granddaughter, Melody Oriole-2 beginning "her incredible journey eastward, ever eastward, in search of her legendary grandfather" (243).

Melody replaces Eliza as Wilbur's Dionysian music and embodies Vonnegut's animating muse or, as he says in the prologue, all that is left of his optimistic imagination and creativeness (19). Even though she is captured "after the Battle of Iowa City" (242), she is able to escape and join her grandfather. It's another of Vonnegut's textual interweavings that when Wilbur realizes who she is, he felt like he "had somehow sprung a huge *leak*. And out of that sudden, painless opening . . . there crawled a famished child, pregnant and clasping a Dresden candlestick" (241). This rebirth of animating imagination is linked to the "leak into another universe" that Vonnegut uses to identify the creative experience in *Breakfast of Champions*. As autobiography, it suggests Vonnegut's own odyssey to Manhattan from the University of Iowa where he was teaching in the mid-1960s when he finally resolved his Dresden novel, *Slaughterhouse-Five*.

The Dresden candlestick carried by Melody functions as a brilliant *mise en abyme*, one of those internal reflecting mirrors that Vonnegut often uses to signal the dual nature of the text as both artifice and an aspect of the larger cultural context: The candlestick "depicted a nobleman's flirtation with a shepherdess at the foot of a treetrunk enlaced in flowering vines" (*Slapstick*, 240). If one reads the Dresden firestorm as a generative paradox symbolic of the many contradictions driving Vonnegut's life and literary career, the candlestick becomes the image here of the *axis mundi* at the core of his work. The vines around the tree trunk are an artistic restatement of the firestorm, transformed into the Dionysian embrace that resolves paradox in Vonnegut's literary inventions. Thus the candlestick becomes an enlightening, life-giving image ironically stemming from the dark, labyrinthian horror of the abyss Vonnegut himself faced as a prisoner of war during World War II. The nobleman's flirtation with the shepherdess surely suggests the interplay of Nietzsche's Apollo and Dionysus, of *Slapstick*'s Wilbur and Eliza, of the "real" Vonnegut and his sister, and of the archetypal Adam and Eve—about to "put their heads together" beneath the mythic Tree for the endless generation of creative imagination in the slapstick dance of life.

As an experiment with parody, *Slapstick* seems to have given Vonnegut renewed interest in developing the metafictional direction of his writing. He would continue to invoke the feminine aspect of Dionysian music as the vehicle for his mimesis of imagination and the restructuring of aesthetic balance, and he seemed confident that the informed reader would undertake the creative transactions his parody signaled.

In his next novel, *Jailbird*, Mary Kathleen O'Looney is the first of a series of "Mary" figures who animate the remainder of his novels. As parodies of the Christian "mother of God" they personify the creative muse called for in *Breakfast of Champions* and reminiscent of Eliza in *Slapstick*. They also echo Nietzsche's view that the Dionysian-Apollonian synthesis opens the way "to the Mothers of Being, to the innermost heart of things" (99–100). They also seem to engender the inventive spirit of the author who links their muse-like qualities to rather inept male protagonists in need of their vitality. All are considerably stronger and more complex than Vonnegut's earlier female characters, although they still suffer the accidents or even death that often afflict his female figures.[6] They all have inwardly strong "earth mother" qualities. Even though they may appear ridiculous at times, they represent the vital force central to Vonnegut's new mythic parodies about the life-enhancing, transformative powers of the androgynous imagination.

Thematically, *Jailbird* resonates with *God Bless You, Mr. Rosewater*'s, concern about political and economic corruption. The social problem it seeks to deconstruct is the "binary opposition" of poverty and wealth, and how this polarity is linked to the political malaise of capitalistic society in the late twentieth century. Structurally, the narrative is a series of flashbacks and "flashforwards" that suggest nothing less than a parody of *The Divine Comedy*. The protagonist,

Walter Starbuck, is the Dante who leaves the dark wood of an "Adult Correctional Facility" where he has been mistakenly imprisoned as a convicted participant in the Watergate scandal. In Manhattan he is guided by a bag lady, Mary Kathleen O'Looney, through the inferno of an underground railroad garage, the "unacceptable air" of New York's purgatorial streets, and its paradise at the top of the Chrysler Building. Mary, a disguised Beatrice in this parody, is also the disguised owner of the RAMJAC Corporation, whose fortune she has inherited and is now secretly redistributing to all citizens who show kindness. Through her Walter finds momentary peace and renewal as a vice president of RAMJAC only to be sent back to prison after Mary's death for concealing her will.

In *Jailbird*, Mary's "divine" comedy is another slapstick story to provide new lenses for a critical look at some ironic cultural effects of the model provided by Dante's esteemed literary masterpiece. The implication is that the structure and goals of free-enterprise systems arise from Dante's medieval vision. However, his poetic model of orderly hierarchical structure and its Scholastic theme of salvation through the active pursuit of faith and reason, have resulted in human disaster in twentieth-century America. Reading *Jailbird* as parody allows the reader to see the chaos lurking beneath the rational Aristotelean order celebrated in Dante's poem. It suggests that capitalism has substituted a pursuit of wealth and power for Dante's pursuit of salvation. The result is an economic structure that in actuality behaves like a "thoughtless weather system" (231) instead of rational heavenly justice.[7]

Like *Slapstick*, the novel's prologue identifies an actual historical context on which the narrative tension builds: the grim effects of the depression on Vonnegut's parents and hometown; the fruitless idealism of Indianapolis labor leader Powers Hapgood and his wife Mary, who had been a vice presidential candidate for the Socialist party; and the judicial travesty of the Sacco and Vanzetti trial in which two Italian immigrants were wrongly executed because of their anti-Socialist sentiments in 1927. The epigraph to *Jailbird* is an excerpt from a letter from Nicola Sacco to his son, Dante.

The first half of the novel develops the ironically interrelated events and people that have shaped Walter's chaotic life up through his incarceration. As parody, one can read his problems with governmental authorities as similar to those of the historical Dante in his fourteenth-century political life. The second half of the novel spins crazily off Dante's poem when an aging Walter is freed from jail, unexpectedly meets his old girl friend, and undergoes his quest for "salvation," temporary though it is, in Manhattan.

Mary is the "Mother of Being" and the Beatrice to the Dante of Walter Starbuck. She is also a looney old lady whose name contains that of a bird; Vonnegut's wordplay posits her as the Dionysian aspect of Walter, the jailbird. But her role in this slapstick parody of Dante's *Comedy* ursurps that of Virgil. In *Jailbird*, Virgil Greathouse is a former Secretary of Health, Education and Welfare who actually takes Walter's place in prison, likewise to serve a Watergate sentence. So in this absurd, fictional world reflecting the Nixon years in America, Mary's compassion takes the place of reason symbolized by Virgil in Dante's allegory.

Her first meeting with Walter on Fifth Avenue is reminiscent of the neanderthaloid Eliza-Wilbur orgies in *Slapstick*. To conceal her identity and protect her fortune in the hazardous jungle of Manhattan, she is disguised as a shopping-bag lady with her valuables stuffed into the toes of her enormous purple-and-black basketball shoes. She grabs Walter and nearly suffocates him with her peanut butter breath before he realizes who she is: his old college sweetheart and circulation manager when he edited a socialist newspaper at Harvard. As metafiction, one reads her as Vonnegut's elusive muse, the creative energy that gives circulation to his ideas, now returning to revitalize him and his doppelganger, Walter. Whimsically reminiscent of Dante's Beatrice, she promises to take care of Walter and help him get back on his feet. It is only later that he learns her real identity—that she is the widow of a famous union organizer and inheritor of his fortune, the RAMJAC Corporation.

In a madcap reversal of Dante's *Inferno*, Walter thinks he must save Mary and get her to his hotel room for food and shelter. She, however, is determined to get him to Paradise, and insists he follow her. In true Virgil fashion she shepherds him through crowds of curious people, naming their sins as she goes: "capitalist fats" and "bloated plutocrats" and "bloodsuckers" (*Jailbird*, 144). In order to throw possible attackers off the track, the paranoid Mary takes him first to her secret catacomb far beneath Grand Central Station—whose grand attraction is that is contains a chamber with row on row of toilets. This is the infernal unconscious of Dante, and Vonnegut's metaphorical source of the primal substance that he reshapes into art worthy of redemption.

The next stop is Paradise, Mary's RAMJAC haven at her American Harp Company atop the Chrysler Building (Vonnegut's favorite), where she tells tells Walter the story of her past loneliness, alcoholism and depression following her husband's death. Against Dionysian music from the warbling songs of myriads of prothonotary warblers who brighten the glassed-in dome, Mary explains how she survived her memory loss from shock treatments in a sanitarium by making up memories "to fill up all the empty spaces" (*Jailbird*, 156). Her story gives Vonnegut the chance to make another statement about the function of literature and myth: to invent meaning and comfort for life's emptiness and absurdity, and to fill the gaps in human reason and intelligence.

It is only after Walter has gone through more Dantean tests and rewards that he realizes Mary is really his benefactor. But by then it is too late. She has been accidentally hit by a taxi, probably one owned by RAMJAC, and is dying in the catacombs under Grand Central Station when he finds her.

As Dante was inspired by his youthful love for Beatrice, and redeemed by her in his poem, so Walter receives atonement from Mary, his first lover, not in Paradise but in a tragicomic scene in the safety of her underground toilet booth. "You couldn't help it if you were born without a heart," she tells him. "At least you tried to believe what the people with hearts believed—so you were a good man just the same" (*Jailbird*, 220).

This final scene with Mary suggests that in the "real" world of chaos, disguised by Dantean pictures of rational order and divine redemption, there is no salvation, only temporary epiphanies that occasionally come from the comfort of loving kindness. It is this kindness that seems to have restored some harmony to Walter's life in the end, even though the RAMJAC fortune is gobbled up by taxes, lawyers, and foreign products, and he is about to be sent back to jail. It also suggests Vonnegut's vision of how novels and stories function as temporary comforts for readers.

But Mary is not the only giver of loving kindness in this novel. Three other women who brought such comfort to Walter's life figure strongly in the first part of the story, and in a way, prepare him for Mary. Not accidentally, one assumes, all four women whom Walter loved have the same biblical names as the characters found at the highest circle of heaven in the thirty-second Canto of Dante's *Paradise*.

Besides Mary, Sarah was a childhood sweetheart with whom Walter could never manage a sexual relationship but with whom he shared joyful laughter and conversation. (The biblical Sarah likewise had a sexually unproductive relationship with her husband, Abraham, in their youth.) The third woman Walter loved was Ruth, his first wife, a Viennese Jew imprisoned by the Nazis and rescued by Walter from near starvation and mental exhaustion. (The Ruth in Dante's *Paradise* also left her native land and was rescued by Boaz, whom she married.) The fourth of his beloved women was his mother, Anna Kairys Stankiewicz, a Russian Lithuanian immigrant who worked as a cook in the home of the millionaire who financed Walter's Harvard education. It was her laughter that was most memorable to Walter, "tiny, pure sounds like a music box—or perhaps bells far away" (*Jailbird*, 204). It was a special joy to Walter that he could imitate this sound, that he could reincarnate the musical laughter of his mother. (Dante gives Anna, mother of the Virgin Mary, a special place of honor from which she sings her hosannas.)

All four women in the novel can be seen as feminine aspects of Walter, just as one can read Eliza and Wilbur as aspects of one character in *Slapstick*. All are linked with music, and seem to function as muselike sustainers of Walter. All are ironically interrelated through him, and through the ironic accidents of their pasts, even as all four women in Dante's *Paradise* are interrelated by the author's vision of their Christian significance. Like Vonnegut's characters, Dante's are awed by the mysterious light of primal love, a paradox in which Dante says he cannot discern the reflected from the reflector. It was a generative, unifying power as mysterious to Dante, whose Christian allegory was critical of fourteenth century corruption, as it seems to be to Vonnegut, whose secular novel takes issue with some of the same corruptions today. A singular message likely inspired both authors: the Sermon on the Mount, a message made more vital and urgent by Vonnegut's parodic defamiliarization.

If Mary doesn't quite make it as a godhead in *Jailbird*, she certainly comes close in *Galápagos*, Vonnegut's zany parody of Darwin's *Voyage of the Beagle*, and his way of inviting Social Darwinists to look more critically at their misapplication of Darwin's ideas to justify greed and exploitation of the weak. The million-year evolution of a "revised" human race in *Galápagos* whimsically echoes Darwin's theory of natural selection, but through ironic defamiliarization the novel reveals how society's polarized view of culture versus nature has functioned to distort Darwin's insights.

In *Jailbird*, as noted above, the aging widow Mary tries unsuccessfully to save humanity by giving the economy back to the people. In *Galápagos*, another aging widow named Mary, a childless, retired biology teacher, takes on even larger mythic dimensions. She is, partly by accident, successful in merely saving the human race and preserving life on earth. Shipwrecked with eight unlikely females and an inept sea captain on a fictional, barren island in the Galápagos archipelago after a foiled "Nature Cruise of the Century," Mary Hepburn becomes a modern scientific parody of the ancient fertility goddess. She employs "certain vital materials on the planet in such a way as to make her, without question, the most important experimenter in the history of the human race" (46). Hyperbole aside, she impregnates her fellow survivors—young illiterate Kanka-bono refugees from a stone age cannibalistic tribe in the Equadorian interior—with semen from the unknowing "latter day Adam" sea captain she lives with on the island. The issue from their impregnations will engender mutated offspring who will eventually evolve into harmless "fisherfolk."

Again, Vonnegut sets this story in a context of global disaster brought on by the ironic success of human inventiveness: a nonnuclear war, famine and deadly pollution, and an unrecognized bacterial epidemic that begins during the International Book Fair in Frankfurt which eventually makes all women (except those shipwrecked on the isolated island) infertile. This modern plague may suggest that world literature, which unknowingly debilitates the feminine, may eventually be the death of us all.[8]

I take it as a sign of Vonnegut's mellowing here that the Mary of *Galápagos* is very like a reincarnation of her nominal predecessor in *Jailbird*. The *Bahía de Darwin* ship—the "Noah's ark"—that accidentally lands the survivors on Santa Rosalia island, was originally supposed to carry world famous celebrities on a hyped "Nature Cruise of the Century." The public relations firm selling the cruise "had just moved into new offices within the hollow crown of the Chrysler Building, formerly the showroom of a harp company which found itself bankrupt" (*Galápagos*, 90). So the failure of Mary O'Looney's RAMJAC fortune in *Jailbird* ironically regenerates this new story. The prothonotary warblers who drink from Mary's teacup in *Jailbird* are parallel to the vampire finch of Santa Rosalia in *Galápagos* which perches on Mary Hepburn's finger to sip droplets of blood from her scratched hand. Both women give sustenance to birds; both are muses animating their stories and male counterparts.

Galápagos is remarkably successful as an intertextual weaving that creates parody but also ironic harmonies with both Darwin's and Vonnegut's voyages. For example, birds animated Darwin's understanding of natural selection: his observation of unique species of finches in the isolated Galápagos Islands gave rise to his discovery of natural selection during his "nature cruise of the nineteenth-century." Not incidentally, Captain FitzRoy, who commanded Darwin's Beagle, is linked by name to Mary Hepburn's first husband, Roy, who was a sailor when they first met, and who had booked their "Nature Cruise" just before his death. Mary first met Roy when she was camping in an Eden-like forest after he awakened her into a blissful morning by whistling an imitation of a whippoorwill.

Birds likewise symbolize the renewing, generative spirit in *Galápagos*. In particular, the island's harmless blue-footed boobies and their comic courtship dance become the metaphor and finally the prototype for human life as the story ends. Early in the novel, Mary as teacher foreshadows the rebirth of a more innocent and gentle humanity when she uses a film of the boobies' clownish dance in her school as an "educational celebration of springtime" (106). The story's narrator, Leon Trout, notes that both he and his lost mother loved to dance, and that he and his father write for the same reason the boobies dance: because they have to. Vonnegut's point is that the human imagination is as irrepressible as the biological life force in choreographing the dance of life. Both are genetically programmed and equally capable of transforming epiphanies or tragic accidents.

This idea is personified in the symmetry of Mary's creative function with that of Leon, the headless ghost "writing" and narrating the story. As noted, Mary is linked sexually with Captain von Kleist, a physical caricature of Kurt Vonnegut (and spinoff of German satirist Heinrich von Kleist), even as Leon is linked genetically with his father, Kilgore. And Kilgore Trout, a favorite character from past novels and likewise a caricature of Vonnegut (or his father), is a ghostly science fictionist who is constantly smoking and admonishing his son from the "blue tunnel to the Afterlife." Thus, in this metafictional narrative, the generative powers of Mary and Leon are both linked to the author, one by sex, the other by genes. Toward the end of the novel as Leon prepares to join his father in the Afterlife, he says, "I have written these words in air—with the tip of the index finger of my left hand, which is also air" (290). A few pages earlier he says he is telling a story that could never have been included in a popular movie: "In it Mary Hepburn, as though hypnotized, dips her right index finger into herself and then into an eighteen-year-old Kanka-bono woman, making her pregnant" (267). So Vonnegut's anima is embodied as two fundamental, creative aspects of humanity—on the one hand cultural, and on the other biological—in the characters of Leon and Mary. For Vonnegut, nurture and nature are inseparable, irrepressible, largely inexplicable aspects of the same generative spirit.

The creative capabilities of humanity in evolutionary history are further deconstructed by this parody to remind us that a misreading of Darwinian evolution can be very destructive to the dance of life. To mistakenly think superior intelligence and technological power can set humanity apart from and above nature or justify exploitative behavior is to misinterpret the story of natural selection and the survival of species. The fittest who survive in *Galápagos* do so as life species always have—because of indifferent genetic programming and mutations, chance accident, and adaptability. Humans in Vonnegut's story survive, in fact, because natural selection deprives them of the big brains and hands with which they did so much damage in the twentieth century.

Survivors of such damage figure strongly in his next novel, *Bluebeard*, published in 1987 and largely misread by critics in the popular press. It is Vonnegut's most ambitious effort to use language to deconstruct the damage language (or any artifact) can provoke despite the artist's intention to create a more humane order. As a means of "getting outside" the medium he seeks to deconstruct, Vonnegut centers on a nonliterary art, the 1950s school of abstract expressionism whose artists sought new ways of responding to the insanity of war. Not incidentally, Vonnegut himself is a painter and print maker of considerable skill, whose pictures are often whimsical self-caricatures. He is self-reflexive in pictoral as well as literary arts.

On one level *Bluebeard* is as a defense of abstract expressionist painters, one of whom is the protagonist, Rabo Karabekian of *Breakfast of Champions* fame. They are one of several cultural groups in the novel who struggle to survive brutal attacks by powerful people who see them as "different," as threatening opposites to what they value. Thus it must have seemed especially ironic to Vonnegut that he was sarcastically attacked by John Ash in the November 17, 1987, *Village Voice* as being "unsettled" by Abstract Expressionist art: "Once painting ceases to depict scenes from mythology or episodes from the life of Christ, it is inevitably about nothing but itself. Vonnegut thinks this is irresponsible"(59).

By taking Vonnegut's metaphorical use of Rabo and his problem as "real," Ash illustates the very problem the author is trying to explore and resolve: Artifacts in the visual arts, like language, shape our sense of reality and value. Vonnegut's novel actually is sympathetic to all artistic endeavors. It suggests that all artists face similar problems in the effort to shape some kind of aesthetic order out of the chaos and conflict that arise in part from people's culturally inborn binary opposition. That is, people whose sense of reality and value is fundamentally shaped by the logic that theirs is the only and unquestionable truth. Vonnegut is in the curious dilemma of not being able to defend his position without insulting critics by suggesting they are the unwitting participants in the very problem he is trying to resolve. This may be one reason why critical response to his work becomes so vitriolic at times. When one's sense of reality is called into question by defamiliarization, one can feel very threatened.

A further irony is that *Bluebeard* satirizes the postmodern deconstructive art of which Vonnegut's own metafiction is a prime example. The protagonist's self-deprecation as he explains how and why he is writing his own story signals Vonnegut's critical look at the nature of both his own and more traditional fiction and its inventive processes.

Parody functions less significantly in this novel, even though an obvious context is suggested by the "Bluebeard" folktale. Women in this novel fare much better than did those wives in the old tale who dared enter the secret room of Bluebeard's castle. The central ironic difference between the two tales is that the secret room (potato barn) of Vonnegut's novel contains Rabo's invention of renewal rather than death. Vonnegut's *Bluebeard* is also enriched by the parodic context of Joyce Cary's *The Horse's Mouth*, whose protagonist, Gulley Jimson, parallels Rabo in his struggles through all manner of adversity to paint his huge masterpiece, "The Creation."

Like Cary, Vonnegut here continues to explore the nature of the creative spirit engendered once again by the eternal feminine. But in this novel, female characters personify a wider range of psychologically energizing powers that have comforted, seduced, and cajoled Vonnegut's fictional survivors into transforming their lives and their inventive ways of adapting to chaos. They all resonate with mythic goddess figures, an indication they are to be read as aspects of the protagonist's Dionysian consciousness which he is trying to transform into a more balanced, androgynous soul.

The Mary of this text is "Marilee," the mistress of the demonic Gregorian (whose Manhattan address is not incidentally the same as Vonnegut's). As the master illustrator to whom Rabo was first apprenticed, Gregorian's severe demands for exact imitation likely represents Vonnegut's foregrounding of the need to look critically at the function of art. Thus, Marilee is linked with Gregorian as the death aspect of Medusa, the goddess whose look could stop the dynamic flow of life and turn men to stone. But her life-giving aspect blooms when she accompanies Rabo to the Museum of Modern Art (MOMA), and when she initiates him sexually, an experience that was for him like a radiant work of art, "never again would the canvas of life, so to speak, help me and a partner create a sexual masterpiece" (*Bluebeard*, 172).

This muse banishes Rabo, however, and he must try to develop his art on his own. In World War II, he becomes a camouflage expert, with great skill at disguising the real. In Vonnegut's exploration of the nature of artistic expression, the realism Rabo learned from Gregorian is equally capable of camouflage or counterfeit. Both cover everything with a false familiarity and thus trick human perception about reality. Both can cause horrendous pain for those who are fooled by their illusion.

The price Rabo pays for his war activities is the loss of one eye. That is, his potentially holistic vision becomes one-sided or polarized, and he is driven to the opposite of realism as an artist. The "white light" he ran into (keying off Vonnegut's experience of the Dresden firebombing) drove him to the new visions of abstract expressionistic painters who became his extended family. Their kind of art will provide no provocative models for those who insist upon dichotomies of the noble warrior versus the foul enemy. Rabo later sells some of their paintings "about nothing but themselves" to Marilee. Her response that they are expressions of genesis, "before subject matter had yet to be created" (241), suggests Vonnegut's philosophical look at the eternal aesthetic dilemma of reconciling the abstract essence or form with the concrete object. Similarly, Rabo's frustrations as an artist stem from his inability to integrate soul into his paintings, as well as into his writing.

Circe Berman is the muse who energizes Rabo into writing about this dilemma in his autobiography at age seventy-one, after his retirement from a failed career as a painter but a successful one as a collector of abstract expressionist art. An aggressive widow in her forties, she strolls across invisible borders onto Rabo's private beach (read mind) in East Hampton and soon moves in with him. She is another Dionysian dancer, a personification of the witch famous for transforming Odysseus' men into swine with her strange drugs and then restoring them improved. Her insistence that Rabo write his life story is the vehicle for Vonnegut's ongoing effort to deconstruct the barriers to wholeness in artistic expression. That effort focuses on Circe's argument with Rabo about her preference for pictoral kitsch art and her disgust with his abstract expressionist collection that fails to "communicate."

This argument personifies the aesthetic problem of the artist who believes the "lesson" taught by realistic paintings or stories can often result in the opposite of its intended effect. To avoid this, Rabo's Barnett Newman–type paintings shied so far away from "meaning" in their effort to express "soul" that they were about "no-thing" but themselves, and were titled with only the name of the shade of paint used. It was like a writer so intent on not distorting reality that he could write only about words.

The aesthetic problem Vonnegut explores here can best be illustrated by tracing the transformations of Rabo's most famous painting, "Windsor Blue Number Seventeen," which literally deconstructed, that is, the paint and tape came unstuck from the canvas. Rabo later recovers the huge canvas which is sixty-four feet long and eight feet high and transforms it into what he thinks will be his last painting, one as close to pure awareness as he can come (thus paralleling his painting in *Breakfast of Champions*). He purges the canvas of color and paints it a dazzling white, then shows it to his wife Edith, another muse who has given him a potato barn studio and mothering comfort after a series of personal disasters. The painting is an an "exorcism of an unhappy past, a symbolic repairing of all the damage I had done to myself and others during my brief career as a painter" (*Bluebeard*, 276). The title is: "I Tried and Failed and Cleaned Up Afterwards, so It's *Your* Turn Now."

But the painting undergoes one more transformation, one apparently impelled by Edith's death to which Rabo's only verbal response was: "Renaissance." (It is useful to note that Edith is the name of Vonnegut's mother who died of suicide when he was twenty-one.) This painting is the secret in the potato barn that Rabo finally shows Circe on the night before she is to leave him. It is a painting that reconciles the binary oppositions of self and other, abstraction and realism, soul and body, language and story. It reveals Vonnegut's own remarkable self-reflexive ability to throw light on the inventive process he is using to engage the reader as a participant in a fictional narrative derived from and interdependent with the cultural context and the author's experience.

It also resolves Circe's demand that Rabo "start a new religion" by painting an explicit picture of the Armenian massacre his parents survived. She had wanted him to paint his mother as she really was: "She is pinned under the corpse of a man, but she is still alive, and she is staring into the open mouth of a dead old woman whose face is only inches from hers. Out of that toothless mouth are spilling diamonds and emeralds and rubies" (24). By pretending to be dead, Rabo's mother had survived to take the jewels from the dead woman's mouth and use them for a rebirth: to get herself and her family to America.

Instead, Rabo has painted a version of the survivors of another massacre—World War II—one that inspirits his epiphanic dance with Circe. When the painting is viewed from one end, it is compressed by foreshortening to appear as a large triangle, an abstract expression with no way to tell what the painting is really *about* (280). Circe says it looks like a "very big fence, an incredibly high and long fence . . . every square inch of it encrusted with the most gorgeous jewelry" (280). This image is enriched when it is read against Nietzsche's sense of the chorus in Greek tragedy as a "living wall against the assaults of . . . that alleged reality of the man of culture" (61).

However, when viewed from the middle, it reveals a frozen moment of paradoxical truth. Rabo says it is a painting of "where I was . . . when the sun came up the day the Second World War ended in Europe. . . . We were standing on the rim of a beautiful green valley in the springtime. By actual count, there were five thousand, two hundred and nineteen people on the rim with us or down below. The largest person was the size of a cigarette, and the smallest a flyspeck" (281). Each of these survivors wears a different uniform, one which functions even as words do to give them separate identity or disguise, and keep them alive and organized into groups so they can fight one another in orderly fashion. In this frozen moment, however, the war is over and their uniforms are not needed.

Again, Nietzsche's context enriches, with his description of the "form of the Greek theatre [that] recalls a lonely valley in the mountains . . . the scene appears like a luminous cloud formation that the Bacchants swarming over the mountains behold from a height—like the splendid frame in which the image of Dionysus is revealed to them" (64).

Rabo's Dionysian picture viewed from the middle is a close representation of Vonnegut's own observations on VE Day, the day he walked out of a schoolhouse in the German countryside near the Czechoslovakian border as a prisoner of war and found that his German guards were gone. "There were lunatics out there, and prisoners from every land, and remnants of the Herman Göering Division—still armed. It was so beautiful. The Russians would not show up for a week. Hi ho."[9]

Thus, viewed from one end the painting abstracts jewel-like souls of the thousands of survivors standing in that valley. It incorporates the diamonds and emeralds and rubies that issued from the dead woman's mouth that made Rabo's life possible. Viewed from the middle it pictures the women and men whose uniforms finally had no relevance to the binary opposition that had structured the war. The dynamic interplay of the two images is a complementarity made possible by the participation of the viewer. It is the *mise en abyme* that resolves opposing dualities. The title of this image of transforming integration? "Now It's the Women's Turn," The painting is the turn/transformation of the jewels/souls of all survivors and outcasts, the mythic energy of the eternal feminine, the muse engendering life's art, despite—or perhaps because of—that life's brutality.

The image is a splendid poetic moment of epiphany for Kurt Vonnegut, one that suggests a long life of learning how to dance with the muse. It is a dance that serves him and his readers well.

NOTES

1. Letter from Kurt Vonnegut to Loree Rackstraw, November 15, 1972.

2. See Rackstraw, "Paradise Re-Lost," for a discussion of this duality. Also see Kathryn Hume's somewhat different, but valuable discussion of Wilbur, Eliza, and Melody as symbolic aspects of Vonnegut in her 1982 article, "Vonnegut's Self-Projections;" and Leonard Mustazza's exploration of the twins and their separation as the Fall from innocence in Chapter 9 of *Forever Pursuing Genesis*.

3. I make this argument even though Lynn Buck says that in 1971 Vonnegut denied any influence by Nietzsche. In "Vonnegut's World of Comic Futility," Buck says she asked him if his sense of the cyclic nature of life was reminiscent of Nietzsche's "eternal recurrence," but Vonnegut responded negatively. However, *Slapstick* was, of course, written after that time. Occasional references to Nietzsche by Vonnegut confirm his familiarity with his philosophy, but I have no explicit knowledge that the parody here discussed was conscious on Vonnegut's part.

4. This is just one of the bizarre and painful accidents that has darkened the author's life experience. He and his first wife, Jane, adopted three of the four children orphaned by this disaster. An autobiographical account of that experience can be read in *Angels without Wings* by the late Jane Vonnegut Yarmolinsky.

5. See Joseph Meeker's *The Comedy of Survival* for an excellent discussion of the cultural effects of the comic and tragic modes in literature.

6. See Charles Berryman's discussion of violence in Vonnegut's novels in "After the Fall: Kurt Vonnegut."

7. See Kathryn Hume, "Myths and Symbols," especially 442, for a discussion of how Vonnegut tries to use a "Christian exostructure" for a secondary plot in *Jailbird*.

8. See a discussion of the effect of destructive images of the female in nineteenth-century literature by Gilbert and Gubar.

9. Letter from Kurt Vonnegut to Loree Rackstraw, May 8, 1976.

WORKS CITED

Alighieri, Dante. *The Divine Comedy*. Trans. Allen Mandelbaum. Vol. 3. New York: Bantam Books, 1982.

Ash, John. "Paint Misbehavin': Kurt Vonnegut Knows What He Wants," *The Village Voice* (November 17, 1987): 59, 63.

Berryman, Charles. "After the Fall" *Critique* 26(2) (Winter 1985): 96–102.

Broer, Lawrence R. *Sanity Plea: Schizophrenia in the Novels of Kurt Vonnegut*. Ann Arbor: University of Michigan Research Press, 1989.

Buck, Lynn. "Vonnegut's World of Comic Futility" *Studies in American Fiction* 3(2) (Autumn 1975): 183–198.

Cary, Joyce. *The Horse's Mouth*. Rev. Ed. New York: Harper & Row, 1965.

Darwin, Charles. *On the Origin of Species by Means of Natural Selection; or, The Preservation of Favoured Races in the Struggle for Life*. New York: Heritage Press, (reprint).

——. *The Voyage of the Beagle*. New York: E. P. Dutton, 1979, (reprint).

Gilbert, Sandra M., and Susan Gubar. *The Madwoman in the Attic: The Woman Writer and the Nineteenth-Century Literary Imagination*. New Haven: Conn.: Yale University Press, 1979.

Hume, Kathryn. "The Heraclitean Cosmos of Kurt Vonnegut," *Papers On Language and Literature*. 18(2) (Spring 1982): 208–224.

——."Kurt Vonnegut and the Myths and Symbols of Meaning" *Texas Studies in Literature and Language*. 24(4) (Winter 1982): 429–447.

——. "Self-Projections: Symbolic Characters and Symbolic Fiction," *The Journal of Narrative Technique* 12(3) (Fall, 1982): 177–190.

Hutcheon, Linda. *Narcissistic Narrative: the Metafictional Paradox*. New York: Methuen, 1980.

——. *A Poetics of Postmodernism: History, Theory, Fiction*. New York: Routledge, 1988.

——. *A Theory of Parody: The Teachings of Twentieth-Century Art Forms*. New York: Methuen, 1985.

Meeker, Joseph. *The Comedy of Survival: Studies In Literary Ecology*. New York: Charles Scribner's Sons, 1972.

Mustazza, Leonard. *Forever Pursuing Genesis: The Myth of Eden in the Novels of Kurt Vonnegut*. London and Toronto: Associated University Presses, 1990.

Nietzsche, Friedrich. *The Birth of Tragedy out of the Spirit of Music* and *The Case of Wagner*. Trans. Walter Kaufman. New York: Vintage Books/ Random House, 1967.

Rackstraw, Loree. "Paradise Re-Lost," *The North American Review* (Winter 1976) 63–4.

Scholes, Robert. *Textual Power: Literary Theory and the Teaching of English*. New Haven, Conn.:London: Yale University Press, 1985.

Vonnegut, Kurt. *Bluebeard*. New York: Delacorte Press, 1987.

——. *Breakfast of Champions* New York: Delacorte Press/Seymour Lawrence, 1973.

——. *Galápagos*. New York: Delacorte Press/Seymour Lawrence, 1985.

——. *God Bless You, Mr. Rosewater*. New York: Holt, Rinehart Winston, 1965.

——. *Jailbird*. New York: Delacorte Press/Seymour Lawrence, 1979.

——. *Slapstick: or Lonesome No More!* New York: Delacorte Press/Seymour Lawrence, 1976.

——. *Slaughterhouse-Five*. New York: Delacorte/Seymour Lawrence, 1968.

——. *Happy Birthday, Wanda June*. New York: Dell, 1970.

"Self-Projections: Symbolic Characters and Symbolic Fiction," *The Journal of Narrative Technique* 12(3) (Fall, 1982): 177–190.

Yarmolinsky, Jane Vonnegut. *Angels without Wings: A Courageous Family's Triumph over Tragedy*. Boston: Houghton Mifflin Co., 1987.

Vonnegut's Invented Religions as Sense-Making Systems

Peter Freese

The strong Puritan heritage of early American literature is still very much in evidence today. The initial religious impetus of American writing has survived the onslaught of Darwinism and psychoanalysis, the political eschatology of Marxism, and assorted philosophies of existential anguish. In diverse stages of secularization, the central plots, motifs, and images of biblical history have turned into shared elements of American fiction, and even those authors who passionately reject fundamental Christian doctrines often do so in the language of the Authorized Version. In the modern American novel, Biblical references proliferate from Ernest Hemingway's *The Sun Also Rises* to William Faulkner's *Absalom, Absalom!* and Nathaniel West's *The Day of the Locust* to James Baldwin's *Go Tell It on the Mountain* and Toni Morrison's *Song of Solomon*. Spiritual brothers of Nathaniel Hawthorne's hapless Arthur Dimmesdale play central roles in countless novels from Harold Frederick's *The Damnation of Theron Ware* and Sinclair Lewis' *Elmer Gantry* to Flannery O'Connor's *The Violent Bear It Away* and Joyce Carol Oates' *Son of the Morning*. Literary transfigurations of Jesus Christ abound from Jim Conklin, the lanky soldier with a wound in his side in Stephen Crane's *The Red Badge of Courage*, and Jim Casey, the migrant preacher killed by vigilantes in John Steinbeck's *The Grapes of Wrath*, to Joe Christmas, the sacrificial victim in William Faulkner's *Light in August*, and James Castle, the prep-school saint in J. D. Salinger's *The Catcher in the Rye*.[1] And the Christian imagery of the apocalypse is endlessly varied from Bernard Malamud's *God's Grace* to Don DeLillo's *White Noise*.[2]

In short, then, in a world in which, for the first time in human history, mankind can annihilate itself by means of its technological inventions, American literature is as concerned as it was in its earlier phases with probing questions about the meaning of existence, the purpose of human life, and the workings of a divine providence. But the erstwhile certainty of belief has given way to the anguish of doubt, the analogies between fictional events and their biblical models have lost their typological significance, the frequent apocalyptic visions no longer imply the promise of a new beginning to come after the end, and the literary transfigurations of Christ are more often than not used in a comical or farcical mood. More and more authors treat traditional Christianity in critical fashion, and, while some have moved toward atheism and nihilism and some have sought solace in religious systems other than Christianity, a growing number of novelists, especially in the field of science fiction, have begun to invent their own religions.[3]

One of the most successful among these is Kurt Vonnegut, who grew up in Indianapolis, Indiana, as the son of a prominent German family. His "first American ancestor, atheistic merchant from Munster" (*Palm Sunday*, 214f.), came to the Midwest as one of the German "Forty-Eighters" and brought with him a long family tradition of *Freidenkertum*, defined by Vonnegut as "the most corrosive sort of agnosticism—or worse" (*Palm Sunday*, 215). Thus, Vonnegut grew up in a climate of profound scepticism, and when the *Playboy* interviewer asked him about his religious background, he answered:

My ancestors, who came to the United States a little before the Civil war, were atheists. So I'm not rebelling against organized religion. I never had any. I learned my outrageous opinions at my mother's knee. My family had always had these. (*Wampeters*, 240)

When the young Vonnegut went to Cornell University in 1940 to study biochemistry and help advance the progress of science, when he survived the atrocious firebombing of Dresden in a subterranean meatlocker in 1945, and when, after his release from a German prison-camp, he went to Chicago to study anthropology, he found his religious skepticism reinforced by all of these experiences. There is ample evidence that his rejection of organized religion became ever more pronounced. About his study of anthropology, for example, he said in his *Paris Review* interview: "It confirmed my atheism, which was the faith of my fathers anyway. Religions were exhibited and studied as the Rube Goldberg inventions I'd always thought they were" (*Palm Sunday*, 101).

Vonnegut, then, is a confirmed atheist who scathingly comments on almost every organized religion from traditional Catholicism to the more recent Born-Againism. But it is this very impassioned agnostic who in novel after novel devises new religious systems and who emphatically argues in his autobiography that "we need a new religion," substantiating such a surprising claim by saying:

An effective religion allows people to imagine from moment to moment what is going on and how they should behave. Christianity used to be like that. Our country is now jammed with human beings who say out loud that life is chaos to them, and that it doesn't seem to matter what anybody does next. (*Palm Sunday*, 198f.)

How, the puzzled reader is bound to ask, can a cynical atheist who calls the "White House prayer breakfasts . . . about as nourishing to the human spirit as potassium cyanide" (*Palm Sunday*, 201f.) devote his creative fantasy to the invention of ever new religions? And how can he, as he did in a sermon he preached in St. Clement's Episcopal Church in New York, call himself "a Christ worshiping agnostic" (*Palm Sunday*, 327)? The obvious conjecture that Vonnegut accepts the Christian doctrine but rejects its institutionalization is far too simple, and only a detailed investigation of his novels will lead to a more appropriate answer.

In all of his eleven novels to date, Vonnegut portrays a world on the brink of a homemade apocalypse, and in most of them he employs what he calls "science fiction of an obviously kidding sort" (*Wampeters*, 262) to put human affairs in a wider perspective, to illustrate his conviction that "there are lots of alternatives to our own society" and to provide some comic relief from the unbearable state of affairs in a world hovering on the verge of destruction. His protagonists are lonely and desperate men faced with the arbitrary atrocities of war and the heartless competition of a money-orientated capitalistic society, with the pathetic uselessness of human beings as they are replaced by ever more efficient machines, with the crumbling of human communities and the ensuing loneliness and despair, with man's ruthless destruction of the planet's ecological balance and the loss of human decency, respect, and consideration.

On the sociopolitical level, then, Vonnegut's oeuvre is a scathing indictment of America as a country that has turned the dreams of its founding fathers into the nightmares of their contemporary descendants. But on a deeper, existential level life in America turns out to be just a paradigm of human existence in general, and at the heart of the protagonists' despair is their inability to understand the cruel workings of a contingent universe that is revealed as a "nightmare of meaninglessness without end" (*Sirens*, 8) and their resulting incapacity to detect a meaning and a purpose for their existence.

In a 1974 graduation speech Vonnegut observed that graduation speakers are usually hired "to answer the question: what is life all about" (*Palm Sunday*, 196). It is this very question that pervades his novels in countless variations and that he answers with his inimitable mixture of cynical pessimism, black humor, and bourgeois sentimentality, creating a contradictory crackerbarrel philosophy of life that thrives on the irritating strategy of the "unconfirmed thesis"and denies his flustered readers any satisfactory answer to the frightening riddles of existence.[4]

In his first novel, the conventional Huxleyan dystopia *Player Piano* (1952), Vonnegut sketches a society in which "machines were doing America's work far better than Americans had ever done it" (65).[5] Consequently, men have become utterly superfluous and robbed of their purpose, their "feeling of being needed on earth" (94), and their sense of human dignity. What motivates the privileged but discontented manager Paul Proteus (who not accidentally bears the name of the Greek god of change) to stage a revolution against the computer-controlled system is his need to understand "Why did it have to happen?"—an outcry defined by the narrator as "the question humanity had been asking for millenniums, the question men were seemingly born to ask" (63). The motley revolutionary band that sets out to fight the omnipotent technocracy is indoctrinated by an unemployed reverend cum anthropologist who predicts that "things . . . are ripe for a phony Messiah" (93). For Paul, who is willing to be that "new Messiah" (97) and who yearns "to deal, not with society, but only with Earth as God had given it to man"

(135), the "big trouble, really" consists of "finding something to believe in" (140), that is, of complementing his entirely rational approach to life with some emotionally satisfying belief.

Predictably, the poorly prepared revolution, which intends "that the world should be restored to the people" (272), fails miserably. The latter-day Luddites, who have just smashed the hateful machines, immediately begin to rebuild them in the tradition of "the American tinker" (243), and "the intemperate faith in lawless technological progress—namely, that man is on earth to create more durable and efficient images of himself, and, hence, to eliminate every justification at all for his own continued existence" (286)—remains unchecked. It becomes painfully evident that the insurgents were just out to replace one kind of "human engineering" with another and that there is no hope that mankind will ever overcome its *Zauberlehrling* syndrome. But when the captured rebels are led to prison, one of them says: "This isn't the end, you know. . . . Nothing ever is, nothing ever will be—not even Judgment Day" (320). It is left to the reader to grasp this concluding statement as a ray of hope against a bleak horizon of despair or to dismiss it as a cynical reference to the endlessly recurring pattern of man's self-destructive hubris.

Vonnegut's first novel shows that he not only uses apocalyptic imagery to infuse secular events with deeper meaning but also concentrates on two essentially religious questions:

1) why do things happen the way they do, and who directs life's seemingly arbitrary course; and
2) what is the purpose of human existence, and what are the values that can make it meaningful?

These questions, which ask for a sense-making structure that can explain the world and man's place in it, have remained at the core of Vonnegut's work from *Player Piano* to *Galápagos*.

In his second novel, the hilariously inventive space opera *The Sirens of Titan* (1959), the jaded playboy Malachi Constant, a latter-day Jonah, has to go through an arduous intergalactic journey of initiation before he can finally realize the value of a simple, self-sufficient existence and of disinterested love and decency. He turns out to be the plaything of Winston Niles Rumfoord, an East Coast aristocrat and fictional rendition of Franklin Delano Roosevelt, who attempts to bring about his 'New Deal' by founding a new religion and who uses Malachi as his unwilling and unknowing Messiah. Here, then, Paul Proteus' sketchily realized Ghost Shirt Society becomes the first full-fledged religious creed in Vonnegut's fictional cosmos, namely, the Church of God the Utterly Indifferent.

The many characters in this "true story from the Nightmare Ages" (8) are all haunted by the question "who was actually in charge of all creation, and what all creation was all about" (7), and they pine for "some kind of signal that would tell [them] what it was all about" (91). The disillusioned tycoon Noel Constant, whose

Horatio Alger career is a biting satire on the connections between Calvinism and capitalism as investigated by Max Weber, can find as little meaning in the world as his intellectual manager Ransom K. Fern, who tries to imitate Aristotle, but attempts in vain to detect some "pattern in what he knew" (68) and searches unsuccessfully for "the vaguest light on what life might be about" (85). Noel's son Malachi, who whiles away his inherited riches with women and drugs and personifies the most thoughtless carpe diem mentality, desperately waits for "just one thing—a single message" (17), and Beatrice Rumfoord, the touch-me-not aristocratic lady, who refuses to become soiled by life, suffers from the despair bred by uselessness and lack of purpose. Thus the ethics of Calvinism, philosophical humanism, hedonism, and isolationism are all shown to be equally inappropriate for a meaningful human existence because they all postulate a transcendental agency to which they ascribe the responsibility for the otherwise inexplicable events of life. Their attempts at explanation reach from the simple concept of luck—Noel is thought to have just been lucky with his speculations—and the intellectual presumption of some hidden order—Fern searches for a 'pattern'—to the assumption of a divine providence—Malachi thinks that "somebody up there likes me" (7; see 20, 46, 215, 319). And it is this very concept of a transcendental agency of whichever kind that is rejected by Rumfoord, and Vonnegut, as the crucial aberration of human thinking and in which both see the ultimate reason for all human sorrow.

Rumfoord decrees that there is "nothing more cruel, more dangerous, more blasphemous than a man can do than to believe that—that luck, good or bad, is the hand of God!" (252), and he argues that the postulation of some God is nothing but an abdication of human responsibility, that throughout history men have killed and tortured each other in the name of their gods and that mankind has suffered endlessly *ad maiorem dei gloriam*. Since the concept of a higher agency intervening in human affairs through punishments and rewards is only an alibi for man's greed and lust for power, Rumfoord creates the Church of God the Utterly Indifferent, which follows the motto "Take Care of the People, and God Almighty Will Take Care of Himself" (180).

Rumfoord's new religion, which Vonnegut unfolds in some detail, might be understood as a variation upon the notion of a *deus absconditus* or as a fictional translation of "God is Dead" theology, but Vonnegut goes a decisive step further when he unmasks the founder of this new creed as a scheming and power-hungry manipulator. Rumfoord, who once drove his private spaceship into a chrono-synclastic infundibulum, a hilarious science fiction equivalent of the astrophysicians' black hole, exists as a wave phenomenon pulsing as a distorted spiral between the Sun and Betelgeuse. As a consequence, he knows about the past and the future and can use his prophetic gifts to establish his credentials: During his first revelation he predicts "fifty future events in great detail" (180) and admonishes his spellbound audience to think about "the Spanish Inquisition" (181). Thus, of course, he becomes guilty of the very manipulation his religion proposes to overcome.

But Rumfoord, who cynically stages a war between Mars and the Earth to make mankind ripe for his teachings and create the necessary martyrs, turns out to be a trickster tricked. The whole history of mankind is revealed as part of a complicated communication system between robots from the extragalactic planet Tralfamadore, with the great buildings from Stonehenge to the Palace of the League of Nations being telecontrolled hieroglyphics that the Tralfamadorians made unknowing earthlings erect to convey coded messages to their fellow robot Salo stranded on Titan. The hilarious unmasking of mankind's greatest achievements as links in an other-directed intergalactic communication system engendered by an immeasurably more advanced civilization of machines, then, is not only the most drastic debunking of man's claim to greatness and importance, but it also provides Vonnegut with a perspective from which to evaluate human follies and aspirations. Rumfoord, who uses Malachi as his tele-controlled Messiah, is himself only a pawn of the Tralfamadorians: man has no free will whatsoever. And Malachi's message, when he comes down to earth in a scene based on the Christian epiphany— "I was a victim of a series of accidents, as are we all" (229)—is reinforced on an all-encompassing universal scale.

The *prima causa* at the center of Vonnegut's complex spiraling plot is not a supreme godhead but a society of robots that are the creations of a manlike species that exterminated itself through its development of ever more advanced technology. And the ultimate message of the novel is that first, scientific attempts at understanding and mastering the universe inadvertently lead to disaster and self-extermination; and second, religious creeds are mendacious but nevertheless necessary inventions that cannot explain the meaning of a world which has no meaning, but that are necessary to provide man with the sense of purpose and direction without which he cannot live. Consequently, man must give up all attempts at understanding the unfathomable workings of an arbitrary universe and must realize, instead, that the meaning of life can only be found in its unconditional acceptance. "A purpose of human life, no matter who is controlling it, is to love whoever is around to be loved" (313) is the sum of Malachi's experience; and Beatrice, who writes a book about *The True Purpose of Life in the Solar System* (308), comes to a similar conclusion.

It is in his fourth novel, *Cat's Cradle* (1963), that Vonnegut presents his most detailed religious system. Most of the action of this highly accomplished tale, which is both a postmodern exercise in storifying and a fictional treatise on the limits of epistemology, takes place on the poverty-stricken island of San Lorenzo. There two strangers, the American Marine deserter McCabe and the Black globetrotter Lionel Boyd Johnson alias Bokonon from Tobago, are shipwrecked, and they decide to turn it into a "Utopia." "To this end, McCabe overhauled the economy and the law, Johnson designed a new religion" (90). It soon becomes obvious, however, that the economy of the godforsaken Carribean island cannot be improved, and thus the new religion becomes "the only real instrument of hope" (118). Consequently, Bokonon works on the assumption that "truth was the enemy of the people, because the truth was so terrible," and he makes "it his business to provide the people with better and better lies" (118).

Like Rumfoord in *The Sirens of Titan*, Bokonon never pretends to receive divine inspirations. On the contrary, he offers his new creed and his continually growing body of holy writ as a system of man made inventions which he calls *foma*, defined as "harmless untruths, intended to comfort simple souls" (*Wampeters*, xv) and recognized by the well-read reader as the spiritual equivalent of Huxley's *soma* in *Brave New World*. Bokonon, whose initials LBJ pun on President Lyndon B. Johnson and his "War on Poverty" and whose complicated life history is charged with analogies to Christ, Jonah, and St. Augustine, bases his religion on the principle of "Dynamic Tension" taken over from Charles Atlas' body-building courses and redefined as "a priceless equilibrium between good and evil" (*Cat's Cradle*, 74). From this principle he deduces the axiom "that good societies could be built only by pitting good against evil, and by keeping the tension between the two high at all times" (*Cat's Cradle*, 74).[6] Therefore, he arranges with McCabe that he become outlawed and that his adherents be threatened with capital punishment to give his religion the lure of the forbidden, and together they create "the living legend of the cruel tyrant in the city and the gentle holy man in the jungle" (*Cat's Cradle*, 119).

The Manichean dualism of good and evil, God and Satan, holy man and evil tyrant thus becomes linked with traditional opposition between country and city, corrupt civilization and pastoral nature, and the exercise of Bokononism turns into an exciting role play full of risk and promise. Since all the inhabitants of the island, including the evil tyrant, are Bokononists, life on San Lorenzo becomes "a work of art" (*Cat's Cradle*, 119), and Vonnegut's warning from the preface to his third novel *Mother Night* (1961), "We are what we pretend to be, so we must be careful about what we pretend to be" (v), fulfills itself. The new religion serves as "opium for the people" by keeping them busily engaged in rituals which make them forget their unbearable reality. Bokononism, then, with its doctrines of the *karass*, the *vin-dit*, the *duprass*, the *wampeter*, the *granfalloon*, and the *zah-mah-ki-bo* and with its central sacrament of *boko-maru*, the mingling of awareness through the rubbing of the soles of the feet (which is, of course, a facile pun on the mingling of souls), is an openly admitted system of "bittersweet lies" (*Cat's Cradle*, 11), an extended spiritual therapy, as it were, that consists of helpful illusions and that works on the assumption that the meaning and purpose without which man cannot live must be invented since they cannot be discovered.

The world is arbitrary, indifferent, and utterly meaningless, and therefore Bokonon invents purposes to explain and make bearable its contingency. Like Walter Starbuck, the hapless protagonist of the later novel *Jailbird* (1979), he knows that we are here for no purpose, unless we can invent one" (*Cat's Cradle*, 232), and thus he teaches his followers that instead of "it happened" they are to say "it was *meant* to happen" (*Cat's Cradle*, 24) or "it was *supposed* to happen" (*Cat's Cradle*, 63), that they have to proceed on the premise that "each of us has to be what he or she is" (*Cat's Cradle*, 178), and that the concept of free will must be abandoned as totally "irrelevant" (*Cat's Cradle*, 128).

Of course, any invented sense-making system is continuously disproved by man's immediate experience of the world, and the arbitrariness of events perpetually defeats any system of alleged causalities. Therefore, Bokonon cautions man against "the folly of pretending to discover, to understand" (*Cat's Cradle*, 13), and he expresses this folly in an ingenious variation of the biblical story of creation:

In the beginning, God created the earth, and He looked upon it in His cosmic loneliness.

And God said, "Let Us make living creatures out of mud, so the mud can see what We have done." And God created every living creature that now moveth, and one was man. Mud as man alone could speak. God leaned close as mud as man sat up, looked around, and spoke. Man blinked. "What is the *purpose* of all this?" he asked politely.

"Everything must have a purpose?" asked God.

"Certainly," said man.

"Then I leave it to you to think of one for all this," said God. And He went away. (*Cat's Cradle*, 117)

Man, however, a species defined in *Player Piano* as seemingly born to ask "Why?" (see 63), cannot think of convincing purposes, although he needs them in order to survive and to not end in self-extermination as did the desperate Tralfamadorians in *The Sirens of Titan*. Therefore, he must pretend to understand, and Bokonon sums up this insoluble conundrum in the most famous of his calypsos, which he offers as Carribean versions of biblical psalms:

Tiger got to hunt,
Bird got to fly;
Man got to sit and wonder, "Why, why, why?"
Tiger got to sleep,
Bird got to land;
Man got to tell himself he understand. (124)

The ineradicable contradiction, then, between man's need to understand and his inability to understand is mirrored by the fact that on an empirical level Bokononism considers man nothing but "sitting-up mud" (*Cat's Cradle*, 150), but that on a spiritual level man forms the center of the universe: The only thing that is holy to a Bokononist is "Man, . . . that's all. Just man" (*Cat's Cradle*, 143). Ultimately, therefore, Bokononism is a desperate answer to "the cruel paradox" of human existence, namely, "the heartbreaking necessity of lying about reality, and the heartbreaking impossibility of lying about it" (*Cat's Cradle*, 189). And it is small wonder that against such a backdrop the Bokononist jungle doctor Julian Castle, with the initials of Jesus Christ, defines *maturity* as "a bitter disappointment for which no remedy exists, unless laughter can be said to remedy anything" (*Cat's Cradle*, 134).

Although Bokononism is a self-avowed system of helpful lies, it proves much more beneficial than its opponent in the novel, namely, natural science. It is this allegedly enlightened science, as practiced by amoral and inhumane experimenters smirking at such superstitions as "God" or "sin," that brings about the end of the world by freezing the earth into a ball of solid ice. And when the illiterate tyrant of San Lorenzo praises science as "magic that *works*" (*Cat's Cradle*, 174), he unknowingly reveals that a belief in technological progress is just another, and terribly dangerous, religion.

Cat's Cradle, which is narrated by one of the few survivors of the apocalypse, uses as its title a children's game. It is this simple and ubiquitous game, that provides the central symbol of man's essential task: The universe he finds himself in is an arbitrary and ever-changing system of meaningless strings, which man, through an act of his creative imagination, has to define as meaningful. If he cannot do that, that is, if he proves unable to invent a meaning that cannot be discovered, he will succumb to the despair of nihilism like the character in the novel who repeatedly observes that there is *"no damn cat, no damn cradle"* (114). But if he bases his imaginative creation of meaning on the helpful lies of religion, he will be much better off than if he grounds his understanding of self and world in the inhumane truths of science. This message, then, which made *Cat's Cradle* a cult book of the youthful counterculture of the sixties with its revolt against technocratic rationality, takes up and unfolds the concerns of Vonnegut's previous novels, and Bokononism can be understood as a combination of Paul Proteus' need to "find something to believe in" (*Player Piano*, 140) and the insistence of the narrator of *The Sirens of Titan* that the universe is "a nightmare of meaninglessness without end" (8) and that everybody has "to find the meaning of life within himself" (7).

Such a reading is corroborated by what Vonnegut said in his famous "Address to Graduating Class at Bennington College, 1970," in which he stated:

A great swindle of our time is the assumption that science has made religion obsolete. All science has damaged is the story of Adam and Eve and the story of Jonah and the Whale. Everything else holds up pretty well, particularly the lessons about fairness and gentleness. (*Wampeters*, 166)

And he implored his young listeners:

I beg you to believe in the most ridiculous superstition of all: that humanity is at the center of the universe, the fulfiller or the frustrator of the grandest dreams of God Almighty.

If you can believe that, and make others believe it, then there might be hope for us. Human beings might stop treating each other like garbage, might begin to treasure and protect each other instead. Then it might be all right to have babies again. (*Wampeters*, 163*f.*)

To Vonnegut, then, all religions—and Bokononism is only the most obvious example so far—are manmade myths or lies, but they provide the sense-making structures necessary for man's survival. And they are more necessary today than ever before because they serve as the essential antidote against the most dangerous "religion" of all, the belief in unbridled technological progress with its alleged objectivity, which is nothing but amorality, and its built-in tendency toward ultimate self-destruction.

This conviction, which might be defined for the time being as agnostic humanism, can also be seen in Vonnegut's next novel, *God Bless You, Mr. Rosewater* (1965), in which the author's alter ego, the unsuccessful and eccentric science-fiction writer Kilgore Trout, who looks "like a frightened, aging Jesus" (134), makes his first appearance. In one of Trout's countless stories, which are summed up in *God Bless You, Mr. Rosewater*, and which will from now on be an essential ingredient of Vonnegut's novels, a man about to commit suicide states that he wants to ask God a single question, namely, "What in hell are people for?" (25). This turns out to be a repetition of a character's request in *Player Piano*, who begs the technician in charge of the central computer, "Would you ask EPICAC what people are for?" (302)

In the America of *God Bless You, Mr. Rosewater*, the Sermon on the Mount (see 140) has been replaced by the hunger for "money as dehydrated Utopia" (141), and a perverted Calvinism is used to justify the distinction between haves and have-nots and to make poor men ashamed of themselves. It is Kilgore Trout who saves the crazy protagonist from being committed to an asylum by the lawyers waiting for "his lunacy . . . to make the great leap into religion" (108) when he defines the essential moral problem of technologically advanced societies as "how to love people who have no use" (215) and when he thus upgrades Eliot's drunken bouts of helpfulness into an advanced philanthropic experiment.

Organized religion, the message of *God Bless You, Mr. Rosewater*, might be summed up, has turned into an instrument of class warfare, and it needs a new Jonah figure like Eliot Rosewater, who is compared several times to the Old Testament prophet, and a new "Jesus figure" (216) in the guise of an eccentric science fiction writer dreaming up "fantasies of an impossibly hospitable world" (24) to redeem a stupid mankind on the brink of self-destruction and to teach humans that it is not progress and success that will save them, but mutual care, love, and common decency.

It is in *God Bless You, Mr. Rosewater* that Vonnegut makes his first oblique attempt to come to terms with one of the traumatic experiences of his life when he makes Eliot read Hans Rumpf's book *The Bombing of Dresden* and has him undergo a hallucinatory vision of Indianapolis "being consumed by a fire-storm" (204). But it is only in his next novel, his generally acclaimed masterpiece *Slaughterhouse-Five* (1969), that Vonnegut squarely faces the holocaust of Dresden and finally manages to exorcise his haunting memories in one of the most accomplished tales of postwar American literature. Here he brilliantly recombines his attack on the hubris of technological progress from *Player Piano*, his playful contrast between a faulty human and an advanced robot civilization from *The Sirens of Titan*, his depiction of the atrocities of World War II from *Mother Night*, his vision of a scientifically induced apocalypse and the innovative narrative stance of *Cat's Cradle*, and the figures of Eliot Rosewater and Kilgore Trout from *God Bless You, Mr. Rosewater*.

One of the artfully intertwined narrative strands of *Slaughterhouse-Five* deals with the passive antihero Billy Pilgrim, an optometrist from Ilium, New York, who acts out his Bunyanesque pilgrim's progress as a contemporary Everyman confronted with and overwhelmed by the cruelties of war and the atrocity of the firebombing that he survives, like Vonnegut himself, in a subterranean meatlocker of the Dresden slaughterhouse. Billy "has come unstuck in time" (23), and the erratic and disjointed narrative follows his uncontrollable time travels, thus providing Vonnegut with a chance to escape the limits of chronology. One of the main destinies of Billy's journeys is the extragalactic planet Tralfamadore, where he learns that it is useless to worry about the future and to cast around for explanations of the incomprehensible events of existence. Appointing himself a missionary, bringing the philosophy of Tralfamadorian fatalism to troubled humans and thereby "prescribing corrective lenses for Earthling souls" (29), Billy attempts to teach his fellow humans that their repeated question "Why?" (see 40, 51, 76, 91, 99) is useless and inappropriate because *"everything* is all right, and everybody has to do exactly what he does" (198) and that they should "concentrate on the happy moments of . . . life, and ignore the unhappy ones" (194*f.*). People therefore should give up being "the great explainers" (85) and abandon their silly concept of "free will" (86).

The Tralfamadorian philosophy with its aesthetics of simultaneity, its rejection of time as succession and its consequent denial of the finality of death (see 26*f.*), its ridiculing of any attempt at causal explanation—"There is no why" (77)—and its stance of fatalistic acceptance of whatever might happen and the ensuing ethics of momentary enjoyment has frequently been misunderstood as an expression of Vonnegut's escapist nihilism. This, however, is a grave misunderstanding caused by the unwarranted identification of Vonnegut, the narrator, with Billy, his hero. Admittedly, Vonnegut is a cynical pessimist, and his black humor shows a streak of deep despair, but as in *The Sirens of Titan*, where the terrible revelation of man's uselessness and folly is counterbalanced by an emphatic plea for courtesy and kindness, and as in *Cat's Cradle*, where the desperate self-betrayal of Bokononism is undertaken in the name of decency and love, in *Slaughterhouse-Five* the facile fatalism of Billy is contrasted with the narrator's defiant altruism.

Through a series of complex narrative strategies, Vonnegut leaves open whether *Slaughterhouse-Five* is a science fiction novel or a novel with a schizophrenic hero haunted by science fiction fantasies. He carefully avoids taking sides and creates numerous unresolved contradictions. He simultaneously makes Billy a latter-day Christ crucified by a world of cruelty and lovelessness and a postlapsarian Adam pining for a return to paradise. These and other strategies deny the reader a quasi-pragmatic reception and force Billy to realize that "there is nothing intelligent to say about a massacre" (19), that appearance and reality indistinguishably intertwine, and that an innovative narrative presented "in the telegraphic schizophrenic manner of the planet Tralfamadore" (title page) does not offer a clearcut message but needs to be coauthored, as it were, by every individual reader against the background of his own experience. This is why the misreading of the novel as an expression of Vonnegut's resigned advocacy of the inevitable can be understood, but a careful analysis of the text leads to a different conclusion.

In the novel's final passage, it is "springtime" and the trees are "leafing out" (215), and Billy drives in a horse-drawn wagon, which is "green and coffin-shaped" (215), through the moonlike landscape of burnt-out Dresden. Like John in *Cat's Cradle*, who opens his tale with "Call me Jonah" (11) and thus invites comparison with Ishmael in *Moby-Dick*, who drifts ashore in a coffin to bear witness to the shipwreck of the *Pequod*, Vonnegut offers *Slaughterhouse-Five* as his testimony to one of the greatest atrocities of modern history. And when he conjures up the annual rebirth of nature and contrasts it with the all-encompassing inferno of human history, he pits the hope for cyclical renewal against the despair bred by linear "progress." While Billy with his resigned fatalism becomes guilty of complicity and self-abandonment and thus inadvertently encourages the repetition of Dresden—his son fights as a Green Beret in Vietnam—Vonnegut tells us that he instructed his sons that they "are not under any circumstances to take part in massacres" (19) and adopts the defiant stance of Lot's wife who, despite God's warning, turned around to look at the destruction of Sodom and Gomorrah: "she *did* look back, and I love her for that, because it was so human" (22).

In *Slaughterhouse-Five*, then, the impassioned pacifist and acknowledged atheist presents no testament of fatalistic acceptance but a passionate plea for resistance against the self-destruction of a mankind that all too often tries to justify its greed and cruelty by references to divine providence. "Earthlings who have felt that the Creator clearly wanted this or that," Vonnegut says in his essay on the American space program, "have almost always been pigheaded and cruel" (*Wampeters*, 87); and Dresden and Vietnam, the Children's Crusade of the Middle Ages, and the race riots of the American sixties are evoked in *Slaughterhouse-Five* as convincing examples of the inhumanity perpetrated in the name of God.

As in Vonnegut's previous novels, the characters in *Slaughterhouse* desperately attempt to find some purpose and meaning for their existence. Billy's disoriented mother, who cannot make up her mind about which church to join, for example, buys a crucifix in a souvenir store, and the narrator caustically comments: "Like so many Americans, she was trying to construct a life that made sense from the things she found in gift shops" (39). When Billy commits himself, after a mental breakdown, to a ward for nonviolent mental patients, he makes the acquaintance of another inmate, Eliot Rosewater, who introduces him to the science fiction of Kilgore Trout. Both Billy and Eliot have "found life meaningless, partly because of what they had seen in the war" (101), and now they use Trout's extrapolations of better worlds to get their bearings again, "trying," as the narrator says, "to re-invent themselves and their universe," a process in which "science fiction [is] a big help" (101).

One of the books of "this cracked messiah" (167) Trout, which Billy reads in the hospital, is *The Gospel from Outer Space* in which a visitor comes to earth and makes "a serious study of Christianity to learn, if he could, why Christians found it so easy to be cruel" (108). He comes to the conclusion that this is due to "slipshod storytelling in the New Testament" (108) because, instead of teaching us to be merciful to the lowliest person, the gospel, by making Jesus the son of God, teaches that *"before you kill somebody, make absolutely sure he isn't well connected"* (109) and thus makes Christians assume that poor and unimportant people can be lynched with impunity. Another Trout novel deals with a time traveler who journeys back to see Jesus and who encounters him as a twelve-year-old boy learning the carpentry trade in his father's shop. Jesus and his father are busy building a cross for a rabble-rouser and "glad to have the work" (202).

These and other direct references to Christianity and its failure to make people behave decently drive home a point that Vonnegut also makes in his expository writings. In his *Playboy* interview, for example, he says: "I admire Christianity more than anything—Christianity as symbolized by gentle people sharing a common bowl" (*Wampeters*, 246). But in his commemoration speech for William Ellery Channing, he states: "I have had even more trouble with the Trinity than I had with college algebra" (*Palm Sunday*, 216f.) and rejects the notion of Jesus as the son of God as an invention of the Council of Nicea.

Vonnegut, then, is "enchanted with the Sermon on the Mount" because "being merciful, it seems to me, is the only good idea we have received so far" (*Palm Sunday*, 325), but he rejects the idea of the divinity of Jesus and of an omnipotent God being his father. He accepts Christianity, that is, as a *"heartfelt moral code"* (*Palm Sunday*, 202) and as an ethics of morally responsible behavior, but he rejects the claim that this code is divine law. This explains why neither Rumfoord, the founder of the Church of God the Utterly Indifferent in *The Sirens of Titan*, nor Bokonon, the inventor of Bokononism in *Cat's Cradle*, ever claim to have been inspired by divine revelations, but why they offer their creeds as manmade ways toward a better and more human life.

Critics generally agree that after *Slaughterhouse-Five* Vonnegut's novels lose their erstwhile power. Their religious implications, however, remain as central as ever. In *Breakfast of Champions* (1973), which attacks the environmental pollution that has brought our "damaged planet" (5) to the brink of uninhabitability, the central idea is the thesis advanced by Trout that "human beings are robots, are machines" (3) powered by chemical reactions. Again we meet desperate people casting around for an understanding of what happens to them: "*Why me?*" for example, is a "common question" (44), and the frustrated protagonist asks in vain "what life is all about" (165).

Although Vonnegut paints a bleak picture of "a planet which [is] dying fast" (7) and of a society that suffers from loneliness, despair, and insanity, he also suggests a means of redemption again. The minimalist painter Rabo Karabekian, who is accused that his nonrepresentational picture of the Temptation of St. Anthony is a fraud, explains that the unwavering band of light on his canvas shows "the immaterial core of every animal," namely, its awareness, and that the picture expresses his conviction that "our awareness is all that is alive and may be sacred in any of us. Everything else about us is dead machinery" (221). This important correction of Trout's thesis about humans as mere robots is just another way of asserting that man has a soul. And Vonnegut, who figures as a desperate and suicidal character in his own novel and is present at this revelation, defines Karabekian's statement as the "spiritual climax of this book" (218) and confesses that by listening to the painter's statement of faith he is "being reborn" (219).

Admittedly, this scene smacks of what Vonnegut himself calls the "almost intolerable sentimentality beneath everything I write" (*Wampeters*, xxv), but apart from its questionable artistic value it provides another instance of a self-avowed atheist's search for the spiritual consolation of a belief in some transcendental link. *Breakfast of Champions*, we know from Vonnegut's biography, is its author's rather desperate attempt at artistic autotherapy in the face of a deep life crisis, and while this fact may account for the novel's aesthetic weakness, it makes Karabekian's assertion and the fictional "Vonnegut's" reaction to it all the more significant.

In *Slapstick or Lonesome No More!* (1976), which is certainly Vonnegut's weakest novel, the creed to become "the most popular American religion of all time" in a country ravaged by changing gravity is "The Church of Jesus Christ the Kidnapped" (142). More important than this grotesque invention is the fact that the novel portrays the growing despair of men and women for whom the American Dream has become a "form of Idiot's Delight" (32), who are "outraged by the human condition in the Universe" (179), and who can find no answer to their question "What does it all mean?" (146). They even have no hope for improvement after death since a scientific experiment has revealed that "the life that awaits us after death is infinitely more tiresome than this one" (72) and should rightly be called "The Turkey Farm" (150) instead of "Heaven" or any other euphemism.

Here, then, where Vonnegut's savage despair and disgust are expressed in a tone reminiscent of Mark Twain's *The Mysterious Stranger*, the meaning of life is reduced to a mere day-by-day survival fight, and Laurel and Hardy are praised as embodiments of the pathetic human task of "bargaining in good faith with destiny" (11). "The low comedy of living" (172) is thus grimly reduced to a mere series of slapstick situations.

In *Jailbird* (1979), a realistic comment on the Watergate affair, the hero-narrator Walter F. Starbuck bemusedly recounts his eventful life unfolding between moral idealism and shameless opportunism. He bears the name of the first mate on Melville's *Pequod*, and his narrative is colored by a curious mixture of Tralfamadorian fatalism with regard to the universe and the history of mankind and a stubborn faith with regard to individual man's daily existence. Finding himself on a "planet, where money matters more than anything" (162), and being surrounded by people who do not give "a damn any more about what's really going on" (234), he chooses to live for his convictions and to hold up courtesy and decency as the only means that make a purposeless life bearable. Patterning his answer before a congressional committee on one given by the labour organizer Powers Hapgood (see 15), he defends his actions with a reference to "the Sermon on the Mount" (236), thus providing an answer to the ubiquitous "Why?" that is a testimony of faith. In spite of the overwhelming proof for his wife's conviction that "human beings were evil by nature" (55), Starbuck asserts, like other Vonnegut heroes before him, that man can learn to be kind and to care for others. If mankind in general may be doomed, individual man is given the chance to live his own life, and as Melville's Starbuck pitted his faith against the monomania of Captain Ahab, so Vonnegut's Starbuck sets his moral convictions against the cynical opportunism of a Richard Nixon.

Deadeye Dick (1982) is another sweeping indictment of "man's festive inhumanity to man" (170) in "an era of pharmaceutical buffoonery" (191) where there are "pills for everything" (165). At the age of twelve, its nondescript protagonist-narrator shoots a pregnant woman. His accidental crime, bred by the foolish irresponsibility of his gun-collecting father, is repeated on a grand scale by the American government when it accidentally drops a neutron bomb on Midland City, Ohio. Individual murder and mass destruction signal the end of the American Dream, and the openly raised suspicion that the dropping of the bomb was no accident but that "Midland City had been neutron-bombed on purpose" (232) because the government needed to test the new weapon, signals the feeling of a bewildered population that they are the victims of some unfathomable conspiracy.

In this novel, again, people ask "that wonderful question . . . 'why, why, why?'" (104), and the apocalyptic motif of the dropping of a neutron bomb, which kills 100,000 people but leaves everything else intact, turns out to be a perfect symbol of a materialistic world. The narrator's resigned question, "Since all the property is undamaged, has the world lost anything it loved?" (34) leads him to the concluding statement, "We are still in the Dark Ages. The Dark Ages—they haven't ended yet" (240).

In *Galápagos* (1985), Vonnegut's latest novel to date, he returns to his outrageous brand of science fiction and employs the son of Kilgore Trout, Leon Trotsky Trout, as his narrator. Leon is a deserter from the Vietnam War, in which he learned that "life was a meaningless nightmare, with nobody watching or caring what was going on" (127). Having been decapitated in an industrial accident in Sweden, he roams the earth as an incorporeal ghost trying to satisfy his "curiosity as to what life is all about" (25), and from a vantage point of a million years hence he tells us what has become the species of *homo sapiens*.

Through a series of wars and famines brought about by the species' ability to think and thus "to make a mess of everything" (184), and through a mysterious bacterium that makes all women infertile, mankind has dwindled in size and finally become extinct. As the result of hilariously funny and cruel accidents, however, a group of ten freakish outsiders, who have been shipwrecked on the desolate Galápagos island of Santa Rosalia, survive and continue procreating. Since most of them are genetically deficient and as their surroundings call for certain abilities and make others superfluous, genetic mutations and environmental influences lead to the "evolution of modern humankind" (287), that is, to seal-like fish-eating beings with flippers instead of hands and with greatly reduced brain powers. These beings are a link in the planet's food chain—they can no longer wield tools, and sharks see to it that there is no overpopulation—and thus Darwin's theory of evolution comes true with a vengeance: "the Law of Natural Selection did the repair job" (291) and sees to it that the faulty "evolution of something as distracting and irrelevant and disruptive as those great big brains of a million years ago" (174) is corrected.

Here Vonnegut's earlier interest in the theory of evolution comes to outrageous fictional fruition. In *Slaughterhouse-Five*, for example, the Tralfamadorians had considered Darwinism much more interesting than the teachings of Christ; and in a 1972 essay Vonnegut had observed that "the two real political parties in America are the *Winners* and the *Losers*" and that "losers have thousands of religions, often of the *bleeding heart* variety," whereas "the single religion of the Winners is a harsh interpretation of Darwinism, which argues that it is the will of the universe that only the fittest should survive" (*Wampeters*, 185*f.*). In *Galápagos* he solves what he had earlier referred to as the "compromise between the need to believe in a traditional paternal God and the contemporary pressures to accept the pronouncements of science" (*Wampeters*, 22) by ingeniously compounding the myth of Noah's ark (see 5) and the alleged facts of evolution theory. Thereby he turns into its opposite the traditional science fiction motif of man's evolution into an ever more perfect species: On the very islands on which Darwin once conceived of his theory, mankind's fate is decided through evolutionary regression, an obvious mistake in the development of the species is corrected, and man is relieved of his destructive brain.

With this outrageous extrapolation of mankind's future history, the climax of despair and pessimism seems to have been reached, but again there is a ray of hope in the sea of desperation. Of the "twenty-thousand quotations from literature" (61) stored by the portable computer Mandarax—a miraculous achievement of human inventiveness that proves to be totally useless on Santa Rosalia—Leon chooses the following statement by Anne Frank as the epigraph for his tale: "In spite of everything, I still believe people are really good at heart." Like John in *Cat's Cradle*, he writes his book although he knows full well that there is nobody left to read it. Thus he asserts his belief in human goodness and his stubborn faith in the importance of art. This faith is obliquely corroborated by a character who dies of a brain tumor and who says to his wife on his deathbed: "I'll tell you what the human soul is. . . . Animals don't have one. It's the part of you that knows when your brain isn't working right" (44). Like Rabo Karabekian in *Breakfast of Champions*, he asserts that man has a soul and thus need not be the helpless victim of his brain, the "only real villain" (270) of human history.

Were men to listen to the advice of their souls instead of following the scheming propositions of their oversized brains—one could interpret the unresolved contradictions of *Galápagos*—the aberrations of "science and progress" (271) could be avoided and Leon's belief that "human beings are good animals" (257) could be confirmed in spite of the overwhelming evidence to the contrary.

The preceding survey shows that Vonnegut does not offer an exclusively pessimistic or even nihilistic view of man. Bosworth's charge that he constantly defeats himself because, "although he abhors our mechanized culture, he believes the world view on which it is based" and thus cannot offer anything but "pessimism, cynicism, resignation, despair"is disproved by a careful reading of his novels.[7] The opposing view, however, is equally inappropriate. Tunnel's assertion that Vonnegut makes "an important contribution to a contemporary understanding of Christian redemption"is certainly unwarranted.[8] The fact that such contradictory readings are at all possible shows that Vonnegut's oeuvre is full of unresolved conflicts and offers anything but a sustained and easily summarized worldview. But there are certain recurring convictions, and with regard to the role of religion in his novels, the following conclusions can be drawn.

A God conceived of as a *prima causa* or a supreme mover of the universe does not exist, or if he does, man is constitutionally unable to discover or understand him. "No one really understands nature or God" (*Palm Sunday*, 11), and anybody who pretends to be in possession of some final truth is a charlatan. This, Vonnegut repeatedly shows in his novels, has been amply proved by history because, whenever people have claimed to act in the name of a divine providence, they have used such claims as an alibi for their greed, cruelty, and lust for power (see *Wampeters*, 87). Consequently, religions can never be divine laws, and any creed that claims to have been established by divinely inspired prophets is a fake. The crucial question, therefore, is not whether a religion is true or false but whether it is useful or not, whether it provides its adherents with a protective sense of community and with helpful *foma*, that is, harmless untruths that make their lives more bearable and their behavior toward each other more decent and more humane.

The most dangerous of all "religions" is the unconditional belief in science and technology because that belief pretends to be based on verifiable premises, facts, and proofs. As is amply demonstrated in each of Vonnegut's novels, science is inherently destructive, has time and again led to "the construction of . . . doomsday machine[s]" (*Wampeters*, 104), has made our planet almost uninhabitable, and has led mankind to the brink of self-annihilation. It has replaced ever more humans by machines and has divided mankind into a great mass of useless people robbed of their purpose and their dignity and a small elite of engineers playing at God and hell-bent on their way to ultimate self-destruction.

It is this very belief in the infallibility of science and the unending progress of technology that makes more humane religions necessary. As the parable of the Tralfamadorians' self-destruction in *The Sirens of Titan* most emphatically demonstrates, the blind trust in science must be counterbalanced by a belief in a human-centered and humanistic set of values. Therefore, humans, who should "pray to be rescued from [their] inventiveness" (*Fates*, 12), need a sense-making system as a means of coping with the meaninglessness of their world. Such a system, however, can only be built on an anthropological fundament, that is, on the fact that a part of man, be it called his awareness by the Bokononists of *Cat's Cradle* or Rabo Karabekian in *Breakfast of Champions* or his soul by the dying man in *Galápagos*, is sacred. Therefore, a religion in Vonnegut's sense is essentially a "*heartfelt moral code*" (*Palm Sunday*, 202). It must not endeavor to explain the inexplicable workings of a contingent universe, but concentrate on the provision of rules for human behavior. Any attempt at a theodicy, then, is bound to fail—and from the Ghost Shirt Society and the Church of God the Utterly Indifferent to Bokononism and the Church of Jesus Christ the Kidnapped, Vonnegut's fictional characters must invent their own purposes, must establish themselves, in true existentialist fashion, as the only available reference points for their world pictures.

The continuously recurring question "What are people for?" which expresses man's search for meaning, purpose, and design, cannot be answered with reference to some transcendental providence. Man, Vonnegut argues, is cursed with a "cruel paradox" (*Cat's Cradle*, 189), that is, with his need to ask for meaning and purpose and his inability to find them. Consequently, he must attempt to discover meaning in himself, and instead of looking for some higher purpose, which does not exist, he must accept the conditions of his life and attempt to fulfill his obligations to himself and his fellow beings. Like Malachi after his strenuous initiation in *The Sirens of Titan* or the Bokononists in *Cat's Cradle*, man must love who is around to be loved, or like Starbuck in *Jailbird*, he must show courtesy and decency to make his purposeless existence bearable.

The danger bred by such a position and the concomitant plea for a stoical acceptance of the unavoidable is the relapse into a resigned fatalism. This position, which Billy Pilgrim in *Slaughterhouse-Five* becomes guilty of, must by all means be avoided. The nonexistence of any external meaning does not allow man to give up and passively drift with the unpredictable flow of events because such an attitude would lead to despair and self-abandonment. On the contrary, it is the very contingency of the universe that makes every individual responsible for his own fate and puts him under an obligation to construct his existence in a meaningful way.

Vonnegut, who can rightly say of himself that "my books are probably more widely used in schools than those of any other living American author" (*Palm Sunday*, 6), is thus certainly an apostate when judged from a dogmatic Christian viewpoint. But instead of being the pernicious blasphemer so many self-appointed censors try to ban, he is a humanist who desperately pleads for love and decency in a world of cruelty and injustice; a novelist who denies the paternal Christian god but proclaims the very message of the Sermon on the Mount; an atheist who holds up Jesus as a person to revere and emulate; and a "Christ-worshiping agnostic" (*Palm Sunday*, 327) who time and again evokes the imminent end of mankind only to alert his readers to the necessity of preventing it through their conversion to a more human "religion."[9]

NOTES

1. See Edwin Moseley, *Pseudonyms of Christ in the Modern Novel: Motifs and Methods* (Pittsburgh: University of Pittsburgh Press, 1962); and Theodore Ziolkowski, *Fictional Transfigurations of Jesus* (Princeton, N.J.: Princeton University Press, 1972). A representative example of a contemporary parodistic Christ figure is Randle Patrick McMurphy in Ken Kesey's *One Flew Over the Cuckoo's Nest* (New York: New American Library,1962).

2. For an investigation of apocalyptic themes, motifs, and images in Vonnegut's oeuvre, see Peter Freese, "Zwischen Dresden und Tralfamadore: Visionen des Weltuntergangs in Kurt Vonneguts Rumanian von *Da hollische System* bis *Schlachthof 5*," in *Apokalypse: Weltuntergangsvisionen in der Literatur des 20. Jahrhunderts*, ed. Gunter E. Grimm, Werner Faulstich and Peter Kuon (Frankfurt/Main: Suhrkamp, 1986), pp. 88–109.

3. Among the growing number of publications that deal with the religious and philosophical implications of science fiction, Robert Reilly, ed.'s *The Transcendent Adventure: Studies of Religion in Science Fiction/Fantasy*, (Westport, Conn.: Greenwood Press, 1984), provides an
informative overview.

4. See Max F. Schulz, "The Unsensing of the Self; and, the Unconfirmed Thesis of Kurt Vonnegut," in his *Black Humor Fiction of the Sixties: A Pluralistic Definition of Man and His World* (Athens: Ohio University Press, 1973), 43–65.

5. Parenthetical dates following Vonnegut's books refer to their original dates of publication. Parenthetical page references following quoted material refer to reprints, which are fully documented in the Works Cited section at the end of this chapter.

6. For a discussion of Vonnegut's inimitable technique of basing transcendental considerations on the most trivial material, see Peter Freese, "Laurel and Hardy versus the Self-Reflexive Artefact: Vonnegut's Novels Between High Culture and Popular Culture," in *High and Low in American Culture*, ed. Charlotte Kretzoi (Budapest: L. Eotvos University, 1986), 19–38.

7. David Bosworth, "The Literature of Awe," *Antioch Review* 37 (1979): 4-26: at 16.

8. James R. Tunnell, "Kesey and Vonnegut: Preachers of Redemption," *Christian Century* 89 November 22, 1972): 1180–1183, at 1183.

9. The number of critical books and articles on Vonnegut's novels is legion, but there is so far no systematic treatment of his religious position. As far as *The Sirens of Titan*, *Cat's Cradle*, and *Slaughterhouse-Five* are concerned, more detailed interpretations and references to the relevant critical literature can be found in my articles "Kurt Vonnegut, Jr., *The Sirens of Titan* (1959)," in *Der Science-Fiction-Roman in der angloamerikanischen Literatur*, ed. Hartmut Heuermann (Dusseldorf: Bagel, 1986), pp. 196–219; "Kurt Vonnegut: *Cat's Cradle* (1963)," in *Die Utopie in der angloamerikanischen Literatur*, ed. Hartmut Heuermann and Bernd-Peter Lange (Dusseldorf: Bagel, 1984), pp. 283–309; and "Kurt Vonnegut, Jr.: *Slaughterhouse-Five* (1969)," in *Der Roman im Englischunterricht der Sekundarstufe II: Theorie und Praxis*, ed. Peter Freese and Liesel Hermes (Paderborn: Schoningh, 2nd rev. and enl. ed., 1981), pp. 414–443.

WORKS CITED

Vonnegut, Kurt. *Breakfast of Champions* (New York: Dell Books, 1974) (first published in 1973).
——. *Cat's Cradle* (CC) (New York: Dell Books, 1970) (first published in 1963).
——. *Deadeye Dick* (New York: Dell Books, 1983) (first published in 1982).
——. *Fate Worse Than Death* (Nottingham: The Bertrand Russell Foundation, 1985) (first published in 1982).
——. *Galápagos* (New York: Delacorte Press/Seymour Lawrence, 1985).
——. *God Bless You, Mr. Rosewater* (London: Panther Books, 1972) (first 1965).
——. *Jailbird* (London: Panther Books, 1980) (first 1979).
——. *Mother Night* (New York: Avon Books, 1970) (first 1961).
——. *Palm Sunday: An Autobiographical Collage* (London: Jonathan Cape, 1981).
——. *Player Piano* (New York: Avon Books, 1968) (first 1952).
——. *The Sirens of Titan* (New York: Dell Books, 1972) (first 1959).
——. *Slapstick or Lonesome No More!* (London: Panther Books, 1977) (first 1976).
——. *Slaughterhouse-Five* (New York: Dell Books, 1979) (first 1969).
——. *Wampeters, Foma & Granfalloons* (New York: Dell Books, 1974).

Bluebeard and the Abstract Expressionists

Cliff McCarthy

Artists should not intrude into others' territory—such as the analysis of literature. (I have considered myself an artist more or less my whole life.) But Vonnegut's *Bluebeard* is about art and artists of the 1940s and 1950s, the period I awakened into, and I am helpless to resist speaking up.

Bluebeard is the autobiography of an Armenian artist named Rabo Karabekian. After Rabo came home from World War II, he associated with the group of New York artists soon to be known as the abstract expressionists. Jackson Pollock was his good friend. He was in his early thirties when he drank with Jackson and the other artists in the Cedar Bar. He is seventy-one when he writes his autobiography.

Rabo Karabekian is a lucky Armenian in many ways. As he writes his story he is living in a mansion in East Hampton, Long Island, that he inherited from his second wife. He also inherited a one-quarter ownership in the Cincinnati Bengals. But his most valuable possession in the mansion is a collection of abstract expressionist paintings, the most extensive still in private hands. They are his by right—another example of his luck. Because his mother found a fortune in jewels spilled from the mouth of an old lady who lay dead on the killing fields of Turkish Armenia, and because the U.S. government paid him a monthly stipend as compensation for an eye he lost in the war, he was able to grubstake the generally poverty stricken artists he chummed with after the war. They paid off their debts to him with their paintings, which weren't selling anyway (*Bluebeard*, 45). But he was unlucky in marriage. His first wife and their two sons moved out on him because he was such a miserable husband and father.

If we are to understand Rabo Karabekian, the most important thing to know is that he can draw like a wizard. He has a gift, but we soon realize that though he is lucky to have such a gift, his ability to draw made him a poor candidate for sainthood as an abstract expressionist. He really didn't understand very well what Jackson Pollock and Mark Rothko and Arshile Gorky and Barnett Newman and the others were into. "I concluded," he says early in his autobiography, "that my mind was so ordinary, which is to say empty, that I could never be anything but a reasonably good camera. So I would content myself with a more common and general sort of achievement than serious art, which is money. I was not saddened about this. I was in fact much relieved!" (*Bluebeard*, 44)

We have met Rabo Karabekian before—before *Bluebeard*. He was an invited guest to the grand Arts Festival planned for Midland City along with Beatrice Keedsler and Kilgore Trout, two important novelists, plus many other important people in the arts as reported in *Breakfast of Champions*. He was in the cocktail lounge of the Midland City Holiday Inn. He had just raised the hackles of the waitress, Bonnie MacMahon, by insulting Mary Alice Miller, Queen of the Festival and Woman's Two Hundred Meter Breast Stroke Champion of the World. She was fifteen and Midland City's most beloved citizen. When Rabo Karabekian learned that Mary Alice's father taught her to swim when she was only eight months old, and made her swim four hours a day, every day, since she was three, he said loudly, so many heard him, "What kind of man would turn his daughter into an outboard motor?"

Bonnie MacMahon blew up. "You don't think much of Mary Alice Miller?" she said. "Well, we don't think much of your painting. I've seen better pictures done by a five-year old" (*Breakfast*, 220).

The painting Bonnie MacMahon was referring to had recently been purchased for the new Midland City Art Center for $50,000. It was sixteen feet high and twenty feet wide. The color was an all-over "Hawaiian Avocado" green. A vertical strip of day-glo orange reflecting tape was located one-sixth of the width from the left edge. Rabo gave it the title *The Temptation of St. Anthony*. Rabo Karabekian seized the moment to render an oration to the hostile locals, a ringing defense of his work:

"Listen. . . . I have read the editorials against my painting in your wonderful newspaper. I have read every word of the hate mail you have been thoughtful enough to send to New York. . . . The painting did not exist until I made it. . . . Now that it does exist, nothing would make me happier than to have it reproduced again and again, and vastly improved upon, by all the five-year-olds in town. I would love for your children to find pleasantly and playfully what it took me many angry years to find.

"I now give you my word of honor that the picture your city owns shows everything about life which truly matters, with nothing left out. It is a picture of the awareness of every animal. It is the immaterial core of every animal—the 'I am' to which all messages are sent. It is all that is alive in any of us—in a mouse, in a deer, in a cocktail waitress. It is unwavering and pure, no matter what preposterous adventure may befall us. A sacred picture of Saint Anthony alone is one vertical, unwavering band of light. If a cockroach were near him, or a cocktail waitress, the picture would show two such bands of light. Our awareness is all that is alive and maybe sacred in any of us. Everything else about us is dead machinery. . . ."

Ecstasy bloomed on the barbaric face of Rabo Karabekian. "Citizens of Midland City, I salute you," he said. "You have given a home to a masterpiece!" (*Breakfast*, 220–221)

But that was years ago. As his biography proceeds we learn that he hasn't painted in decades. He is, by his own words, only a museum guard who does nothing more than a paid guard would do, that is, answer the question asked by visitor after visitor, "What are these pictures supposed to mean?"

His good-for-nothing life of indolence is interrupted by a pushy widow who accepted a casual invitation to live with him—in a completely platonic arrangement. Her name is Circe Berman. She is a recent widow of a Baltimore brain surgeon and in her own right a world famous writer of straight-from-the-shoulder books for young adults. Her pen name is Polly Madison. Circe persuades Rabo to write the story of his life—since he doesn't seem to have anything better to do. Then she launches into her agenda to rearrange both the mansion and old Rabo. She noses into every nook and cranny of the house and into every detail of Rabo's life. She knows everything that could be known about Rabo Karabekian, the old war veteran and ex–abstract expressionist, except one thing. The one thing he would not reveal was what he referred to as "the worthless secret of a silly old man." Not Circe Berman nor anyone will find out what was in the long, narrow, windowless potato barn on the back of his property until after he had gone to the "great art auction in the sky" (*Bluebeard*, 40).

Rabo Karabekian, our fabricated abstract expressionist, achieved several notable successes before his career was halted by a chemistry catastrophe which destroyed all his work. His most famous creation was an eight foot by sixty-four foot painting entitled, *Windsor Blue Number Seventeen*, bought by GEFFCo and installed in their headquarters building on Park Avenue. The Guggenheim Museum bought another large canvas called *Hungarian Rhapsody Number Six*.

It certainly was an attack of bad luck that Sateen Dura-Luxe, a new paint touted as eternally durable and which Rabo bought hook, line and sinker, should carry a fatal flaw. An unforeseen reaction between the paint and the primed canvas caused the Sateen Dura-Luxe and the vertical tape strips to peel off. What happened to Rabo Karabekian's paintings was soon known throughout the art world. He became a laughing stock. Art history teachers showed their students before-and-after slides of his paintings. Nosey Circe Berman found sixty-three gallons of Sateen Dura-Luxe still stored in the mansion basement.

Rabo Karabekian's *Temptation of St. Anthony*, which he defended so stoutly in the cocktail lounge of the Midland City Holiday Inn, resembles a painting by a real world abstract expressionist, Barnett Newman. *Midnight Blue*, which Newman painted in 1970, the last year of his life, is an overall dark, royal blue. It contrasts sharply in color with *St. Anthony*, which is *Hawaiian Avocado*, a warm green, but compositionally, they are remarkably similar. Rabo has placed his vertical strip of orange tape on the left of his canvas while Newman's single stripe of light cerulean blue is located on the right; merely a detail of preference, I presume.

About 1946, Newman reached the point of simplifying his compositions wherein a single stripe divided the canvas. Curves and diagonals were eliminated. His first fully resolved postwar work, *Onement I*, was declared finished by him after studying it through the winter, spring, and summer of 1948. The rather ragged vertical stripe of cadmium red light is exactly in the middle of the vertical canvas. The background color is a deep red-brown shaded slightly darker toward the top. It is surprisingly small, only twenty-one inches high and sixteen inches wide. Newman used five vertical stripes in *Vir Heroicus Sublimis*, (Man Heroic and Sublime) one of his masterpieces in the Museum of Modern Art. It is eight feet high by seventeen feet, nine and a quarter inches long. He finished it in 1951.

If Karabekian had been a successful husband, if he had been Jewish rather than of that tragic clan from Armenia, and if he had never drawn a recognizable image in his born days, his status as a Barnett Newman clone would have been established. But that was not to be. While Rabo was a lonely recluse in his mansion on Long Island, Barnett Newman was a confident, productive and, as far as I know, happy man in Brooklyn. Barney Newman and Annalee Greenhouse had a June wedding in 1936 and lived happily ever after. He ran for mayor of New York City in 1933, on an "Art for the People" platform, for heaven's sake (Hess, 24). He was a businessman, botanist, ornithologist. He was knowledgeable in law and geology, and he wrote aggressively on the current art scene in New York and as an apostle of his own artistic faith. If his family had fled from genocide in a past time, the memory was buried in their New World experience, in their Brooklyn citizenship, that Barney treasured. No one in his family had ever seen a dead old woman with uncut gems falling from her mouth. The final, bitter discrepancy between Rabo Karabekian and Barnett Newman is that the Brooklyn abstract expressionist was not an old veteran. He had no war stories to tell because he had never seen a field strewn with dead and dying; he had no war wounds. He was excused from serving in World War II on grounds of conscience. He did not mind shooting Nazis, he said, but he would rather not shoot people because some second lieutenant told him to (Hess, 26).

Rabo Karabekian's life has its counterpart in the real world but in another of the abstract expressionists, an Armenian. Arshile Gorky was eleven years old when his family was forced to leave their home in Van, Turkish Armenia. The year was 1915. Like Rabo's parents (who had not yet met) they were doing their best to avoid being slaughtered by the Turks. On their journey toward survival Arshile's mother died of starvation—in his arms, it is said. Arshile and his sister Vartoosh, with the help of an uncle, eventually made their way to the Land of the Free where Gorky enrolled in high school and attended the Rhode Island School of Design (Waldman, 256).

Gorky's real name was Vosdanik Adoian, but soon after he arrived in the new land, he told people he was Russian, the nephew of Maxim Gorky, the great Russian writer. Some sources still list his nationality as Russian. Perhaps he changed his name because he had Survivor's syndrome, like Rabo Karabekian's father, and didn't want to be Armenian any longer. Survivor's syndrome is a trauma that attaches itself to those still living after severe disasters such as holocausts. It makes them feel guilty that they are still alive after others, perhaps loved ones, have died. Perhaps Vosdanik was burdened with the knowledge that his mother had starved herself to death so he could live, and he imagined if he could become another person he would feel better.

Rabo had a similar desire to escape from his Armenian skin. Near the town of San Ignacio, California, where Rabo grew up, was a Luma Indian reservation, and sometimes people passing through town would mistake him for a Luma boy. "I liked that a lot," he tells us in his autobiography. "At the time I thought it certainly beat being Armenian" (*Bluebeard*, 36).

Like Rabo Karabekian, Arshile Gorky apparently was unsatisfactory as a husband and as a father. And he suffered a series of bad luck events: a barn burned with twenty-seven paintings, drawings and books in it; an auto accident; the onset of cancer; and, like Rabo, his wife left him. Finally, in 1948, in defeat and despair, he committed suicide. That was thirty-nine years before Rabo Karabekian was badgered by Circe Berman into writing his tragic story.

The startling difference between Arshile Gorky and Rabo Karabekian is in their work. Although they both emerged from the frightful tragedy of World War I Armenia, their painting took opposite paths. Karabekian adopted the planar minimalist surface interrupted by a few static vertical stripes as exemplified by Barnett Newman. Gorky's painting was all curved forms, like viscera, in strong, cleanly recited color. *Biomorphic* is the word critics use to describe Gorky's form.

The central mystery of Rabo Karabekian's artistic life is, why would he throw aside his vast natural gift for detailed representational drawing to adopt a mode of such extreme sparseness? My answer is that he bought the wrong ideal.

The Guggenheim Museum and GEFFCo must have seen value in Rabo's work since they bought large paintings from him, but the average person considered his paintings mostly empty. Circe Berman detested his work, and she positively despised his valuable collection of abstract expressionist painting. When he sold one to the Getty Museum for a million and a half dollars she said, "Good riddance . . . now give the rest of them the old heave-ho" (*Bluebeard*, 36). His cook had never seen any of his paintings because they had all disappeared due to the Sateen Dura-Luxe disease, but if one were resurrected she would have said to him, "It just doesn't mean anything to me. Maybe if I went to college I would understand it" (*Bluebeard*, 34). We know that is what she would say about his painting because she said it about his collection of Pollocks, Rothkos, Stills and Motherwells. She complained to him that he had sold the only picture in his collection she liked. As it turned out, that painting had not been painted by one of his abstract expressionist friends but by his mentor and former role model, Dan Gregory, world famous, superrealist illustrator. It was about two little black boys and two little white boys trying to decide whether they should play together or go their separate ways.

Circe Berman, a very clear-headed woman, urged Rabo to use his own life story as the subject of his work rather than the abstract expressionist style which, she said, was about nothing at all. She detected that something was wrong in his life and she wanted to redirect him. The very first thing she said to him when they met on the beach was, "Tell me how your parents died" (*Bluebeard*, 111). It was her first shot to convince him he should somehow use his own life in his work.

Like Gorky, Rabo had such an interesting life, even though it was tragic. He had so many images in his head, so many details, so many facts! He had stories to tell, yet he chose to join the abstract expressionists who would be no help at all in storytelling. If they had stories to tell, they did not want to tell them *explicitly*. They chose to encode their messages in an abstract and, they hoped, meaningful form.

The abstract expressionists were after an invisible thing. Barnett Newman was talking and writing about reaching out to the sublime. This is what he wrote in his essay, "The Plasmic Image":

The present painter is concerned not with . . . his own personality but with the penetration into the world mystery. His imagination is therefore attempting to dig into metaphysical secrets . . . his art is concerned with the sublime. It is a religious art which through symbols will catch the basic truth of life which is its sense of tragedy. (Hess, 38)

Elsewhere he wrote, "We are reasserting man's natural desire for the exalted" (Rose, 159).

In the middle of World War II, two prominent abstract expressionists wrote what is now regarded as a manifesto of their creed. It appeared as a letter to the editor in the *New York Times* on Sunday, June 13, 1943. The letter is signed by Mark Rothko and Adolph Gottlieb, but Barnett Newman helped write it. Here are some of the things they say:

To us art is an adventure into an unknown world which can be explored only by those willing to take the risks. . . . This world of the imagination is fancy free and violently opposed to common sense. . . . We favor the simple expression of the complex thought. We are for the large shape because it has the impact of the unequivocal. . . . We are for flat forms because they destroy illusion and reveal truth. . . . It is a widely accepted notion among painters that it does not matter what one paints as long as it is well painted. This is the essence of academism. There is no such thing as good painting about nothing. We assert that the subject is crucial and only that subject-matter is valid which is tragic and timeless.

Imagine, the *Times* piece and Newman's discussion of the sublime in "The Plasmic Image" were both written in 1943, while Rabo Karabekian was still with his camouflage platoon doing important work for Uncle Sam—forty-four years before Circe Berman told Rabo that all those paintings by his friends were about nothing at all.

I wonder if Karabekian knows that Arshile Gorky, a fellow Armenian artist, conducted courses in camouflage in the early 1940s. Gorky wrote in a course announcement that the purpose of camouflage is to "confuse and paralyze" the vision of the enemy. He believed the modern artist was best suited to do this because he already knew the language of making things visible, so hiding things would be no problem for him. Gorky offered his services to the U.S. Army, but they refused him because he was overage (Waldman, 264). He was thirty-eight. He gave himself six more years to live.

If I may make an observation, I think Rabo Karabekian traveled with the wrong crowd. The sadness we feel for Rabo as we read his autobiography lies in our realization that his friends at the Cedar Bar did not try to understand him, and he certainly was not permitting himself to tune in clearly on what they were all about. After all the drinking and art blather sessions where he knew the excitement and warmth of comradeship, he could not be honest with himself and admit that he should be drinking in another bar.

Yet he was loyal and had the heart to defend them when necessary. We heard his rousing speech to the crowd in the Holiday Inn cocktail lounge. Even the author of the story, who was in the lounge at the time and who of course wrote the speech Karabekian gave, was surprised by his courage in standing up to that crowd of noisy Philistines (*Breakfast,* 220). But Rabo was defending someone else's turf.

What was it that Rabo Karabekian, the transplanted Armenian artist who could draw like a wizard, did not understand? He didn't understand that the abstract expressionists were impatient with hay fields and silos, with counting fingers and toes. They wanted to leapfrog backwards out of the horrors of present time to an early age when there was no history, merely oneness with universal innocence. He did not understand how abstract forms could have power to move a viewer, and he did not understand, or he preferred not to believe, that artists could work without images, could create meaning from a void, so to speak, like the Creator Himself.

Proof of this sad fact about Karabekian lies in his effort to explain the meaning of the stripes that were the only interruption on the otherwise featureless plain of his canvases. "I had a secret," he tells us in his autobiography, "which I have never told anybody before . . . each strip of tape was the soul or the core of some sort of person or lower animal—once an illustrator, always an illustrator!" (*Bluebeard,* 221). The eight foot by eight foot canvas he sold to the Guggenheim Museum had six strips toward the left edge and a red vertical band on the right. The vertical tapes were laid over a thoroughly even, rolled-on coat of greenish burnt orange labeled *Hungarian Rhapsody* sold by the Sateen Dura-Luxe Company, hence the title of the painting, *Hungarian Rhapsody Number Six.* Karabekian explained the meaning of the painting this way. The six colored strips to the left were six deer in a forest glade. The lone red strip on the right was a hunter taking aim at one of them. In another of his paintings a white strip is the soul of a polar bear attacking a lost explorer. At the funeral of his beloved second wife, Edith, he had this vision of the mourners: "There was this hole in the ground, and standing around it were all these pure and innocent neon tubes" (*Bluebeard,* 277).

It is interesting to note that there is an artist working today who uses neon tubes as his primary material. He is descended from Barnett Newman and Rabo Karabekian, artistically speaking. His name is Dan Flavin. The remarkable thing about Flavin's work is he does not use canvas or a panel of any kind to mount his neon tubes (Auping, 149–150). We, the viewers, and his neon tubes, are standing in the same contiguous space. We and the art are one: a twentieth-century art and technology miracle.

Barnett Newman was not an illustrator. The rumor is that he drew not a single recognizable image in his entire life. He wanted us above all to measure our presence by his painting, to know our own scale, our core of meaning in time and space, and so approach the oneness with self that he called the sublime. Harold Rosenberg, a critic who wrote sympathetically of Newman, said he could be called a "mystic through whose canvasses the onlooker levitates into cosmic pastures where emptiness and plenitude are the same thing." Newman offers us a "shortcut to the unattainable" (Rosenberg, 169). That's tall talk about a mere painting. Would Karabekian welcome with open arms such an explanation?

Newman's vertical stripes, which he called "zips," are not the gap between elevator doors as they close or open, as a jokester suggested (Rosenberg, 173), nor are they are neither hunters nor polar bears. They are more like the first division in a cell that must become two before it can become one again, or the moment of epiphany when God and you or I, if we are lucky, accomplish oneness with Him, or, perhaps, when a man and woman join in sublime satisfaction.

Rabo Karabekian stopped painting in the early 1960s. He writes that it was a "postwar miracle" that "wrecked" him, an acrylic wall paint that was supposed to ". . . outlive the smile of the Mona Lisa" (*Bluebeard*, 20). Such an unlucky event certainly could discourage even a stout-hearted artist, but Rabo had other ego-breaking events attack him about the same time. He came to understand that his abstract expressionist family loved him for his money and not his painting. Jackson Pollock died in a car crash; his best friend, Terry Kitchen, committed suicide; and his first wife and their two boys left him for good. He now was beginning to believe that he had nothing to say in paint, certainly not anything as imageless as what his friends at the Cedar Bar were talking about.

The foremost tragedy Rabo had to accept among the variety that came his way was the burden of his heaven-sent gift of drawing. He could draw anything at the drop of a hat and he proved it on several occasions when challenged to do so, like the moment in an argument when his first wife, Dorothy, was after him for not getting a proper job with a dependable income. She said, hoping to wound him into action, ". . . you guys all paint the way you do because you couldn't paint something real if you *had* to" (*Breakfast*, 266). To prove her wrong he grabbed a green crayon lying on the table and drew portraits on the kitchen wall of their two boys who were asleep in the other room. She was amazed. "Why don't you do that all the time?" He answered, using the four-letter word for the first time in their married life, "It's just too fucking easy." Six years later when she left him she cut the two portraits out of the wall and took them with her.

Another example: As a proof-of-ability test before admitting him to full apprenticeship, Dan Gregory, the world famous illustrator (formerly Gregorian, another Armenian) required that Rabo paint a picture of his studio. The painting of the infinitely detailed room, filled as it was with weapons, tools, hats, models of all sorts, stuffed animals, fifty-two mirrors and six fireplaces each with its own fire, took Rabo six months to complete. So meticulously was it painted that each droplet of "water dripping from the skylight in my painting was not only the wettest you ever saw: in each droplet, if you used a magnifying glass to look at one of them, the whole damn studio!" (*Bluebeard*, 146) Gregory said, "Not bad, not bad" and placed the painting on the burning coals in the fireplace.

Karabekian had to endure the depressing truth that his incredible drawing skill was useless. He had an old world, past-century skill in a postwar body. He had tried to be a part of the New World's artistic experiment, its idealism, its transcendentalism, but he was not equipped. Now at the age of seventy-one he was resigned to being a lonely old man, content that his secret in the potato barn would be revealed only after he was dead. He would not have to face the music.

The point of his autobiography is to reveal to the reader and the world that Circe Berman changed all that for Rabo Karabekian. She put him right on some things.

But there was no Circe Berman for that other Armenian abstract expressionist, Arshile Gorky. On a July morning in 1948, he wrote, "Goodbye My Loveds," in white chalk on a picture crate in his Sherman, Connecticut, studio and then hanged himself from a rafter (Waldman, 267). It cannot be confirmed, but Rabo Karabekian would probably agree with me when I say I believe Gorky might have died of Survivor's syndrome.

Circe, the pushy enchantress, persuaded Rabo Karabekian to write his life story, and most spectacular of her accomplishments, she talked Rabo into showing her his "worthless" secret in the barn. This is how she brought off that miracle: She called him a coward and told him that would be the way she would remember him if he persisted in his refusal to let her see what he had in the barn. He searched out the keys and asked her to follow him.

It is not my place to describe what was shown in the barn that night except perhaps to give you the size of it and a few necessary facts. What Circe saw under the brightness of a row of floodlights was a "jewel-encrusted fence" eight feet high and sixty-four feet long. The eight panels used for this "fence" were the very same that GEFFCo bought almost thirty years earlier as *Windsor Blue Number Seventeen*, Rabo's most famous creation. They had been locked in the third basement below the Matsumoto Building (formerly GEFFCo) after shedding their Sateen Dura-Luxe and tapes. This painting, a failure of technology as measured by its own promise to outlive the *Mona Lisa*, is discovered by safety inspector Mona Lisa Trippingham. She calls Rabo to see if he has any desire to claim the remains. Rabo resurrects the canvases, moving them to his potato barn where he repaints the panels into a visual extravaganza containing 5,219 people, some as small as a fly speck. He had not painted for so many years and this thing was so unique, so different, and so completely from the core of himself that he hesitated calling it a painting. Weeks later, when his "whachamacallit" became so popular with common people that they were trooping through the barn by the hundreds, Rabo called it a "tourist attraction," a "gruesome Disneyland" (*Bluebeard,* 270).

That first night in the barn, under the floodlights, Rabo Karabekian, with Circe's help, became a whole Armenian American artist who could draw like a wizard. He stopped being ashamed of himself or any part thereof!

POSTSCRIPT:

An exchange of letters I had with Kurt Vonnegut between 1980 and 1987 revealed an aspect of his attitude toward drawing skill and especially representational drawing that I would like to pursue for a moment. Vonnegut was writing *Deadeye Dick* when the correspondence began. He had asked me if I could help him through an information void about Ohio artists who were active in the early decades of this century. Whether I actually moved his project even a jot is wide open to question, but I enjoyed our brief chat by mail.

I believe our references to art, and drawing in particular, began when I presumed to compare *Deadeye Dick* with the painting of Philip Guston. This is what I wrote to him the 30th of July, 1982:

If you will permit me further comment on *Deadeye Dick*—I see a strong correspondence between your latest writing and the third period in the work of the painter, Philip Guston. He died two years ago. You both employ bitter humor, much of it directed at yourselves (and so at the reader or viewer). You both have evolved a simple and powerful form which excludes horseshit of any kind; and you both refer to the sinister forces, the beasts in ourselves and in our society which perpetuate cruelties, injustice and absurdity. Guston's Hoods emerged out of the briarpatch form that was Abstract Expressionism, and give image again to his social consciousness which was so much part of his pre-AE work. . . . He is also a hero of mine.

Vonnegut's response to my bringing Guston into the conversation is contained in a letter dated August 11, 1982. He devoted two paragraphs to the subject. The first paragraph said this:

I saw Philip Guston's last works—at the Whitney. I must say, you painters find that stuff a lot more exciting than the civilians do. To a painter, those pictures show a man's being reborn, I guess. To me they show contempt for skills developed over a lifetime. I would just as soon hear Benny Goodman play a clarinet with a broken reed, missing pads, and so on.

For purposes of clarification, permit me to insert a short monograph on Philip Guston. He was born in 1913, so was one year younger than Jackson Pollock. He and Pollock attended Manual Arts High School together in Los Angeles before they migrated to New York. He is one of the dozen to eighteen members of the first generation abstract expressionists group that Rabo Karabekian knew and traveled with after World War II until about 1955.

Guston was unique among artists active before 1940, because he was financially successful when most of the others were struggling through the birth stages of the style that would dominate Western painting through the 1950s. His resolved style in the 1940s was based upon renaissance perspective and traditional drawing with a cubist structure. It earned him mural assignments, exhibitions, and fellowships. In short, he had a gift for traditional drawing and he used it well during that first mature period of his career.

As the fifties approached, his work became abstract and flat. The image and traditional drawing disappeared from his canvases as he committed himself to the canons of abstract expressionism. His work through the fifties was delicate, quiet in contrast to most of the others. Through the 1960s Guston's brush strokes began to come together to form bulks, even ominous shapes. Beginning about 1968, the brutish, comic strip figures Vonnegut expressed regret over appeared. His central comment in this last of his three periods is "mea culpa." We are to blame for pollution, crime and injustice. Yes, even the artist is. *I* smoke and drink too much. *I* contribute to the world's ugliness and misery. It is a pretty hopeless message he delivers. He kept at it until he died in 1980.

I was crushed a bit to read that Vonnegut could not accept my comparison of his recent writing, especially *Breakfast of Champions* and *Deadeye Dick*, to Guston's last work. Of course I meant to commend him for the power of it and for his courage in resorting to innovative forms to accomplish his felt objectives. I continue to believe there is a "mea culpa" quality in his writing that places him in a significant and, in my mind, welcome, avant-garde. I continue to admire Vonnegut's power and freshness, perhaps I should say, his contemporaneousness with Guston's last twelve years' work. It is those same qualities many of us admire unstintingly in Kurt Vonnegut's writing.

We must accept Vonnegut's hypothetical situation that Benny Goodman playing with a damaged clarinet would most certainly be cacophonous. I guess my response is that Guston's instrument, however characterized, was not damaged. He simply chose to leave off the sweet notes. Jackson Pollock had so much confidence in his own airborne gestures that between 1947 and 1950 he gave up his brushes.

I said some of the above in my next letter (January 1, 1985):

A re-read of your last note reveals you didn't take kindly to my comparison of the forms in your present fiction to the forms Phil Guston used in his last dozen years of painting. I'm still convinced of the usefulness of the comparison. It is meant to help describe the kind of power *Breakfast of Champions* and *Deadeye* contain. At least the comparison helps me to understand. There is more but I'll get off that horse.

He answered promptly in part as follows (January 7, 1985):

I forget whatever you may have said about me and Guston's last works. Any unease I expressed had to do with Guston, not me. I envy anyone who can really draw, and so it seems wasteful and rude when someone so gifted turns his back on the gift. I felt the same way when Artie Shaw said he really didn't like playing the clarinet all that much. At least he took up with women instead of the kazoo.

A year later he wrote (January 7, 1986):

I say again that Guston's purposely primitive responses to modern times seemed abuse of wonderful machinery.

Rabo Karabekian got into our discussion when he reached a conclusion about his own and his famous mentor's potential for greatness:

What kept him from coming anywhere near to greatness, although no more marvelous technician ever lived? I have thought hard about this, and any answer I give refers to me, too. I was the best technician by far among the Abstract Expressionists, but I never amounted to a hill of beans, either, and couldn't have . . . .

But let's forget me for the moment, and focus on the works of Gregory. They were truthful about material things, but they lied about time. He celebrated moments, anything from a child's first meeting with a department store Santa Claus to the victory of a gladiator at the Circus Maximus, from the driving of the golden spike which completed a transcontinental railroad to a man's going on his knees to ask a woman to marry him. But he lacked the guts or the wisdom, or maybe just the talent, to indicate somehow that time was liquid, that one moment was no more important than any other, and that all moments quickly run away.

Let me put it another way: Dan Gregory was a taxidermist. He stuffed and mounted and varnished and mothproofed supposedly great moments, all of which turn out to be depressing dust-catchers, like a moosehead bought at a country auction . . . . (*Bluebeard,* 82–83)

Those harsh words spoken by an artist who has been through the mill, so to speak, should give Vonnegut pause to reflect. At the very least, Rabo is saying that perhaps more than a gift for drawing is necessary for greatness. Rabo should know, don't you think?

Perhaps not so coincidentally, Kurt Vonnegut produced a mini-gallery of drawings to illustrate his script for *Breakfast of Champions*. Many of them have the very quality he complains of in Guston's painting: they are simple and display a touch of crudeness (if I may so observe), yet many of them are sensitive, completely effective in their communication, and all of them hit the mark. He may protest that they are not drawings at all. They are merely a part of his experiment in writing. Speaking for all his readers, I can only say this: they look like drawings to us!

At the beginning of this postscript I omitted a second paragraph from Vonnegut's August 11, 1982, letter. Here it is:

I was in Washington, D.C. this morning, and saw the El Greco show—about a fifth of his work, they say. He believed in the Devil, I'm sure, but never tried to show him in a picture. Maybe that's what Philip Guston was trying to do. Maybe he even succeeded.

Unless Vonnegut objects to revealing the Devil in all his mischief we have hope, after hearing those words, that the Grand Conversation will continue.

So it goes.

WORKS CITED

Auping, Michael. *Abstract Expressionism: The Critical Developments.* New York: Abram, 1987.

Hess, Thomas B. *Barnett Newman.* New York: The Museum of Modern Art, 1971.

Rose, Barbara. *Readings in American Art Since 1900.* New York: Praeger, 1968.

Rosenberg, Harold. *The Anxious Object.* New York: Horizon Press, 1966.

Sandler, Irving. *The Triumph of American Painting: A History of Abstract Expressionism.* New York: Praeger, 1970.

Vonnegut, Kurt. *Bluebeard.* Delacorte Press, New York, 1987.

——. *Breakfast of Champions.* Dell, New York, 1980.

——. *Deadeye Dick.* Dell, New York, 1982.

Waldman, Diane. *Arshile Gorky.* New York: Abrams, 1981.

Hartke's Hearing: Vonnegut's Heroes on Trial

Lawrence Broer

The world's fundamental lunacy so burdens the mind of Eugene Debs Hartke that he agrees that human beings are "about 1,000 times dumber and meaner than they think they are" (*Hocus Pocus*, 55), then consoles himself with the thought that "at least the world will end . . . very soon" (13). In the land of the free and the home of the brave, the forces of stupidity, cruelty, and injustice appear so irresistible—on the order of tidal waves or earthquakes—that the split personae of *Hocus Pocus*—Vonnegut the novelist and Hartke the teacher-narrator—offers this dose of sobering iconoclasm: "I see no harm in telling young people to prepare for failure rather than success, since failure is the main thing that is going to happen to them" (60).[1]

Such expressions of despair prompt a majority of reviewers to conclude, as always, that Vonnegut is a novelist of "pessimistic" or "defeatist" novels, that, in fact, futility—charting the planet's helpless drift toward apocalypse—is the primary subject of *Hocus Pocus*. According to Pauline Mayer, Vonnegut seduces us again with an "irresistible message of pessimism and doom"—a "fable of hopelessness" about injustice, greed, war, the destruction of our planet, and our "inability to do much about these and other calamities" (D6). For Jay Cantor, the depressed memoirs of Eugene Debs Hartke offer Vonnegut an opportunity to "model his despair." For the reader, they provide "a long education in the unchanging senselessness of life, unlikely to be transformed except for the worse" (C15). Dan Cryer, agreeing, writes of "descent into disillusionment" (C9). "Society's obituary" (H2) echoes Lisa Anderson. Even if Vonnegut *used* to be the "canary-in-a-coalmine," Anderson concedes, offering "not-too-late-to-wake up parables of the perils of war, technology, pollution, and other 20th century horrors," the author's present view of a crumbling American civilization is a "nightmare from which there is no hope of awakening" (H1).

So it goes. Such unfortunate readings (this is Vonnegut's thirteenth novel) continue the tedious argument of critics from David Goldsmith to Josephine Hendin that those "crazy lunkers" (Hendin, 190) from outer space, Vonnegut's infamous Tralfamadorians, are at it again, projecting the author's own sense of the futility of the human condition.[2] Eugene Debs Hartke does appear to follow a long line of susceptible Vonnegut protagonists for whom the supposed consolations of Tralfamadorian fatalism seem irresistible. Early childhood trauma; deforming experiences in Vietnam; and public humiliations that include family insanity, being fired late in life as a college physics teacher, and imprisonment for treason suggest to Eugene that human beings are so dumb and aggressive that the planet's destruction as imagined by the science fiction writer, Kilgore Trout, is inevitable.[3] According to the story Eugene reads in *Black Garterbelt* called "The Protocols of the Elders of Tralfamadore"(*Hocus Pocus*, 188), the Tralfamadorians will render the earth "as sterile as the moon" (192), first by making the planet a hell of hatred and aggression through a rewriting of the Genesis myth, and second by populating the universe with microscopic spacemen—self-reproducing germs that earthlings will appropriate as new chemical weapons. The elders instruct the writer of the Genesis story to encourage humans to "fill the Earth and subdue it: and have domination over the birds of the air and over everything that moves on the Earth" (189). Believing that the Creator Himself thus wants them to "wreck the joint" (190), earthlings proceed to make the deadliest weapons and poisons in the universe, annihilating "strangers" as if doing "Him" a big favor (192).

After the war, rife with guilt and self-doubt, Eugene is understandably anxious to assign the calamities of his life to the Tralfamadorians—or to the two "prime movers" in the universe—"Time and Luck" (30), suggesting that Tralfamadorian fatalism does indeed, as Goldsmith and others say, help Vonnegut and his psychically scarred protagonists cope with their wartime nightmare. To wit, the sardonic logic of the Tralfamadorians that events are inevitably structured to be the way they are assists Vonnegut's "mature acceptance" of the horrors of life as something it does no good to worry about (Goldsmith, 26). Appropriately, Jay Cantor notes that while Eugene repeatedly counts the cost of being a Vietnam veteran, he "sounds more like a sad, wised-up WWII dogface than a Vietnam desperado" (C15). If I were a fighter plane," says Eugene, "instead of a human being, there would be little pictures of people painted all over me" (*Hocus Pocus*, 284).

At the age of thirty-five, Eugene has seen so much death and destruction that a potentially paralyzing fatalism prompts him to forsake all hope of improvement in the human condition, causing him, as with Malachi Constant and Billy Pilgrim before him, to drug himself to reality—to make himself "dissolute with alcohol and marijuana and women" (59) and to dream dangerous escapist fantasies such as Tralfamadore. "What a relief it was," says Eugene,

to have somebody else confirm what I had come to suspect toward the end of the . . . war . . . particularly after I saw the head of a human being pillowed in the spilled guts of a water buffalo . . . that Humanity is going somewhere really nice was a myth for children under 6 years old, like the Tooth Fairy and the Easter Bunny and Santa Claus. (194)

But rather than providing a saner or more "mature" perspective, the pain-killing philosophy of Tralfamadore reinforces Eugene's cynicism, threatening him with the same fate that claims Billy Pilgrim at the end of *Slaughterhouse-Five* (1969)—a form of moral paralysis that precludes responsibility or action. "I did not realize at the time," Eugene explains, "how much that story (Tralfamadorian) affected me. . . . Reading it was simply a way of putting off for just a little while my looking for another job and another place to live at the age of 51, with 2 lunatics in tow" (*Hocus Pocus*, 194). It is this same emotional malaise—a tendency toward paralysis and withdrawal—that separates Paul Proteus from his sanity, that lands Eliot Rosewater in an asylum, and that leads Howard Campbell to suicide.[4] As with Billy Pilgrim, each of these early protagonists crawls into a kind of schizophrenic shell—a deliberate cultivation of a state of death-in-life existence that isolates and divides him against himself. But if Pilgrim's flight from the responsibility of "wakeful humanity" leads directly to what John Tilton calls a "spiritual oubliette" (*Cosmic Satire in the Contemporary Novel*, 101), it is precisely Eugene Debs Hartke's willingness to face the painful complexities of human identity and the anguish of choice that separates him from these former fragmented heroes.

Like Christopher Lehmann-Haupt—Vonnegut's most hostile and uncomprehending critic—those who see Vonnegut as a fatalist and view pessimism as the subject of *Hocus Pocus* do so without understanding its affirmative function in the psychological plot central to this novel and to Vonnegut's career as a whole. Lehmann-Haupt is precisely right that Eugene "loathes" himself for all the killing and lying he did in Vietnam, observing, "If there's anything you don't like about Eugene, he has probably beaten you to it" (16).[5] But failing his own counsel, that is, thinking "as carefully about the pessimism as Mr. Vonnegut seems to want you to do," Lehmann-Haupt concludes that Eugene's acrid self-criticisms mean an increase in Vonnegut's own "darkness and despair," and warns the reader against succumbing to the author's unreal "nuclear apoplexy."

Failing to understand the nature of Vonnegut's divided fictive selves—a self that affirms and a self that denies—Lehmann-Haupt hears Eugene's nihilistic voice, the Eugene who feels powerless and despised, but ignores altogether its spiritual twin, the efforts of a healthier, yearning, creative self to brave the life struggle and to determine its own identity in a world of mechanistic conformity and anonymity.[6] No Vonnegut protagonist since Howard Campbell, in fact, has chosen to explore his shadowy inner world so directly, or to nurture awareness and moral responsibility more avidly than Eugene Debs Hartke, whose potential as a healer of self and then a healer of others distinguishes Vonnegut's protagonists after the spiritual transfiguration of *Breakfast of Champions*.[7] Whereas each of Vonnegut's earlier heroes become increasingly successful at confronting the dark side of his personality and combatting defeatism,[8] Eugene joins ranks with Wilbur Swain, Walter Starbuck, Rudy Waltz, Leon Trout, and Rabo Karabekian, emergent artists who not only conquer pessimism, but who work out an "aesthetics of renewal"[9]—the existential possibilities of authoring one's identity in life as in art.

It is the essential narrative structure of *Hocus Pocus*—a retrospective vision in which Eugene puts his own troubled soul on trial—that keys the novel's creative affirmation. While Eugene awaits a literal trial for treason for supposedly masterminding a mass prison break at the New York State Maximum Security Adult Correction Institute, his lawyer seizes upon Eugene's remark that he is addicted to older women and housekeeping as credible grounds for a plea of insanity (109). Since in his own mind a history of killing and dying, and of invented justifications he calls "lethal hocus pocus" (148), leave his sanity much in doubt, Eugene determines to conduct a kind of pretrial, an inquiry both moral and psychological, in which he weighs the sane things he has done—the hopeful, caring, merciful side of his nature, against his insane deeds, the cruel and aggressive acts of an unfeeling, cynical, or indifferent self. As if, he says, there really was a "judgment day" and "a big book" in which all things were written (150), he will compile a kind of moral account book that he hopes will prove his sanity—"that I could be compassionate" (290)—in which he records his "worst sins," the lives he has taken, the lies he has told, but also his life-enhancing deeds. When his lawyer sees Eugene's tortured marginal notes about this or that damaged human being, this or that corpse (150), he observes: "The messier the better . . . because any fair minded jury looking at them will have to believe that you are in a deeply disturbed mental state, and probably have been for quite some time" (150).

When imprisoned and awaiting trial, Eugene declares, but "I haven't been convicted of anything yet" (18, 19), effectively inviting the reader turned psychologist to become his coanalyst and judge, probing his culpability and his sanity. As with Vonnegut's former heroes on trial—Paul Proteus, Howard Campbell, Eliot Rosewater, Kilgore Trout, Walter Starbuck—the interpretive challenge is complicated by the ambiguity of Eugene's psychological condition and by the fact that, as Eugene's lawyer demonstrates, notions of sanity are inescapably tied to the ideological assumptions of the speaker, often simplistic, inhumane, and manipulative.[10] Eugene's lawyer knows that Eugene's accusers will judge him insane, stating, "They believe that all you Vietnam veterans are crazy, because that's their reputation" (150). When "hallucinated by the flying saucer people or the CIA," his lawyer sighs, "all the same—all the same." Vonnegut discourages, and Eugene learns to resist, easy categorizations. "All subjects," Eugene insists, "do not reside in neat little compartments" (143). In fact, "people are never stronger than when they think up their own arguments for believing what they believe" (143). Such problematizing stimulates a more intimate and creative relationship between reader and text. The resulting instability requires the reader not only to rethink routine assumptions about and definitions of reality but also to grow aware of the way meaning and value are constructed and therefore challenged or changed. In *Metafiction: The Theory and Practice of Self-Conscious Fiction*, Patricia Waugh observes that Vonnegut's novels are fictional mythologies, which, like Roland Barthes' work, aim to unsettle our convictions about the relative status of truth and fiction.[11]

At age sixty-one in the year 2001, from Eugene's prison-home in the Tarkington library bell-tower, Eugene's self-inquiry indicates that by war's end he was indeed a "seriously wounded man both physically and psychologically" (116)—a potential "burned out case" (103) prone to "psychosomatic hives" (290, 299) and dangerously tempted by "good old oblivion" (119). The computer Griot finds him so unsalvageable it projects him as hopelessly depressed, dying of cirrhosis of the liver on Skid Row (105).

While it is the "entire last half of the 20th Century" (115, 116) that has potentially unbalanced Eugene—the spiraling brutality of childhood, West Point, Vietnam, and humiliating experiences at Tarkington College and Athena prison—Eugene locates the most immediate source of the "something wrong with me" (149) in what he calls his "family image problem" (34): a father "as full of excrement as a Christmas turkey" (14) and a "blithering nincompoop" (15) of a mother so vacuous she agrees with "every decision" his father ever made.[12] So "deeply troubled" (34) by his parents' lack of integrity, Eugene fantasizes that his father was actually a war hero and that both parents were killed heroically on safari in Tanganyika (35). Ultimately, he suggests that an appropriate epitaph would be, "OK, I admit it. It really was a whorehouse" (206).

In the mold of Felix Hoenikker, whose coldness turns his children into "babies full of rabies" (*Cat's Cradle*, 47), Eugene's father is a research scientist who whores for Dupont, a manufacturer of "high explosives" (*Hocus Pocus*, 32). Eugene reflects that during the war, which was about "nothing but the ammunition business" (14), he may have done his father's bidding when calling in a "white-phosphorus barrage or a napalm air strike on a returning Jesus Christ" (14). His father's success at finding new synthetic plastics to make lighter weapons earns him the company's vice presidency in charge of research and development, which in turn earns one of Tarkington's trustees a fortune when Dupont is sold to I. G. Farben of Germany, the same company that manufactured cyanide gas "used to kill civilians of all ages, including babies in arms, during the Holocaust" (37). The greed and human indifference that Dupont and Eugene's father represent transform Dupont's employees into robots unaware of the "miracles" they package and label (39). And, says Eugene, "Never mind what he did to the environment with his nonbiodegradable plastics. Look what he did to me!" (15).

Specifically, Eugene refers to the embarrassment he feels when his father forces him to cheat on a high school science project about crystallography for the County Fair. Eugene has so little to do with the exhibit his father constructs that when he inquires what his father is doing, he is told to be quiet. "Don't bother me," his father scolds (42). The unfair competition makes Eugene so literally sick he throws up. Thinking back to when they were caught, Eugene discerns ominous spiral-like connections between his father's aggression and absence of conscience—the desire to win at any costs—and that of the Vietnam War:

"Generals George Armstrong Custer . . . Robert E. Lee . . . and William Westmoreland . . . all come to mind" (44). Disclaiming guilt, his father declared that they were not about to go home with their "tails between their legs" (45).

About the "spider web" of guilt and futility his father has fashioned, which Eugene likens to "a microscopic universe"(119), he concludes, "at least it wasn't a hydrogen bomb" (118).[13] Yet he emerges from the war zone of childhood with psychological wounds so severe that only "a whole new planet or death" (48) would cure them. The planet, perhaps, is Tralfamadore; the "death" is the death of the spirit for those who succumb to Tralfamadorian fatalism as a defense against pain. After all, Eugene says, "If my father was a horse's fundament and my mother was a horse's fundament, what can I be but another horse's fundament?" (142). References to having been "zapped" during the "darkest days" of childhood (40), to both childhood and Vietnam as "battlefields" (35), and to Eugene's reliance on drugs to survive both ordeals, effectively merge Eugene's childhood nightmare with that of his war experience. He concludes that "at the age of 35, Eugene Debs Hartke was again as dissolute with respect to alcohol and marijuana and loose women as he had been during his last 2 years in high school. And he had lost all respect for himself and the leadership of this country, just as, 17 years earlier he had lost all respect for himself and his father at the Cleveland, Ohio Science Fair" (59).

The oblivion of drugs—turning his "brains to cobwebs" (41) with marijuana, alcohol, and their philosophical counterpart, Tralfamadorian fatalism ("failure is the norm," he decides [41])—entraps Eugene further in the web of lovelessness and aggression he seeks to escape. His withdrawal is a natural reaction to very real terrors from which he does well to shrink. His crisis, however, is that the aesthetic of fatalism may condemn him to what R. D. Laing in *The Divided Self* describes as "existential gangrene" (82).[14] Withdrawal from an outer world of people and things into one of phantom fulfillment may lead to a total inability to act and finally to a state of nonbeing and a desire for death. That is precisely the moribund condition that threatens Eugene through "habits" of masking or distorting reality, which he "develops very young" (*Hocus Pocus*, 36), and which leave him as dangerously "unprepared" (41) for complex experience as the brain-damaged victims of Athena or Tarkington.

It is here that Eugene's father exerts his most destructive influence, creating that separation of Eugene's several selves that Howard Campbell calls schizophrenic (136), a split between the protagonist's aspiring, creative self, and the isolated, moribund side of his character. As Eugene ignores or lies about unpleasant experience, he buries or hides his youthful idealisms, that part of himself that wants to tell the truth, so that his hopeful voice, the voice of conscience, the spirit of the man he is named after, Eugene Debs, is neutralized by his father's voice, the voice of Tralfamadorian futility.[15]

Just as Rudy Waltz's father in *Deadeye Dick* counsels Rudy to "plug your ears whenever anybody tells you you have a creative gift of any kind" (112), Eugene's father thwarts Eugene's deepest creative instincts. Eugene's happiest, even ecstatic moments, come as a musical innovator with his high school band—"cutting loose" on the piano with "never-the-same-way-twice" music (*Hocus Pocus*, 15), which resembles Rudy Waltz's love of scat singing or tinkering with imaginative recipes. But, like Rudy, Eugene's parents turn him into their family servant, who does most of the family marketing after school, and most of the housework and cooking, leaving him little time to nurture the artist within. Eugene's father also subverts Eugene's literary ambitions by deflecting him from the school of journalism at the University of Michigan to the school for homicidal maniacs (14) at West Point. His father believes that the prestige of a son at West Point may atone for Eugene's mediocre high school career, letting those four years go by without scoring a touchdown or doing anything but making "jungle music" (37). So just as Rudy's father turns Rudy into a druggist, and the father of Rabo Karabekian delivers his son into the hands of the artist of mechanical creations, Dan Gregory, Eugene's father makes an unholy alliance with West Point recruiter, Colonel Sam Wakefield (Eugene sees them "laughing and shaking hands" [51]), who desperately wants Eugene's body "to mold, no matter what it was." In the manner of such previous false tutors as Niles Rumfoord, Bokonon, Frank Wirtanen, and Kilgore Trout, fatalistic father figures whose supposed authority the protagonists are too will-less to resist, Sam Wakefield represents the cynicism that tempts past heroes to moral suicide. Eugene had hoped to take courses in English, history, and political science, and to "serve John Q. Public's right to know" (33) by working on the school paper. Instead, because his father considers West Point "a great prize," something "to boast about" to simple-minded neighbors (15), Eugene's creative energies are diverted into the deathly business of making war, Eros converted to Thanatos.[16] By graduation, his identity is so effectively perverted from music-maker to death-maker—his father's role at Dupont—he wonders, "Can this be me?" (60). Rather than a free thinker or innovative musician (he hoped to play at peace rallies and love-ins), Eugene is "turned into a homicidal imbecile in 13 weeks" (15). Cadets at West Point "did not make music" (33), or if they did, they were under orders to play as written, and never as they felt about the music. More ominously, West Point regimentation creates such an emotional void that the cadets, like the unfeeling sociopathic computer game, Griot, feel nothing at all. "There wasn't any student publication at West Point," Eugene says, "so never mind how the cadets felt about anything" (34). Thus Eugene concludes about the forbidding presence of Sam Wakefield: "Incredibly, the spectacularly dressed man with the paratrooper's wings and boots" was "what I would become" (48, 49) for the next 14 years," a professional soldier programmed to kill "Jesus Christ himself . . . if ordered to do so by a superior officer" (14).

What Eugene appears to become, by his own definition, is "insane," so numb or indifferent to reality that fact and illusion become indistinguishable. West Point so extends the job Eugene's father has begun of numbing Eugene's conscience and perverting his artistic identity that at one point the doped up soldier feels no difference between the playing of bells and the lobbing of shells—both of which seemed to him "very much like music, interesting noises . . . and nothing more" (81). Used to dulling his wits with drugs and cynicism, he finds scenes of mutilation and death "no more horrible than ultrarealistic shows about Vietnam" on television (124), a desensitized condition that allows him to commit unspeakable acts of violence and cruelty.[17] Referring to the corpses he has seen and "in many cases created" (173), he remembers strangling someone with piano wire (261), throwing a suspected enemy agent out of a helicopter (203), and killing a woman, her mother, and her baby by throwing a grenade into the mouth of a tunnel (236).

But Eugene's freakish parents, with the help of West Point, have spawned not only a temporarily insane, psychopathic killer, but an expert liar whose "elaborate" (36) destructive fantasies carry over to his role as public relations officer in Vietnam. As a "genius of lethal hocus pocus," the effects of which he likens to mood modifying drugs (36), Eugene's justification for "all the killing and dying" become "as natural as breathing" (36). The representation of deceit as normal suggests the perversion of Eugene's life instinct by the instinct to aggression and death. Vonnegut continues here his concern first highlighted in *Mother Night* and *Cat's Cradle* with fiction as a form of play that can be constructive or destructive. In the editor's note to *Mother Night*, Vonnegut writes that lies told for the sake of artistic effect can be the most beguiling form of truth (9). Eugene's essential challenge—a problem for every Vonnegut protagonist—is to learn to distinguish good from bad "lies" or fictions that, as David Ketterer says, either encourage the forces of aggression and death or abet the forces of life—of courage, compassion, and engagement (308). Ultimately this is Eugene's perception—that both forms of aggression, killing, and lying about killing were equally insane, typical of people who rendered themselves "imbecilic or maniacal" (*Hocus Pocus*, 36). Such was the fate of the students at Tarkington and the prisoners at Athena. The crippled human potential of the students with "learning disabilities," passed on to them by materialistic parents, and by the romantic success myths—stories of "supposed triumphs" (41)—that dominate Tarkington's library, equates with the dazed and hopeless condition of the convicts. The melodramatic success stories, the puerile and absurdly outdated impressions of reality displayed on prison T.V. reruns like "I Love Lucy" and "Howdy Doody" (218), create a mental prison for both populations, effectively isolating them from complexities within and from each other. Underscoring their common plight, Eugene observes that the two communities, so close geographically, yet so socially and economically divided, both name their main street "Clinton Street" (243). He notes too that teaching at the prison was "not all that different from what I had done at Tarkington" (243). The point is that the ease with which the college eventually converts to a prison merely literalizes the intrinsically oppressive nature of both institutions.[18]

Like such previously father-persecuted, war-scarred protagonists as Howard Campbell, Eliot Rosewater, and Billy Pilgrim, Eugene's sense of estrangement after the war is so great he wonders, "What is this place, and who are these people, and what am I doing here?" (242). Beyond the routine effects of bombings he has witnessed, memories of "orgies" (299) of death and suffering that he labels "Unforgettable!" (297) fill Eugene with such guilt and moral uncertainty that, again, like Billy, like Eliot, he seeks relief for blame or responsibility in anonymity ("I wanted nothing more than to be left strictly alone with my thoughts" [237]) or in the imagined sanctuary of affairs with off-balanced, middle-aged women who would make everything "all right" (120).[19] No wonder that like the hallucinating Billy Pilgrim and Eliot Rosewater, who share a room in a mental hospital because of what they had seen in war (*Slaughterhouse-Five*, 101), Eugene should be tempted by the same pain-killing philosophy of life for refuge—the "morphine paradise" (*Slaughterhouse-Five*, 99) of Tralfamadore. Eugene likens the feeling that he is the plaything of enormous forces of control to that of his student who gets trapped in a Bloomingdale elevator. The student's sense of isolation and helplessness is magnified by the fact that as with returning Vietnam veterans, no one cares, no one apologizes, and no one takes responsibility (*Hocus Pocus*, 158–159).[20] In *Sirens of Titan*, Vonnegut calls such spiral-like systems of control a "dynamite bouquet" (290), defined in *Cat's Cradle* as "what looked like a wonderful idea then—what looks like a hideous idea in retrospect" (55). Such mechanistic traps, which may be economic, religious, philosophic, militaristic, psychic, or biological cures, are symbolized by Vonnegut throughout his work as fountains, clocks, cones, webs, roller coasters, staircases, mountain rims, and mind-numbing cocoons. Demonstrating that these insidious spirals lead to violence and cruelty rather than the paradise they promise, Eugene notices, for instance, the swirling "spirals of dust" (218) present when his friend Hiroshi Matsumoto was atom-bombed, that it is the belfry of a spiral-like tower that the college president, "Tex" Johnson, turns into a "sniper's nest" (77), and that Athena and Auschwitz are similarly "ringed" with barbed wire and watchtowers (226). Even the TB germs inside Eugene's body exist in spiral-like shells. To show his contempt for liberal ideas, jingoist talk-show host Jason Wilder covers them in "spit" and throws them back with "a crazy spin" which makes them "uncatchable" (266). Earlier it was noted that Eugene refers to his wife's insanity as a "spider web" (118), and, linking her madness to the maniacal aggression of Sam Wakefield, the rabid West Point lieutenant who "blows his brains out," Eugene observes that it is "a clock that made them sick" (164).[21]

Because like Griot, the computer that does not care about anything, especially "hurting people's feelings" (103), these hellish mechanisms appear either superficially benign and alluring or too pervasive and powerful to escape (103); they lock the unwary individual into cycles of action indifferent to individual will or aspiration, engendering robotlike aggression, or the passivity that allows aggression to happen, at both the top and the bottom of the spiral. The convicts particularly hate Griot because when they punch in their race and age and what their parents did, how long they had gone to school and what drugs they used, Griot sent them straight to jail (104). Feelings of futility create in turn the sociopathic madness of the age—the trustees' complete indifference to the suffering at Athena, the absence of "remorse" of Alton Darwin (78), the lunatic laughter of Jack Patton, who has "the same untightened screw" (77) and for whom all disasters are funny (57), and even Eugene's apathy at Tarkington until he is made to empathize with the suffering of the prisoners across the lake. Thus it is that for years to come, believing that the loveless, inhumane spirals of his life are beyond his ability to resist, Eugene becomes a potential moral sleepwalker, threatened by the same petrification of will and conscience that dooms the prisoners at Athena and the students of Tarkington College. Eugene marries unknowingly into a family with a history of madness, saddling himself with a crazy wife and mother-in-law (84), then lives with dread that his two children, who hate him for reproducing, will go as crazy as their mother and grandmother. It is a short distance, Eugene says, to "where I am now" (142)—to getting fired by Tarkington, to teaching the unteachable at Athena, and to eventual imprisonment for treason (50). He might have avoided all this, he reflects, if his "exit" had not been "blocked by Sam Wakefield" (50). It is another of Wakefield's recruits, the morally dead Jack Patton who preaches pessimism, who introduces Eugene to his crazy sister and bride-to-be.

Of course Eugene's psychological odyssey brings him also to the realization that his "exit"—to journalism, to music-making, to a more courageous and independent identity ("saying and wearing what I goshdarned pleased" [50])—was torpedoed by the father who, upon reflection, Eugene says tried to blame him entirely for his troubled past (36, 37). It is Eugene's present ability to see both his own involvement and his father's responsibility in creating the horrors he has seen and committed—in effect, their common humanity, or inhumanity—that liberates him from paralysis and guilt and that allows the long pent-up artist to emerge.

In his search for the compassionate self that would prove him sane, he had hoped that the names of the women he has loved would prevail over the list of people he has killed; at the same time, he worries that by war's end he had become the unfeeling machine ("an electrical appliance . . . a vacuum cleaner" [147]) that his wife and mother-in-law see upon his return—manifesting that absence of feeling that Griot represents and that both Eugene and Griot share with the sociopathic mass murderer Alton Darwin (149). What Eugene discovers, however, is that the contending proofs on his imagined epitaph are "enigmatic" (38), that is, "virtually identical" (195). Not only do they suggest a precarious balance between the forces of kindness and cruelty, aggression and restraint, but each list is itself ambiguous—the impulses of the soldier/lover inextricably mixed, military kills mitigated by acts of mercy, irresponsible seductions counterbalanced by genuine compassion. This is the "argument" (64) within himself that he experiences when the music he makes as a carillonneur at Tarkington echoes off the prison walls and Scipio's empty factories, returning to him as if a second carillonneur were mocking him from across the lake. While the prospect of an equivocal nature invites futility, Eugene's inquiry brings him instead to that grace of awareness Vonnegut calls "sacred" in *Breakfast of Champions* (221), an understanding that fragmentation is the universal human condition. Though he playfully observes that "if there is a Divine Providence, there is also a wicked one" (120), he recognizes that such antagonisms are never absolute, but a complex potential of the human spirit for good or for evil, and that by understanding and controlling their heart of darkness human beings, not Griot, not the mechanical Tralfamadorians, may shape their lives for the better.

From the ironically regenerated perspective of his bell-tower prison, Eugene visualizes the contrary "possibilities" (105) of love or aggression within himself through such psychic projections as Jack Patton and Paul Slazinger, each of whom has grown coldly cynical and apathetic, and through the aware and morally courageous figures of Eugene Debs and Helen Dole. The psychopathic tendencies of Patton, Eugene's "equal" (57), and of Slazinger, who was "echoing" him (115), reflect the Eugene who killed with his bare hands and laughed about it afterwards. On the other hand, Helen Dole, the feisty little black woman who teaches physics at Tarkington and the pacifist/healer Eugene Debs equally represent Eugene's humanitarian instincts. When the Tarkington trustees try to turn Helen into an uncritical teaching machine, she defies not only the trustees but also Griot, who finds her so independent and assertive that it can describe her destiny only as "unpredictable" (264). Multilingual and versed in science, history, literature, music, and art, Helen challenges racist stereotypes as well as Tarkington's totalitarian structures, accusing the trustees of being as exploitative as modern-day plantation owners (264).

As Eugene sorts out the tangled debris of his troubled past, he is surprised to learn that he was never as dispossessed of the Helen Dole or the Eugene Debs in himself as he had thought. He finds marked evidence that while even after the war he succumbed to ingrained habits of lying and evasion to assuage shameful or embarrassing experience, his youthful idealistic and creative self had never ceased to function, the self who identifies with Eugene Debs' credo of love and humanitarian service. Eugene notes, for instance, that whereas Alton Darwin had murdered innocent people for money, he "had never stooped to that" (72). And while as a soldier in Vietnam he had seen mutilations, he "hastens" to say that under his command that would never have been tolerated (52). Eugene's role call of good and bad deeds reveals not only a painfully active conscience but also a disposition to kindness and moral courage that often prevails over his worst self. If he has been a "gung-ho" warrior (164), his final soldierly act was not militant but merciful—the rescue of American personnel from the rooftop of the U.S. Embassy in Saigon.[22] Eugene's eventual colleague at Tarkington, Muriel Peck, reminds him of how "kind and patient" he has been with his "worse than useless relatives" (210), remaining so loyal to his unbalanced wife and mother-in-law that Andrea Wakefield calls him a "saint" (164). When Eugene's estranged, out-of-wedlock son Rob Roy assures Eugene that he intends to make no demands on his father's emotions, Eugene welcomes the relationship, insisting, "try me" (286), determining to behave "as though I were a really good father." "I like life to be simple," he says, "but if you went away that would be much too simple for me, and for you, too, I hope" (288).

If caring for his troubled family, even as he himself battles tuberculosis, Eugene succeeds, as is said of Wilbur Swain, in "bargaining in good faith with destiny" (*Slapstick*, 2), it is as a teacher that he keeps faith with his grandfather's belief that the greatest use a person could make of his or her lifetime was to "improve the quality of life for all in his or her community" (*Hocus Pocus*, 176). First, at Tarkington College, an oasis of white in a community dominated by 10,000 black inmates at Athena prison, Eugene is persecuted by the college's dim-witted, mean-spirited trustees for daring to tell the truth even about "things nice people shouldn't want to see"—the horrors at Athena or Vietnam, for instance, to which the trustees remain smugly oblivious. When Eugene tells one of the trustees about the agonies of prison life, and about the mental illnesses and feelings of futility of the prisoners, Jason Wilder "closed his eyes and covered his ears" (225). The trustees believe that the government's first responsibility was to protect them from the lower classes (226), while Eugene's sympathies are those inscribed on the tombstone of his namesake, Eugene Victor Debs: "While there is a lower class I am in it. While there is a criminal element I am of it. While there is a soul in prison I am not free" (9).[23]

Accordingly, when Eugene's efforts to free his students from "ignorance and self-serving fantasies" are dubbed unpatriotic, and he is fired for being not just un-American but also anti-American, he continues at his new teaching post at Athena to make the lives of the inmates "more bearable" (228), however uphill the struggle. Though the inmates are kept literally and figuratively "drugged" to reality (coked to the gills on Thorazine, or rendered docile and unaware by TV reruns [243]), he raises their literacy level by 20 percent.[24] When the convicts stage a massive prison break, overrunning the college, and the campus becomes a prison for the recaptured prisoners, Eugene does his best as temporary warden to humanize conditions. "Let it be recorded," he says, that "when Warden of this place . . . I moved the convicted felons out of tents . . . into the surroundings of buildings. They no longer had to excrete in buckets, or in the middle of the night, have their homes blown down" (295). Eugene personally houses and feeds three infirm old men serving life sentences.

Even when following the insurrection Eugene returns to a soldierly role as military commander of the Scipio District, he continues using his authority to combat rather than foster aggression. He turns soldiers into firemen,[25] personally supervises the exhumation of bodies, notifies next-of-kin, and sees that the dead are given decent burials (276, 277). However chaotic his life or disruptive the bizarre changes of career, Eugene continues to find proof positive of his compassionate self. Not only does he oppose the sociopathic indifference to the suffering of people like Alton Darwin or the trustees at Tarkington, he demonstrates, as Kathryn Hume says, "what an individual can do to alleviate the pain inherent in the human condition" ("Kurt Vonnegut and the Myths and Symbols," 442). We see that rather than being guilty of the "pessimism" for which he is fired at Tarkington, or of the "treason" for which he is imprisoned for sympathizing with Athenian prisoners, both charges implicate the ignorance and duplicity of his accusers. "I wouldn't be under indictment now," he says, "if I hadn't paid a compassionate visit to the hostages" (148). Not only does Eugene directly repudiate his reputation for pessimism at Tarkington ("that was twice within an hour that I was accused of cynicism that was Slazinger's, not mine" [115]), but he also says that all he ever wanted to do as a teacher was to encourage his students to think for themselves and perhaps to raise questions about the moral contradictions of Vietnam, capitalism, and organized religion, for which he is judged "unpatriotic." The real betrayal here is the suppression of honest inquiry by an economic system so corrupt that it calls a concern for others "un-American" if it threatens the status quo. "What could be more un-American," Paul Slazinger says sarcastically, "than sounding like the Sermon on the Mount" (97).

But Eugene's greatest evidence of sanity, he hopes, will be his salubrious relationships with women. Just as the words on his namesake's tombstone reflect decency and caring, Eugene projects as his own epitaph the names of the women he has loved. He ponders that if at times he has used women irresponsibly, women too "full of doubts" (120) to make emotional demands (Marilyn Monroe would have been perfect, he muses [120]), he believes that rather than exploitative or superficial, these relationships have been soulful and intellectual ("not another infernal device") as well as ardent or libidinal (17).[26] Hence, when artist-in-residence Pamela Hall asks Eugene why he has come to visit her, he replies, "I wanted to make sure you were O.K." (121, 122). And when Marilyn Shaw, also a Vietnam veteran who had "a rougher war than I did" (164) lapses into despair after the war, it is Eugene who rescues her "drunk and asleep on a pool table" (105) and who apparently nurses her back to health.

Appropriate to Kathryn Hume's observation that the increased affirmation of Vonnegut's protagonists after *Breakfast of Champions* correlates with their more sympathetic relationships with women, Eugene's connection with this community of female fellow sufferers is, as is said of Zuzu Johnson, not only "deep" but "thoroughly reciprocated" (102).[27] Just as Eugene's final thought is of their well-being (38), *their* courage and love proves cathartic and liberating to Eugene, opening him emotionally and helping him form a more holistic and creative self. Hence Eugene finds himself "spilling his guts" (123) to Pamela about the Vietnam War, confessing his nightmares to Harriet Gummer (124).

So the chief irony of Eugene's suspect sanity is not that he feels so little but that he feels so much once he discovers the "equation" (298) that brings all spirals into being: the age-old impulse to cruelty and aggression that perpetually threatens human life. It is not the Eugene who killed with his bare hands and laughed about it who writes these memoirs, but the long-repressed artist for whom this act of creative exorcism and renewal has been so humanizing and illuminating that he can say, that was "the old me . . . I think" (180) . . . "the soldier I used to be" (253). Whereas he once found it easy to mask or distort the truth, he determines no longer to "play hide-and-seek" (119),which "wasn't my natural disposition" (78), but, however painful the exposure, to openly acknowledge his crimes.[28] He speaks of the corpses "I created" (173), of the slaughters "I myself had planned and led" (246, 247), and when assigning responsibility for the strafing of a village in which innocent women and children were killed, he makes clear that the chief transgressor was himself, not his father, not Sam Wakefield, not West Point, and certainly not the Tralfamadorians. "You know who was the Ruling Class that time?" he asks. "Eugene Debs Hartke was the Ruling Class" (236).[29]

The new Eugene conveys his contempt for the totalitarian designs of others by ridiculing the notion that Tralfamadorian-like forces control his fate. Determining to combat the TB germs that have invaded his body (metaphorically speaking, Tralfamadorian agents), he declares, "If any of these germs are thinking of themselves as space cadets, they can forget it. They aren't going anywhere but down the toilet" (194, 195). Eugene's reference to the box containing Trout's story of Tralfamadore as "a sort of casket" (187) presages both the dangers of Tralfamadorian fatalism and Eugene's rejection of such a philosophy along with the rest of his dead past, "the remains of the soldier I used to be" (187). But like Vonnegut's other emergent artist-heroes, Wilbur Swain, Walter Starbuck, Leon Trout, and Rabo Karabekian, Eugene learns not only that such inhuman mechanisms as Griot, Dupont, or West Point can be resisted, but that they can be reconstituted through the fabulating power—the "hocus pocus"—of creative imagination. Just as he had once used the "ammunition" of language (148)—his "lethal" hocus pocus—to foster violence and death, he will now put his "genius" for elaborate fantasies to work for constructive rather than destructive purposes. Recognizing that life and art, reality and illusion, are mutual fictional constructs—products of mind, as Rabo Karabekian says in (*Bluebeard*, 153) or tricks of imagination, Eugene uniquely stylizes his memoirs in ways that defy static or arbitrary language conventions, and thus assert the power of imagination to restructure or reinvent reality.

Eugene's venture in self-creativity abounds with references to fact and illusion as interchangeable or indistinguishable realities, so that like Warden Matsumoto, the reader finds himself "among structures and creatures both real and fantastic" (*Hocus Pocus*, 227). Eugene's war memories are like "old movies" (149), his childhood "all a dream" (38). Dead American soldiers are "manufactured" beings, "curious artifacts" (39), and Vietnam is a "hallucination" (85), so much "show-biz" (253). For Eugene, playing the bells at Tarkington, which "might have been mistaken for an emerald-studded Oz or City of God or Camelot" (250), has "absolutely no basis in reality" (64), and for the convicts at Athena, there is no distinction at all between TV and "what in the real world might be going on" (252).

To demonstrate further that reality is largely the product of imagination and will, as fluid and dynamic as dreams, Eugene provides countless examples of experiences whose fluctuating meanings are determined not through their intrinsic value, but through the perception or invention of the viewer, shifts in language convention, or changes in historical or cultural context. Scipio becomes "Pompeii" (140); escaped convicts, "Freedom Fighters" (204); the Christian cross, the Nazi's "swastika" (128); and "champagne cases" in Scipio, "cartridge cases" in Vietnam (198). An Italian racing bike might have been a "Unicorn" (196); "stogies" could be called "mogies" or "higgies" instead (21); "Petrograd" is renamed "Leningrad," then "Petrograd" again (281); and "The Mohiga Valley Free Institute" becomes Tarkington College.[30] What people call themselves, says Eugene, was not "reality" (204). Thus, Arthur Clarke the "fun loving billionaire" (166) was not Arthur Clarke "the science fiction writer," and Herbert Van Arsdale, a president of Tarkington, bore no relation at all to Whitney Van Arsdale, the "dishonest mechanic" (183). Eugene doubts that "Donner" was really the last name of the "John Donner," the "pathological liar," who appears on "Donahue": "He could have made that up" (214).

By noting the unreliability of signs as verifiers of objective reality, Eugene is encouraged to reevaluate the status of "truth" and "fiction" and to appreciate their interchangeability—that reality can be made over by imagination for better or worse.[31] He observes that whereas Scipio's citizens "daydreamed" of shooting escaped convicts (249, 250), Damon Stern envisions that the "tidy checkerboard . . . streets and old stucco two-story shotgun building" of Auschwitz "might have made a nice enough junior college for low-income or underachieving people in the area" (280). Sam Wakefield transmogrifies from a rabid military man to a Christ-like being, with "eyes full of love and pity," who speaks against the war (156). That human beings and machinery alike may be put to creative as well as destructive purposes, we see that Tarkington's carillon bells are cast from mangled Union and Confederate rifle barrels and cannonballs and bayonets (63), and that the mobile field kitchen invented by one of Tarkington's founders, Aaron Tarkington, was adopted both by the German Army during World War I and by the Barnum and Bailey Circus (22).

It is finally Eugene's ingenious narrative, or magic act, that signifies his personal transformation from jailbird to canary bird: a brilliant fabrication that illustrates his awesome, redirected powers of invention. Demonstrating the possibilities of existential authorship in life as in art (that it is he rather than Sam Wakefield, Griot, or Tralfamadore who was "the helmsman of my destiny" [162]), Eugene and the "editor" who helps arrange his text continuously identifies Eugene's memoirs as "pure fiction" (9), a "game" (50, 296) or "trick" (130) or "joke" (22) whose truths are personal, elusive, and multifaceted. Eugene's editor knows that while Eugene had hoped to amass absolute proofs of "humility" *or* "insanity," what he "is doing is writing a book" (7), an imaginative reconstruction rather than an objective representation of so-called actual events or objects in the real world. "Bear with me," Eugene explains, "this is history" (21). But it is history whose truths are problematized by imperfect memory, recapitulated impressions from second or third-hand sources, and from Eugene's and his editor's own selective storytelling. Past events are pieced together from old newspapers, letters, and diaries, and from the *Musketeer*, the Tarkington

College alumni magazine, dating back to 1910 (62), and from the *Encyclopedia Britannica* (215), and *Bartlett's Familiar Quotations* (146). At best, Eugene and his editor can only "speculate" (7) can know only "what is likely" (7), or what "supposedly" happened (270, 271), what happened, for instance, "according" to the "story," the "legend," of Adam and Eve (189) passed on to Eugene from Jack Patton and passed on in turn from "the nameless author" of "The Protocols of the Elders of Tralfamadore" (190).

The creative idiosyncrasies of Eugene, his editor, and of course Kurt Vonnegut, remove the reader still further from representational reality. With references such as, "Before I tell about that" (207), "there is more I want to tell" (271), "that will seem to complete my story" (271), and, "I will carry on as though I hadn't heard the news" (271), Eugene establishes himself as a subjective storyteller who will delete or embellish as he chooses. The editor explains that he himself has attempted to improve the "disreputable appearance" (7) of Eugene's text (what else has he tampered with?) by setting in type what did not reproduce well on the printed page (8), but though we have only his editor's word on this, or his editor's editor, it is Eugene's artistic contrivances that compel our attention.[32] The editor explains that the book was written on everything from brown wrapping paper to the backs of business cards (7), that "for reasons unexplained" (8) Eugene capitalized words that should have been in lowercase, that he let numbers stand for themselves rather than put them in words, for example, "2 instead of two" (8), and that he drew lines across the page to separate passages within chapters.[33]

If Eugene's grammatical or literary deviations puzzle his editor, the reader sees that such linguistic liberties correspond precisely with Helen Dole's defiance of the repressive moral strictures at Tarkington. Since he had been used as a government propaganda machine to create the horrors of Vietnam, he will now use the "ammunition" of language to expose rather than produce such deceptions—realities uniquely his own. "The expression *I* will use for the end of the Vietnam War," he says, "will be when the excrement hit the air conditioner" (272).

Pondering the speed with which such linguistic and spiritual hocus pocus may be performed, Eugene marvels that whereas "only 3 hours before, I had been so at peace in my belltower . . . now I was inside a maximum-security prison with a masked and gloved Japanese National who insisted that the United States was his Vietnam!" (220). Yet how different are the bars that imprison the body of Eugene Debs from that mental cage that holds Billy Pilgrim prisoner on Tralfamadore—a fatalistic dream that assures Pilgrim's descent into madness, but whose repudiation signals Eugene's freedom from self-imprisoning spirals, or "self-serving fantasies," and allows the creative artist to ascend.[34] Contrasts between the world as rational and humane and the world as a slaughterhouse of ongoing violence and cruelty become too unbalancing for Billy Pilgrim to endure. Such a symbolic moment occurs in *Slaughterhouse-Five* when Billy's friend Edgar Derby is shot by a firing squad for taking a teapot. Derby's loyalty to the sacred civilized graces of family, love, God, country, leads Billy to believe that Derby must be the greatest father in the world. Yet none of this exempts Derby from the stupidity and absurdity of death. Such horrors, which Tralfamadorian philosophy argues are random or causeless and hence indefensible, cause Billy to call upon the consolations and the alleged wisdom of the Tralfamadorians as never before. Caged in a zoo, turned into a puppet for the entertainment of mechanical creatures whose own world is both physically and morally sterile, seduced into removing whatever vestige of free will he has left, Billy Pilgrim becomes the very embodiment of what Vonnegut has warned against for years. Insulated from pain, Billy has traded his dignity and integrity for an illusion of comfort and security, becoming himself a machine.

In a similarly climactic scene in *Hocus Pocus*, Eugene is threatened by the same maddening contrasts between sanity and insanity, and the same feelings of futility, that doom Billy Pilgrim. His friend Hiroshi Matsumoto, like Edgar Derby, inordinately innocent and kind, nevertheless commits the "trick" (130) of suicide out of guilt and remorse for horrors for which he appears blameless. The answer to Eugene's question, "But why would I care so much?" (294) is complexly revealing of Eugene's quest for the meanings of sanity, his and his world's. Eugene identifies both with Hiroshi's tormented childhood (Hiroshi was a boy when the atom bomb was dropped on Hiroshima) and by the fact that someone so relatively blameless ("He never shirked his duty, never stole anything, and never killed or bombed anyone" [295]) should yet hold himself responsible for a legacy of "burning and boiling" (219) before even he was born. The spiritual bond between Eugene and Hiroshi is that both recognize that however subtly related, the smallest or most personal acts of aggression are connected to the world's larger, bloodier deeds. The impulse that boils lobsters alive, or that allows Eugene to kill with his bare hands, emanates from the same heart of darkness that creates the "Rape of Nanking" (297), that drops bombs on Hiroshima (118), that commits the "vainglorious lunacy of Vietnam (219), and that has turned the entire planet "into an Auschwitz" (226). Hence the trustees of Tarkington "had a lot in common with B-52 bombardiers" (226), and the escaped convicts at Athena "were like a neutron bomb" (28). Eugene and Hiroshi know too that like the Carib Indians (264), the victims of Hiroshima were "burned alive" (218). Just as Jews and Romans crucified their enemies, Tex Johnson is crucified with spikes through his palms and feet. American forests are in fact being looted by Mexican laborers using Japanese tools under the protection of Swedes to sell to the Japanese. Eugene and Hiroshi, both reformed warriors, see finally that it is the denial of responsibility for such violence that makes the deadly spiral of aggression circular and unending. But what most disturbs Eugene (he experiences an "attack of psychosomatic hives" [299]) is the fact that self-destruction, the equivalent of Billy Pilgrim's withdrawal into the "morphine paradise" of Tralfamadore (99), should become Hiroshi's only recourse to the world's suffering and pain. The notion so demoralizes Eugene that he is glad he had not shown Hiroshi a copy of "The Protocols of the Elders of Tralfamadore," which might have hastened Hiroshi's suicide. Hiroshi might have left a note saying, "The Elders of Tralfamadore win again" (299). "Only I and the author of that story," Eugene concludes, "would have known what he meant by that" (299).

What Tralfamadorian fatalism "means," to Eugene Hartke, and to Kurt Vonnegut, is central to our decision about Eugene's sanity, but more importantly, to Vonnegut's view of the sanity of his readers and critics. Do these "crazy lunkers" who delight in pain (193), who are, "to say the least," indifferent "to all the suffering going on" and who foster the kind of suicidal futility that causes Hiroshi to kill himself, that threatens Eugene with "existential gangrene" after the war, and encourages the people of the earth to "wreck the joint," speak for Eugene and his author?

Since, as with Eugene's purpose as a teacher, Vonnegut writes more to encourage reflectiveness than to offer specific reforms, we must decide for ourselves whether Vonnegut uses such fantasies as Titan, Shangri-La, or Tralfamadore to warn against or affirm such a philosophy.[35] Yet Eugene's own final judgment appears to be a direct rebuke on the author's part of critics like Josephine Hendin or Jack Richardson, who join in calling Tralfamadorian fatalism "a higher order of life" or a philosophy that teaches "unenlightened earthlings" a tolerance for pain.

Contemptuously, Eugene calls "dumb" and "humorless" those "earthlings" who find "acceptable" the "series of sidesplitting satires about Tralfamadorians arriving on other planets with the intention of spreading enlightenment" (191). It is hardly coincidental that Eugene's aspirations as a teacher, to expose "self-serving fantasies" (92) correspond with those of Vonnegut the novelist, and that both Eugene and Vonnegut should be called "pessimists" or "defeatists" by "imbeciles" (36) and charlatans. It appears that both Tarkington's trustees and critics who read Eugene's memoirs as a "model" of despair project their own apathy and cynicism and thus fail Eugene's primary criteria for sanity.[36] It is they, after all, who have been on trial.

As his own new identity attests, Eugene knows that it is belief and its linguistic formulations that determine reality, that what we are therefore sane enough—aware and compassionate enough—to imagine the future to be will influence what it becomes. Indicating *his* belief that destiny will be shaped by human beings, not machines, Eugene observes that "any form of government, not just Capitalism, is whatever the people . . . sane or insane . . . decide to do" (96). "When it came to dreaming up futures for ourselves," says Eugene, "we left Griot in the dust" (178).[37] Whether we view Eugene's text through the cynical, unfeeling eyes of Griot, or the Elders of Tralfamadore, or "like life," see it as consisting of better "possibilities" (105), will decide whether we imagine and create for ourselves the sociopathic future of Alton Darwin and Jack Patton or the more humane and responsible world of Helen Dole, Eugene Debs, and Eugene Debs Hartke.

NOTES

1. See Lisa Anderson (H2). This reference by Vonnegut highlights the author's frequent use of drowning imagery to represent loss of moral identity. Characters see themselves as "deluged," overwhelmed by "tidal waves" sucked into whirlpools or sewers.

2. Hendin says that Vonnegut "celebrates" the themes of detachment and meaninglessness as devices for diminishing the emotional change of painful experience (259). Goldsmith and Patrick Shaw argue that the Tralfamadorians unclog Billy Pilgrim's vision, helping him to realize the fallacies of history and earth time.

3. While Vonnegut's self-projections as Kilgore Trout are complex, Trout's role in Vonnegut's later fiction is decidedly sinister. It is Trout's pessimism in *Breakfast of Champions* that drives his son Leo from home, and who then, in *Galápagos*, encourages Leon Trout to self-destruction. Leon calls his father "nature's experiment with cynicism" (82).

4. In my book, *Sanity Plea: Schizophrenia in the Novels of Kurt Vonnegut*, I show that, on the one hand, insanity becomes Vonnegut's most graphic and compelling metaphor for a society hell-bent upon self-destruction. But Vonnegut also uses the imagery of schizophrenia to describe the psychic malaise of protagonists who range from the severe depression of Paul Proteus to the dangerously withdrawn if not catatonic state of characters like Eliot Rosewater and Billy Pilgrim. I have tried to demonstrate that it is this psychic dimension—what Kathryn Hume calls "the infernal subdepths"—of Vonnegut's function ("Kurt Vonnegut and the Myths and Symbols of Meaning," 444) where Vonnegut's art functions most ingeniously and where he achieves his most compelling emotional effects.

5. "I am reminded," says Vonnegut, "of the late sculptress Louise Nevelson, who told me that she was seventy years old before people 'realized that I really meant it.' 'People won't pay attention,' she said, 'until they realize that you really mean it.' Chris Lehmann-Haupt said to me a couple of years back that he was sorry, but that he could no longer read me. . . . As far as the *Times* is concerned, and the *Washington Post*, too, I have nothing to mean" (personal letter, June 11, 1989).

6. It is the fierce combat of these warring identities that Sigmund Freud refers to in *Beyond the Pleasure Principle* as a battle between the forces of Eros, the life instinct, and Thanatos, the death instinct. This dichotomous struggle of simultaneous assertion and denial of the value of existence, in which the individual is torn between the yes of the will to live and the no of the will to cease, has baffled critics, leading them to allege self-contradictions and philosophical inconsistencies in Vonnegut's work. How the protagonist resolves these opposing forces of optimism and pessimism is the fundamental concern of every Vonnegut novel.

7. The author tells us in *Breakfast of Champions* that twin forces, which we may assume are those of optimism and pessimism, were at work in his own soul, struggling for control of his creative imagination. The very act of recognition suggests the presence of an imaginative faculty capable of resisting submission by the machine within and without. Vonnegut comes to see this awareness according to the vision of Rabo Karabekian as an

"unwavering band of light," a sacred irreducible force at the core of every animal (221). From this faith comes his decision to cleanse and renew himself for the years to come by setting free all his literary characters, including the omnipresent Kilgore Trout. The symbolic liberation of Trout, which amounts to the author's repudiation of his most pessimistic voice, is a necessary act of exorcism that both prepares for and explains the author's rebirth, the emergence of "a new me" (218) who determines to steer his life and work is a more sane and vital direction.

8. Billy Pilgrim is the notable exception. The earlier heroes' gains in awareness and moral courage fail Billy entirely—by design—for Billy, like Kilgore Trout in *Breakfast of Champions*, becomes Vonnegut's scapegoat, carrying the author's heaviest burden of trauma and despair.

9. This term is employed by Ernest Suarez in his doctoral dissertation, "James Dickey: Culture, South, and Contemporary American Poetry," University of Wisconsin, Madison, Wisconsin, 1989.

10. Distinctions between sanity and insanity, between the schizoid individual and the psychotic, are problematical. It is difficult to say, for instance, when the schizoid manifestations of characters like Paul Proteus, Eliot Rosewater, Billy Pilgrim, or Malachi Constant cross the borderline into psychosis--that is, when they can no longer control their split with reality and thus become a danger to themselves or others. While most of Vonnegut's protagonists drift into psychosis at some point, it is better to call them pre-psychotic or schizoidal—persons especially vulnerable to psychosis but whose isolation and angst may engender a more honest and creative way of living in a world of uniformity and aggressive madness.

11. Involving us in a matrix of contradictions, ambiguities, and inconsistencies, Vonnegut forces us into an active dialogue with the characters themselves—challenging us to finish the text by providing new definitions of what is sane or not sane.

12. In *Sanity Plea*, I propose that in *Slapstick, Jailbird, Deadeye Dick,* and *Galápagos,* Vonnegut summons up deeply repressed childhood experiences—a legacy of coldness, morbidity, guilt, and suicide—which needed to be faced as Vonnegut had faced the traumatic experience of war in *Slaughterhouse-Five*. In *Hocus Pocus,* Vonnegut continues to work out tensions between himself and parents who he says in *Galápagos* "made psychological cripples of their . . . children" (78), described in *Breakfast of Champions* as "that saddened worn out father and that suicide mother who babbled of love, peace, war, evil, and desperation" (113). The author encourages an autobiographical reading, writing to me first that he finds what I say about his work "perfectly okay," (personal letter, June 11, 1989), then more emphatically, "You have me dead to rights. It seems to me that you have solved what has long been to me a mystery. Why my work is so offensive to some readers . . . I thought maybe the issue was my quite conventional religious skepticism or my undying love for the National Recovery Act. . . . I now understand that it is my violation of the commandment that we honor our fathers and mothers (personal letter, Feb. 12, 1990).

13. Part of Vonnegut's critical success is the achievement of a story whose message of psychic and social trauma is perfectly fused. Eugene's personal suffering reflects the nation's larger decline. As Eugene battles tuberculosis, sees his wife and mother-in-law put into an asylum, and is imprisoned for treason, the country is swept by the plague of aids, oil spills, radioactive waste, poisoned aquifers, looted banks and liquidated corporations. The warden of Athena prison wonders whether "the whole place was finally going insane" (235).

14. Laing likens such a fate to living in "a concentration camp," in which the imagined advantages of safety and freedom from the control of others is tragically illusory.

15. Eugene adopts the "false self system" of previous heroes, or what in psychiatry is called a "mask," that is a deliberate strategy of maintaining personal freedom by withdrawing behind a protective shield, and putting another false self forward. Sigmund Freud, R. D. Laing, Jacques Lacan, and Carl Rogers warn that the tendency to hide behind elaborate facades, masks, or false selves, to withdraw into narcissistic fantasies and daydreams that distort or exclude the real world, may create a perpetually equivocal nature and render the individual unable to participate in real life. In this light, a significant moment for Eugene comes when he achieves what Carl Rogers calls "the stripping away of false facades." "It was as though you took off a mask," Muriel Spark tells him, "and you seemed as though you were suddenly all wrung out" (*Hocus Pocus*, 209). Refusing to wear "gloves and a mask" at Athena, Eugene remarks, "who could teach anybody . . . while wearing such a costume" (117).

16. The perversion of creative or sexual energies by such unfeeling, mechanistic activities as characterize the impersonal world of Tarkington, Athena, Dupont, West Point, and Griot represents the basic psychic disturbance of protagonists from Paul Proteus to Eugene Hartke. Eugene's personal dilemma is symbolized by the "bell clappers" on the library wall of Tarkington identified as "petrified penises" (127).

17. What West Point does to Eugene resembles what Martian brainwashing does to Malachi Constant in *Sirens of Titan*, causing Malachi to murder his best friend in a test of loyalty to his Martian puppetmasters.

18. Vonnegut's most ingenious imaginative hocus pocus comes in the form of numerous linguistic tricks that connect these two communities, showing that while to the Athenian prisoners Tarkington appears as a "paradise" (83) of harmony and love, its life is only visibly less futile than that of the prison. Each year, 30 inmates die for every student who graduates from Tarkington, the number of sloops (thirty) the college is given by a parent who had "cleared out the biggest savings and loan bank in California" (264). A major irony is that neither community recognizes its mirror reflection in the other or that their tragic alienation is self-induced. When Robert W. Mollenkamp loses his fortune, Eugene notes that "he and his wife were as broken as any convict in Athena" (109). The worlds merge again when a son of one of Tarkington's Trustees is sent to Athena for strangling a girlfriend behind the Metropolitan Museum of Art (216).

19. Eugene's interest in middle-aged women appears at least partly Oedipal in nature, a continuance of what Paul Proteus describes as the "unpleasant business between me and . . . my father" (*Player Piano*, 97), what Eliot Rosewater's psychiatrist calls "crossed wires" (*God Bless You, Mr. Rosewater*, 73), "the most massively defended neurosis I've ever attempted to treat" (28), and what Eugene identifies as "the something wrong with me" (*Hocus Pocus*, 149). Jacques Lacan explains that to escape the Oedipal relationship with the mother and constitute his own identity, the subject must accept the name ("the paternal metaphor") of the father, but Vonnegut's protagonists are frustrated in the attempt by fathers who are coldly aloof, mechanical, and unloving (Bice Bennenuto, *The Works of Lacan*, 53–58).

20. In contrast to those who see "randomness" at the center of Vonnegut's worldview, Vonnegut continues in *Hocus Pocus* to explore what Doris Lessing calls "the ambiguities of complicity" (135), which cause the reader to think carefully about degrees of responsibility for violence and injustice. As John Leonard notes, we take leave of *Hocus Pocus* "feeling . . . reflective, as if emerging from the vectors of a haiku" (421). The kind of complacency that prevents readers from establishing causal relationships in Vonnegut's fictional world characterizes as well a society whose self-righteousness blinds it to the criminality of racism, illiteracy, greed, or the suffering of the homeless. Eugene reflects that the American rich "had managed to convert their wealth . . . into a form so liquid and abstract . . . that there were few reminders . . . that they might be responsible for anyone outside their own circle of friends" (225). "Being an American," Paul Slazinger says, "means never having to say you're sorry" (95).

21. In *Breakfast of Champions*, Vonnegut writes that he felt like a syphilitic machine standing underneath the "overhanging clock" that his father had designed (3), and in *Palm Sunday*, he expresses his contempt for mechanistic structures by saying that in writing this book about his personal history he was "driving my [his] fists into the guts of grandfather clocks" (xv).

22. The situation was, in actuality, morally compromising. The American lives Eugene saves are at the expense of Vietnamese left behind.

23. Eugene Debs inspires the protagonist's sympathies for those without political power or great wealth just as Sacco and Vanzetti does for Wilbur Swain in *Jailbird*. For both Eugene and Wilbur, rebirth comes through an acceptance of the "agony" of all human beings as their own—showing "pity" for "unhappy strangers" (225).

24. In an apparent jibe at the inability of critics to read his works seriously or attentively, Vonnegut has Eugene remark that "the lesson I . . . learned was the uselessness of information to most people, except as entertainment." Suggesting that such a failure of critical perception and sympathy is a major subject of *Hocus Pocus*, Vonnegut interweaves intertextual references to his own stories and novels throughout Eugene's narrative, for example *Wanda June*, the "Shah of Bratpuhr" (289), "Mark Rothko" (209), "Ed Bergeron" (138), "James Watt" (191), "Midland City" (250), "slapstick comedies" (142), etc. A reference to "the rise of the Vonnegut Memorial Fountain" (137) suggests the identity of Vonnegut's novel as an ironic "memorial" to the career-long obtuseness of critics as "comatose" or just "plain stupid" as the learning-disabled students at Tarkington.

25. Calling these fire fighters "the last shred of faith people have . . . an amazing instance of civic responsibility" (276), Vonnegut repeats his career-long belief that volunteer firemen are humanity's purest expression of disinterested charity, that is, sanity.

26. Prior to the appearance of Rabo Karabekian, the hero's inability to experience sex as a positive act is a major symptom of his general emotional malaise. This affirmation of Eros in *Hocus Pocus*—a fusing of flesh and spirit—marks a degree of psychic healing that distinguishes Rabo Karabekian and Eugene Hartke from all of Vonnegut's previous heroes.

27. In reference to *Jailbird,* Hume perceives that having exorcised the mother who "so contaminated his inner picture of women," Vonnegut can now accept the female principle in himself and espouse "a more active response to the hurts of the world" ("Vonnegut's Self-Projections," 184).

28. This reference calls to mind the "Nation of Two" in *Mother Night,* a form of moral retreatism that reduces life to an endless game of hide and seek.

29. It is Howard Campbell's belief that the ability to imagine the "cruel consequences" (74) of his lies determines that he is sane and hence morally responsible. Eugene's moral accounting corresponds with Campbell's view that in an amoral world, the moral man must create order and meaning and justice where none seems to exist.

30. The novel's most telling example of realities that transform for better or worse is the grotesquely alienated world of Scipio, a microcosmic representation of American democracy. As imagined by its founding fathers, the utopian community of 1869, with Tarkington its democratic hub, would offer a free education to either sex, of any age, regardless of race, or religion, and a modest fee to those farther away (24, 25). Even the prison across the lake was intended to improve the bodies and souls of youthful offenders—a mystic work camp for criminals from big city slums. With the passing of time, materialistic lusts bankrupt the society's spiritual ideals, turning the once sympathetic relationship between Scipio's haves and have-nots to distrust and hatred. Both societies are duped by the promise of paradise at the end of the Capitalistic rainbow, and dehumanized by the indifferent machinery of free enterprise and the vicious class system it breeds. Eugene attributes the misery of the "poor and powerless" (67) of Athena directly to the greed of the American rich, no better themselves than "robbers with guns" (264). For the exploited convicts, Athena becomes the terrible alternative to accepting whatever their "greedy paymasters" gave them in the way of subsistence or working conditions. Many of the prisoners are there, in fact, because of the social irresponsibility of the American business community. When they were little, Eugene says, they had eaten chips or breathed dust from old lead-based paint, the brain damage from lead poisoning had made them capable of the "dumbest crimes imaginable" (201). At the same time, reminiscent of the rebellion of *Player Piano*'s "reeks and wrecks" or the futility of Pissquonit County's disinherited in *God Bless You Mr. Rosewater,* the desperation of poverty and social inferiority causes Scipio's social rejects to reciprocate in kind—meeting cruelty and insensitivity with the bloodbath of terror and death that follows the Athenian insurrection. Suggesting that, to the last, Athenians and Tarkingtonians are alike victimized by capitalistic "delusions of grandeur" (96), Alton Darwin inspires the attack on Tarkington with promises of glory and riches, dreaming of using his freedom to restore Scipio's

industry. During the siege, the escapees slaughter teachers and trustees but are careful not to damage the physical campus since they believe that its treasures would be theirs for generations to come (28).

31. Eugene's socialist grandfather refers to the foolishness of those who believe that every word is "true" in a book put together by "a bunch of preachers 300 years after the birth of Christ." "I hope," he says to Eugene, "you won't be that dumb about words . . . when you grow up" (98).

32. In reference to several sketches, Eugene's editor informs us that Eugene has made only one such drawing; the others are but "tracings" of the "original" (7, 8). Such superimpositions correspond to the multiple layers of reality that constitute the telling of Eugene's story.

33. Eugene's numbering of pages to create the illusion of sequentiality (7), and the self-conscious framing of passages, further foreground the text as an artifact, a purely human construction. John Leonard notes that Eugene's scraps of paper remind one of those odds and ends of thoughts that Dr. Reefy in Sherwood Anderson's *Winesburg, Ohio* scribbled on bits of paper and then stuffed away in his pockets to become "little hand rubber balls," or self-created truths (421).

34. Tralfamadore, by anagram, is "Or Fatal Dream."

35. Eugene sees himself as a "sort of non-combattant wiseman" (91), and Vonnegut views himself as a "shaman," a "canary bird in the coalmine" who provides spiritual illumination.

36. According to the testimony of Leon Trout in *Galápagos*, it is fatalism and apathy—the failure "to give a damn" (80)—that steers the characters of *Galápagos* into an apocalyptic nightmare.

37. The autobiographies of Wilbur Swain and Walter Starbuck are cast in the form of dreams, realities re-formed and humanized through the creative imagination. As with these heroes, Eugene's story is "a game our dreams remade" (*Slapstick*, 230).

WORKS CITED

Anderson, Lisa. "Vonnegut Gives Up Laughing. So it Goes." *Tampa Tribune* (23 September 1990): H1, H2.

Bennenuto, Bice. *The Works of Jacques Lacan: An Introduction*. New York: St. Martin's Press, 1986.

Broer, Lawrence. *Sanity Plea: Schizophrenia in the Novels of Kurt Vonnegut*. Ann Arbor: University of Michigan Research Press, 1989.

Cantor, Jay. "Vonnegut's Unique Brand of Good-Humor Morality." *Tampa Tribune* (27 July 1990): C15.

Cryer, Dan. "Vonnegut's Strangest Book in Years." *The Miami Herald* (2 September 1990): C9.

Goldsmith, David. *Fantasist of Fire and Ice.* Bowling Green, Ohio: Bowling Green University Popular Press, 1972.

Hendin, Josephine. *The Harvard Guide to Contemporary American Writing.* Daniel Holfman, ed. Cambridge: Belknap Press, 1979.

Hume, Kathryn. "The Heraclitean Cosmos of Kurt Vonnegut." *Papers on Lanauage and Literature* 18 (1982): 208–24.

——. "Vonnegut's Self-Projections: Symbolic Characters and Symbolic Fiction." *The Journal of Narrative Technique* 12 (Fall 1982): 177–90.

Ketterer, David. *New Worlds for Old: The Apocalyptic Imagination, Science Fiction, and American Literature.* Garden City, N.Y.: Anchor Books, 1974.

Laing, R. D. *The Divided Self.* New York: Random House, 1969.

Lehmann-Haupt, Christopher. "Familiar Characters and Tricks of Vonnegut." *New York Times* (8 September 1990): Arts and Leisure section, 16.

Leonard, John. "Black Magic." *The Nation* (15 October 1990): 421–423.

Lessing, Doris. "Vonnegut's Responsibility." *The New York Times Book Review,* (4 February 1973): 35.

Mayer, Pauline. "Mixing Hope and Cynicism." *St. Petersburg Times* (26 August 1990): Books section, D6.

Richardson, Jack. "Easy Writer." *New York Review* (2 July 1970): 7–8.

Shaw, Patrick. "The Excremental Festival: Vonnegut's *Slaughterhouse-Five.*" *Scholia Satyrica* 2(3) (Autumn 1976): 3–11.

Suarez, Ernest. *Politics, Culture, and the South in Literature.* Doctoral dissertation, University of Wisconsin, Madison, Wisconsin, 1988.

Tilton, John. *Cosmic Satire in the Contemporary Novel.* Lewisburg, Pa.: Bucknell University Press, 1977.

Vonnegut, Kurt. *Breakfast of Champions.* New York: Dell, 1973; reprintt. ed., 1975.

——. *Cat's Cradle.* New York: Dell, 1963; reprintt. ed., 1975.

——. *Deadeye Dick.* New York: Delacorte Press/Seymour Lawrence, 1982.

——. *Galápagos.* New York; Delacorte Press/Seymour Lawrence, 1985.

——. *Hocus Pocus.* New York: G. P. Putnam's Sons, 1990.

——. *Mother Night.* New York: Dell, 1961; reprint. ed., 1974.

——. *Palm Sunday.* New York: Dell, 1981.

——. *The Sirens of Titan.* New York: Dell, 1959; reprint. ed., 1971.

——. *Slapstick or Lonesome No More.* New York: Dell, 1976.

——. *Slaughterhouse-five.* New York: Dell, 1969; reprint. ed., 1972.

Waugh, Patricia. *Metafiction: The Theory and Practice of Self-Conscious Fiction.* New York: Methuen, 1984.

Appendix: The Graphics of Kurt Vonnegut

Peter J. Reed

Kurt Vonnegut's grandfather and father were both architects; therefore both drew professionally but both were also amateur artists. The writer's interest in the visual arts has been evident almost throughout his career. First of all there is his talent for very visual comedy in his fiction—the sort of comedy he associates with early film comedy of the Laurel and Hardy style—or that he describes sharing with his sister, where the door of the streetcar opens and the first passenger comes out horizontally. Many of those jokes that he has described as being like the tiles in the mosaics of his texts succeed by visualization. He has emphasized that quality in his technique: for example, presenting the ludicrous figures and events of the short story "Harrison Bergeron" as viewed on a television screen; defamiliarizing the bombing of Germany in *Slaughterhouse-Five* by portraying it in a film run backwards; or by the insertion of observed "playlets" in *Deadeye Dick*. Most obvious of all, of course, are those simple felt-tip pen drawings scattered throughout *Breakfast of Champions*.

It was the drawings in *Breakfast of Champions* that first drew any sort of public attention to Vonnegut as a graphic artist. They were variously regarded as illustrating the ludicrous disparities sometimes existing between words as signifiers and what it is they signify; as debunking some sacred cows; as "pop art" deflating "high art" in the same way that his simple prose and irreverent diction do; as funny; or as simply not very good. Those drawings certainly accorded with Vonnegut's mood at the time, where having confessed to being overwhelmed by what could be achieved visually in the film version of *Slaughterhouse-Five* he declared himself through with "spooks on paper"; embarked on the play, *Happy Birthday, Wanda June*; and contributed to the television screenplay, *Between Time and Timbuktu*. Vonnegut has continued to collaborate with visual presentations of his work, such as the 1979 stage production of *God Bless You, Mr. Rosewater* by his daughter Edith Vonnegut or the 1995 filming of *Mother Night*, with screenplay by Bob Weide and directed by Keith Gordon.

The drawing continued, as exemplified by striking, heavy-lined doodles drawn on pages of a discarded manuscript. "It is my custom to doodle on superseded drafts, and to sign and date the doodle," he said, and examples of these appeared in the 1978 *Dictionary of Literary Biography*, "American Novelists Since World War II." More formalized drawings, similar in style to the doodles but composed to a much larger scale on parchment, using colored felt-tip pens, followed soon afterward. Some thirty of these were exhibited at the Margo Fiden Gallery in Greenwich Village in 1983, where a number were sold while others were presented as gifts. Soon after this, Vonnegut experimented with smaller etchings. In these his penchant for self-portraiture, usually profiles with bushy hair and drooping cigarette, is sometimes amplified by the presence of an answering face from a mirror or reflecting surface.

The graphics appearing in this appendix are more recent, having their origin in an event that brought Vonnegut together with Kentucky artist, Joe Petro III. In 1993, the novelist responded to a request by an old friend from his days at General Electric to assist in the dedication of a new library at Midway College in Lexington, Kentucky. Ollie Lyon, who well remembers the day when Vonnegut had his first short story accepted, had gone on to reside in Lexington and become chair of the Development Council for the college. Vonnegut not only agreed to perform one of his "How to Get a Job Like Mine" evenings as a fund-raiser, but he also provided one of his self-portraits for a poster advertising the event and the opening. Another friend of Ollie Lyon, bookseller John Dinsmore, provided the connection with Joe Petro III, who silk screened the drawing for the poster. Since then, Vonnegut has continued to produce images painted on acetate, and by the end of 1995 Petro had silk-screened some fourteen.

Vonnegut quickly points out that his painting began much earlier. While living on Cape Cod in the 1950s, he painted in oils landscapes and seascapes, some of which may still exist in the houses of acquaintances there. Somewhat later, freelancing in public relations, he also did some art for advertisements— mostly either representational or what he calls "neo-cubist still lifes." The present graphics are painted on acetate that he buys in twelve-foot rolls. They are usually composed in black, with color filled in later. Sometimes the color is added by Petro at the silk-screening stage, and some of the pictures have been produced in multiple color combinations. Both Vonnegut and Petro like the use of "negative space," heightened by small areas of color that increase attention to the blank spaces. For the same reason, the image is sometimes silk-screened onto gray stock with the white areas painted. Both like to use white as a color, and this technique also intensifies the sense of space given by the white areas.

There is little doubt that Vonnegut finds a release in graphic art from the rigors of writing. Typically, he writes in the morning and paints in the afternoon. He has been very open about finding writing increasingly arduous, and ambitious undertakings like *Galápagos* and the as yet unfinished *Time Quake* have presented scientific as well as literary challenges. The paintings, on the contrary, are fun. Writing is hard, and the writer's joy comes in the moment when he or she hands the manuscript to the editor and says, "It's yours." The painter, Vonnegut says, "gets his rocks off while actually doing the painting. The act itself is agreeable." Frequently, he says, it is a matter of drawing a line across the acetate, then dipping the brush in the India ink and letting it follow the inevitable development of forms.

At the same time, Vonnegut is not only very sensitive to form and color, but also to art history. He reminds one that his original masters degree thesis, rejected by the University of Chicago, was about artists. He is also frank to admit derivative elements in his painting that acknowledge the influence of Paul Klee and Georges Braque. The latter is "a special hero," and Vonnegut particularly admires what the cubists did in "breaking up the chaotic into geometric forms, pleasing shapes." For him there is no sense that art is lessened by being derivative. "The notion that someone can make a big discovery and then nobody can make use of it would be very poor science," he says, once more alluding to his scientific training. He can look at pictures by Paul Klee, say "I can do that sort of thing," and give himself "an enjoyable way to pass the time." And Vonnegut repeatedly emphasizes the element of fun, of enjoyment, in this art.

Turning to the graphics in this appendix, Vonnegut insists that the titles are always afterthoughts applied when the image is complete. He does not begin with a subject or theme. Secondly, there appears to be some uncertainty about the exact chronology of their creation.

"Sphincter" obvious owes its origin to the notorious "asshole" of *Breakfast of Champions* that Vonnegut has subsequently incorporated into his autograph. Joe Petro made up a portfolio of eight "Sphincters" in different colors with a black on gray coversheet and a black on black bottom sheet. This was produced at the time of the Midway College dedication, and both single autographed silk-screens and portfolios were offered for sale at that time.

"One Eyed Jack" is a variation of very similar drawings dating back at least to the time of the Margo Fiden Gallery exhibition of 1983. Some profiles resemble Vonnegut's trade-mark self-portrait profile more closely than does "One-Eyed Jack," and there are variations in the floral decorations around the eye and, sometimes, around the mouth. This drawing has been treated in varying colors. An early version was in orange and green, a combination that Vonnegut seems to like but according to Petro's judgment, "the colors don't play off each other well." The original for the one illustrated here has gold and dark blue around the eye, a gold upper lip or mustache, and a yellow lower lip. More difficult to perceive is a dark blue line down the length of the upper lip, imposed on the black background. Characteristically, Vonnegut lets the background show through by using black to set the profile in relief. This, like the rough and irregular borders and the fact that the images often protrude beyond the borders, is a whimsical touch that calls attention to the medium and to the art as artifice.

"Self Portrait #1" is a variation of many earlier self-portrait caricature profiles. There is a playful formality in this one in the way the repeated curls of the hair take on pattern; the nostril is elaborated into a counterbalancing coil; the mustache has a severe straight edge; and the lips, the eye, the mustache and even the eyebrow repeat the circles and semicircles announced by the curls. This was the first colored self-portrait, with gray hair, mustache and eyebrow, and red and blue shirt. Again the black background lets the parchment peep through, and the coloring of the hair stops short of the border, producing the same tone of off-handedness as the overlaps in other pictures. The original silk-screen measures 30 by 22 inches.

Vonnegut regards "Wasp Waist" as a picture of a picture in the sense that it is based on art history, being a version of a familiar subject. To capture that perception he says that he has emphasized surface and that, combined with having the image overlap the drawn frame, forces the picture to be looked at as picture. In effect, the figure is posed in front of a framed picture of the background. Once again gray stock is used, with the white and beige of the background painted on it. And once again artifice is emphasized in having the gray show through the black hair and black floor.

There is obvious whimsy in "Wasp Waist." The curlicues of the buttocks, the electrical sockets set in the baseboard rather than above in the wall, and the fact that the "nude" can also be seen as a face with a shock of black hair and protruding nose. Originally the room had floorboards like those in "Trio" and "Vasectomy," but the black gives a more dramatic effect and counterbalances the black hair. Of interest are the small (gold) triangle between the back of the head and the border and the partial sun seen through the window, both motifs recurrent in the later pictures. The geometric shapes of walls, door and window set off the curves of the figure.

The figure in "Wasp Waist" was originally flesh colored, but was changed to gold, with some corresponding changes in the background colors, too. It has also been made the subject of a portfolio in six variations of color (chrome yellow, scarlet red, brilliant blue, green, blue, and purple). Furthermore, Petro has also made a sculpture in relief etched in quarter-inch thick aluminum alloy and standing approximately 24 inches high. After the initial test cast, three proofs and nine finished castings of the sculpture were made and marketed.

In "Egyptian Architect" the interest in coils at eyes and nostrils continues, and the play with triangles, pyramids and things Egyptian comes to the fore. The minimal use of color emphasizes whiteness and negative space, pushing the two faces right up into the framing of the border and elongating the distance to the pyramid in the background. The pyramid is black and pale gold; the background sky is aqua, and the seven colored panels in the eye of the left-hand figure are alternating pale gold and aqua. Other triangles are formed between the two heads and between the right-hand head and the border. As in some of Vonnegut's earlier etchings, the faces are presented in such a way that they might be the reflection of one face, with some distortion. The line dissecting the right-hand face intersects the line of the horizon—a line that is continued in the straight mouth of that face. There is consequently a counterpointing of the curling and the straight, as in "Wasp Waist." The faces are at once startling and amusing, and the total effect is to imply the self-conscious brilliance and perhaps smugness of the architects in the context of linear desert space and architectural regularity.

"Vasectomy" seems playfully literal. Once again we see wall, window and sun, while there is the emergence of the wood-grained floorboards that Vonnegut finds amusing to draw. He suggests that the origin of the idea is in seeing paper bags with eyes and mouth cut out, and he is fascinated with how easily humans can make distinctions between very simplistic variations of eyes and mouth. Just as dogs are able to distinguish between and identify an enormous number of scents, he says, humans can recognize and recall a seemingly infinite number of faces from the barest perception of features. Thus he can see at a distance down the street a former classmate whom he has not seen for years and still recognize him when only outlines of eyes and mouth are distinguishable. "Vasectomy" is obviously a vase that has been cut into *vase-ectomy,* but is also a face. There is both word play and visual play.

The background is unusually detailed and literal, but the continuation of the flat part of the windowsill over the window frame seems designed to undercut the literalness. The black in front of the floor boards seems to push the image back from the surface. The wall is gray, the sky and the interior of the vase a lighter gray, the sun and two flowers red, the other flower pink, and the hillside green.

"Three Madonnas" brings together the intersecting lines of "Egyptian Architect" and the impression of reflections noted elsewhere. Looked at with the small (yellow) corner square at bottom left, the picture might represent a surrealistic Madonna face with a smiling face. Joe Petro thinks this abstract face resembles a Howdy Doody face, too, and admires the resemblance of "Three Madonnas" to a stained glass window, appropriate to the subject. Turn the picture so that the small square is top left and one sees a Madonna and child and their reflection in a horizontal surface in the foreground. Reverse it again (small square bottom right) and there is another Madonna and child with an elongated reflection. The colors are black, yellow and red, with the gray partial rectangle enclosing the small yellow square. Vonnegut explains that he is interested by the arcs involved here, and has played with making Madonna figures out of these before. In this case he began with the dividing line across the middle and worked out from there. The fact that it can be looked at three ways is happy serendipity.

"Cheops" is the most geometric of the graphics. The abstraction of the face seems to stand in contrast to the solidity of the pyramids while echoing their triangles. One can play "count the triangles" with this one. Vonnegut will only comment that he finds the triangle a pleasing shape; Joe Petro recalls hearing him speak of triangles and pyramids as the strongest structural forms. Who knows if the three sides are a visual pun on Joe Petro III? As in his fiction so in his drawing, Vonnegut constantly experiments and plays. It is art to entertain viewer and creator alike.

Vonnegut does not offer any explanation for the Egyptian motif in this collection, insisting that he does not work with a theme in mind and that the titles are considered, and then rather casually, only after the painting is finished.

"Cheops" would appear to be another that is begun with intersecting lines. This time two lines dissect the image both vertically and horizontally. The horizontal lines produce startling affects, among them the impression of two horizons. Over the upper of these the face appears as a huge supernatural presence with commanding eyes thrown up against the sky. Perhaps adding to the affect of vast desert mirage is the downward pointing pyramid, which can be looked at as hovering over two pyramids standing on the second, lower horizon. The two solid blocks of color at the bottom, yellow and red, have a solidity that invites the eye into the deep blank spaces above. To say this is simply to play with the possibilities of this compelling image and probably to treat it too literally, for it is, as Petro suggests, the most geometric or formulaic of these graphics. Petro's impression is that it is perhaps Vonnegut's favorite.

"Trio" invokes the number three again, but the superimposed faces appear to owe much to the doodle faces of the 1970s. It makes unusually bold use of color, however, with heavy blocks of crimson, purple, gray and black brightened by yellow rimmed eyes. Is it three heads, or a multiracial, androgynous compilation of one being? Once more the simple features of eyes and mouth command. The wood grain floorboards balance the lighter right-facing profile; the block of black floor on the left balances the deep red in the upper left, so that the features (are they laughing or are they slightly predatory?) of the left face are thrust to the viewer's attention.

"Nostalgia" returns again to the "negative space" of open white areas, the whiteness intensified by being painted on gray stock. There is pale yellow in the two dissected circles at the very center of the image, and green-yellow-green-red in the four small squares in the lower right corner. The rest is black and white. The heaviness of some of the black lines may be gauged by the fact that this is the largest of Vonnegut's images, measuring approximately 35 by 28 inches. Its scale, the bold simplicity, and the compelling eyes make this an exceptionally strong image. Vonnegut reports that "Nostalgia," like "Three Madonnas," was begun with a line across the center and then sweeping arcs that bear some resemblance to distorted reflections.

The baleful expression of "Nostalgia" contrasts with the tranquil soulfulness of "Helen." Once again expression rests in simply delineated eyes and mouth. At the time of writing, this was the latest product of the Vonnegut-Petro collaboration, being screened in the Fall of 1995.

Meanwhile Vonnegut continues to work on more images obviously finding this new form of expression stimulating, relaxing and just plain fun. He tends to talk of it lightly, as he often does of his writing, but clearly it embodies his life-long interest in visual art and his critical senses continue to exert themselves on his own efforts. Understandably for someone whose career as a novelist covers such a long span, Vonnegut has found decreasing stimulation in writing of late. This new medium provides a welcome outlet for his creative energies, and he brings to it the same experimentation, play with form, and humor to be found in his fiction.

IN 1993 JOE PETRO III AND I BEGAN COLLABORATING ON PRINTS. I PAINTED PICTURES ON ACETATE. JOE PRINTED THEM. K. VONNEGUT.

"Foreword"
1993–1994. Ten portfolios each containing ten 30 x 22 inch silk screen prints in ten colors.

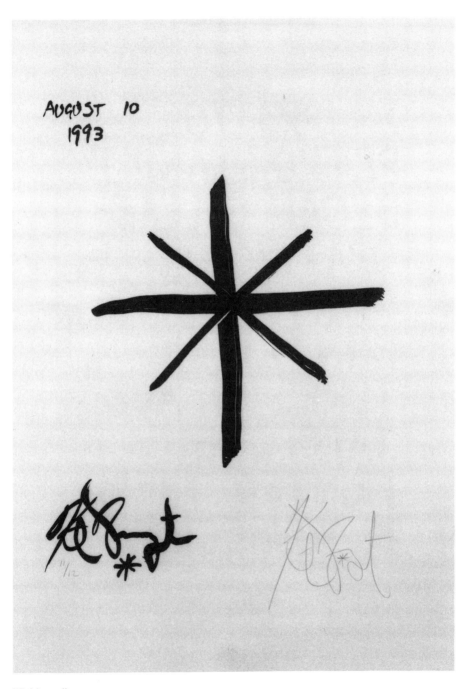

"Sphincter"
August 10, 1993. 30 x 22 inches. Edition of twelve on white. Signed in pencil by Kurt Vonnegut.

"Self-Portrait # 1"
1993. 30 x 22 inches. Edition of 235. In the tradition of self-portraits dating back to that at the end of *Breakfast of Champions* (1973).

"One-Eyed Jack"
1993 (though various editions were drawn from the 1980's onward). 30 x 20 inches. Four colors, ten in the red edition.

"Egyptian Architect"
1993. 26 x 20 inches. Four colors, an edition of ten. Vonnegut's father and grandfather were architects.

"Three Madonnas"
1993. 26 x 22 inches. Five colors, an edition of fifty. The picture that can be hung three ways.

"Cheops"
1993. 26 x 20 inches. Three colors, an edition of forty. Vonnegut enjoys the strength of the
triangular form.

"Trio"

1993. 26 x 20 inches. Five colors, an edition of forty. The first appearance of wood grain, which Vonnegut enjoys. See also "Vasectomy."

"Nostalgia"
1993. 30 x 22 inches. Six colors on gray paper. Edition of twelve.

"Vasectomy"
1993. 26 x 22 inches. Five colors, an edition of fifty. The pun is both visual and verbal.

"Wasp Waist"
1993–1994. 30 x 22 inches. Ten portfolios of six silkscreen prints on gray folio paper in tan, yellow, fire red, cobalt blue, burgundy red, and cerulean blue. Also the subject of a 24 inch bas relief sculpture.

"Helen"
1995. 22½ x 13½ inches. Five colors, an edition of ninety–nine. Vonnegut is
interested in how simple features of eyes and mouth convey identity and expression.

A Selected Bibliography, 1985–1994

Compiled by Peter J. Reed and Paul Baepler

This bibliography is intended to supplement chronologically two earlier comprehensive Vonnegut bibliographies, *Kurt Vonnegut, Jr.: A Descriptive Bibliography and Annotated Secondary Checklist*, by Asa B. Pieratt and Jerome Klinkowitz (Archon Books, 1974), and *Kurt Vonnegut: A Comprehensive Bibliography* by Asa B. Pieratt, Jerome Klinkowitz, and Julie Huffman-Klinkowitz (Archon Books, 1987). It is not as inclusive as those excellent bibliographies, excluding for example translations and dissertations, and is not annotated. It should prove of assistance, however, in keeping track of the rapidly growing body of secondary works on Vonnegut and the major reviews of his most recent work.

WORKS BY VONNEGUT

Books

Bluebeard. New York: Delacorte Press, 1987; London: Jonathan Cape, 1988.
Fates Worse Than Death: An Autobiographical Collage of the 1980s. New York: Putnam, 1991; London: Jonathan Cape, 1991.
Hocus Pocus. New York: Putnam, 1990; London: Jonathan Cape, 1990.

Articles and Essays

"The Boy Who Hated Girls." *Saturday Evening Post* 260 (September 1988): 42.
"Can't We Even Leave Jazz Alone?" *New York Times*, sec. 4 (14 December 1986): 23.
"The Courage of Ivan Martin Jirous." *Washington Post* (31 March 1989): A25.
"A Dream of the Future (Not Excluding Lobsters)." *Esquire* 104 (August 1985): 74.
"50 Years Later: Hoosiers Remember WWII: Kurt Vonnegut, Jr., Frank Klibbe, Madge Minton, Alex Vraciu. . . ." *Traces of Indiana and Midwestern History* 3(4) (Fall 1991): 43–45.

"Frank Conroy: The Triumph of the Arch." *GQ: Gentlemen's Quarterly* 60(9) (September 1990): 37.

"From the Desk of Kurt Vonnegut." *Mother Jones* 11 (January 1986): 26.

"The Fundamental Piece of Obscenity." *Publishers Weekly* (31 June 1986): 263.

"The Gospel According to Vonnegut." *Guardian* 28 (August 1991): 28.

"Great Beginnings: In Praise of the Incomplete." *Architectural Digest* 43 (May 1986): 170–175.

"He Leadeth Us From Porn: God Bless You, Edwin Meese." *Nation* 242(3) (25 January 1986): 65.

"Heinlein Gets the Last Word." *New York Times Book Review* (9 December 1990): 13.

"The Hocus Pocus Laundromat." *Swords and Ploughshares*. Nottingham, England: Bertrand Russell Peace Foundation, 1987.

"Kurt Vonnegut on Ernest Hemingway." In *Blowing the Bridge: Essays on Hemingway and For Whom the Bell Tolls*, ed. Rena Sanderson. Westport, Conn.: Greenwood, 1992.

"The Lake." *Architectural Digest* 45(6) (June 1988): 27.

"Lie," *Saturday Evening Post* 253 (November 1991): 50–51.

"My Fellow Americans: What I'd Say If They Asked Me." *Nation* 247 (16 July 1988): 53.

"My Visit to Hell." *Parade Magazine* (7 January 1990): 16–17.

"My Visit to Hell." *Washington Post* (7 January 1990): WSP16.

"Notes from My Bed of Gloom: Or, Why the Joking Had to Stop." *New York Times Book Review* (22 April 1990): 7, 14.

"One Hell of a Country." *Guardian* (27 February 1992): 21.

"Requiem: The Hocus Pocus Laundromat." *North American Review* 271 (December 1986): 29–35.

"Runaways." *Saturday Evening Post* 263(5) (July 1991): 28–34.

"Skyscraper National Park & Musings on New York." *Architectural Digest* 44(11) (November 1987): 76+.

"Slaughter in Mozambique." *New York Times* (14 November 1989): A31.

"Something's Rotten." *New York Times* (11 April 1991): A24.

"This Son of Mine." *Saturday Evening Post* 255 (October 1983): 74–76.

"War Preparers Anonymous," *Harpers* 268 (March 1987): 4.

"Why My Dog Is Not a Humanist." *Humanist* 52(6) (November 1992): 5–6.

"Why We Need Libraries." *The Utne Reader* 64 (July 1994): 139.

Articles Coauthored by Vonnegut

Vonnegut, Kurt, Edward Albee, Jules Feiffer, John Irving, John Knowles, Arthur Miller, and William Styron. "Can Great Books Make Good Movies? 7 Writers Just Say No!" *American Film* 12 (July–August 1987): 36–40.

——, John Kenneth Galbraith, Thomas E. Goldstein, and Peter MacKinnon. "Nietsche Might Have Applauded Bombing of Libya." *New York Times* (1 May 1986): 28.

——, Karen Kennerly, Sharon Olds, Tillie Olsen, and Susan Sontag. "The Case of Daud Haider." *New York Review of Books* (24 October 1985): 57.

——, Rose Styron. "If Warsaw Wants Normal Relations," *New York Times*, sec. 1 (7 July 1986): 17.

INTERVIEWS

Abádi-Nagy, Zoltán. "Serenity, Courage, Wisdom: A Talk with Kurt Vonnegut." *Hungarian Studies in English* 22 (1991): 23–37.

Allen, William Rodney, ed., *Conversations with Kurt Vonnegut*. Oxford, Miss.: University of Mississippi Press, 1988.

Carman, John. "Kurt Vonnegut, Couch Potato." *San Francisco Chronicle* (28 July 1992): D1.

Denison, D. C."Kurt Vonnegut." *Boston Globe Magazine* (2 September 1990): 8.

Dviy, E. "Posie Nar Khot Potop?" *Literaturnaia Gazeta* (23 October 1985): 43.

Imamura, Tateo. "Vonnegut in Tokyo: An Interview with Kurt Vonnegut." *Eigo Seinen* 130 (1984): 260–266.

"A Kurt Post-Mortem on the Generally Eclectic Theater: Kurt Vonnegut Interviewed." *Film Comment* 21(6) (November–December 1985): 41-44.

McCabe, Loretta Leone. "Kurt Vonnegut." In *On Being a Writer*, ed. Bill Strickland. New York: Writer's Digest Books, 1989: 132-138. Reprinted from *Writer's Yearbook—1970*: 92–95, 100–101, 103–105.

Mallory, Carole. "The Joe and Kurt Show." *Playboy* 39(5) (May 1992): 86-88.

Mirchev, A. *Interviu*. Niu-Iork: Izd-vo im. A. Platonova, 1989.

Nuwer, Hank. "Kurt Vonnegut Close Up." *Saturday Evening Post* 258 (May–June 1986): 38–39.

———. "A Skull Session with Kurt Vonnegut." *South Carolina Review* 19(2) (Spring 1987): 2–23.

Plimpton, George. "Hanging Out." *Esquire* 115(2) (February 1991): 42–44.

Schumacher, Michael. "Vonnegut on Writing." *Writer's Digest* (November 1985): 22–27. Reprinted from *On Being a Writer*, ed. Bill Strickland. New York: Writer's Digest Books, 1989: 139–143.

Shenk, David. "Duty to One's Country." *CV Magazine* 1(2) (April 1989): 57–59.

Streitfeld, David. "Vonnegut, from Cradle to Grave." *Washington Post* (29 August 1991): C1.

Szichman, Mario. "Bitter American Not Looking to the Future, Vonnegut Says." *Houston Post* (23 December 1990): C5.

Weimarer, B. "?" *New Fiction* 33 (1987): 379.

Writers at Work: The Paris Review Interviews, sixth series. London: Secker and Warburg, 1985.

WORKS ABOUT VONNEGUT

Reviews

Bluebeard

Book World 17 (4 October 1987): 9.

Booklist 83 (August 1987): 1699.

Books (April 1988): 16.

Clute, John. *The Times Literary Supplement* (29 April 1988): 470.

Deveson, Richard. *New Statesman* 115 (27 April 1988): 24.

Kirkus Reviews 55 (1 August 1987): 1113.
Listener 119 (5 May 1988): 29.
Los Angeles Times Book Review (4 October 1987): 10.
Minneapolis Star-Tribune (11 October 1987): G10.
Minneapolis Star-Tribune (30 August 1987): G3.
Moynahan, Julian. *New York Times Book Review* 92 (18 October 1987): 12.
Observer (2 April 1989): 45.
Observer (8 May 1988): 42.
Publishers Weekly 234 (16 September 1988): 80.
Publishers Weekly 232 (25 September 1987): 95.
Rackstraw, Loree. *North American Review* 273(1) (March 1888): 65–67.
Rieben, Cynthia. *Voice Youth Advocates* 11 (April 1988): 31.
Spectator 260 (30 April 1988): 36.
Stand 30 (Winter 1988): 77.
Time 130 (28 September 1987): 67.
Times Educational Supplement (3 June 1988): 26.
Village Voice 32 (17 November 1987): 59.
Wright, A. J. *Library Journal* 113 (January 1988): 101.

Fates Worse than Death

Anderson, Doug. *"Fates Worse Than Death." New York Times Book Review* (15 September 1991): 26.
Clark, Ross. "Just a Few Quick Ones before I Go—*Fates Worse Than Death* by Kurt Vonnegut." *Spectator* 267(8523) (16 November 1991): 45.
Coates, Joseph. "Truly Subversive Vonnegut." *Chicago Tribune* (1 September 1991): 4.
Edmiston, John. "Writers Focus on Daredevils, the Wilderness." *Houston Post* (4 October 1992): C9.
"Fates Worse Than Death." Atlanta Journal Constitution (22 September 1991): N10.
Heard, Alex. "Vonnegut on Vonnegut, Again." *Washington Post* (29 August 1991): C3.
Hiltbrand, David. "Picks and Pans—*Fates Worse Than Death* by Kurt Vonnegut." *People Weekly* 36(9) (1991): 29.
Holt, Patricia. "Vonnegut on Why the World Is Doomed." *San Francisco Chronicle* (25 September 1991): E1.
Hughes, Glyn. "Sermon for the Entirely Unsanctimonious." *Guardian* 7 (November 1991): 27.
Kirsch, Jonathan. "Vonnegut's Dark Oracle Speaks Plainly." *Los Angeles Times* (25 September 1991): E2.
Morton, Brian. "American Graffiti—*Fates Worse Than Death: An Autobiographical Collage of the 1980s* by Kurt Vonnegut/*A View from the Diners Club: Essays: 1987-1991* by Gore Vidal." *New Statesman* 4(177) (1991): 43–44.
Olson, Ray. *Booklist* 87(21) (July, 1991): 2010.
Shreve, Jack. *Library Journal* 116(13) (August 1991): 102.
Stuttaford, Genevieve. "Nonfiction—*Fates Worse Than Death: An Autobiographical Collage of the 1980s* by Kurt Vonnegut." *Publishers Weekly* 238(29), (1991): 51.

Wood, James. "The Wrecked Generation—*Fates Worse than Death: An Autobiographical Collage of the 1980s* by Kurt Vonnegut." *Times Literary Supplement* (15 November 1991): 8–9.

Galápagos

Avallone, Susan. *Library Journal* 110 (15 October 1985): 104.
Berry, Neil. *Encounter* 66(5) (1986): 57–58.
Best Sellers 45 (December 1981): 332.
Book Report 4 (March 1986): 31.
Book World 15 (22 September 1985): 1.
Booklist 82 (1 September 1985): 5.
Brians, Paul. *Bulletin of the Atomic Scientists* 42 (March 1986): 50.
Christian Century 103 (19 November 1986): 1037.
Deveson, Richard. *New Statesman* 110 (15 November 1985): 31.
Disch, Thomas M. *Times Literary Supplement* (8 November 1985): 1267.
Economist 297 (9 November 1985): 104.
Fantasy Review 8 (October 1985): 22.
Gerrity, Mary T. *School Library Journal* 32 (April 1986): 106.
Kirby, David. *America* 154 (8 February 1986): 104.
Kirkus Reviews 53 (1 August 1985): 751.
Lehman, David. *Newsweek* 106 (21 October 1985): 80.
London Review of Books 7 (7 November 1985): 24.
Los Angeles Times Book Review (29 September 1985): 1.
Moore, Lorrie. *New York Times Book Review* 90 (6 October 1985): 7.
New York Times Book Review 91 (19 October 1986): 50.
New York Times, (25 September. 1985): 21.
North American Review 270 (December 1985): 78.
Observer (3 November 1985): 25.
Publishers Weekly 230 (29 August 1986): 393.
Publishers Weekly 228 (30 August 1985): 413.
Punch 289 (23 October 1985): 88.
Science Fiction Review 15 (February 1986): 48.
Sheppard, R. Z. *Time* 126 (21 October 1985): 90.
Stand 30 (Winter 1988): 77.
Towers, Robert. *New York Review of Books* 32, 19 December 1985: 23.
USA Today 4 (4 October 1985): 4D.
Wall Street Journal 206 (6 November 1985): 30.

Hocus Pocus

Adams, Phoebe-Lou. "Brief Reviews: *Hocus Pocus.*" *Atlantic* 266(4) (October 1990): 137.
Ahearn, Barry. "It's Always Something." *Times-Picayune* (16 September 1990): F14.
Anderson, Lisa. "Vonnegut's Vision." *Chicago Tribune* (2 September 1990): p. 5:1.
Barron, John. "Very Vonnegut." *Detroit News* (3 October 1990): H3.
Berry, Michael. "Magic from the Inimitable One." *San Francisco Chronicle* (26 August 1990): Review Section 1.

Buchan, James. "Any Old Irony." *Spectator* 265(8467) (1990): 31–33.

Cantor, Jay. "Kurt Vonnegut: So It Still Goes." *Washington Post* (19 August 1990): The Week in Books p.1.

Carroll, Jerry. "Kurt Vonnegut: Prince of Pessimism." *San Francisco Chronicle* (25 April 1989): B3.

Danziger, Jeff. "Kurt Vonnegut, Quirks and All." *Boston Globe* (2 August 1990): B41.

Diehl, Digby. "Books." *Playboy* 37(9) (Sept. 1990): 36.

Garrett, George. "A Long-Awaited Return." *Chicago Tribune* (19 August 1990): 14:6.

Graf, Tom. "Back Before 'Twin Peaks,' There Was Kurt Vonnegut." *Denver Post* (26 August 1990): D8.

Graham, Keith. "Vonnegut Is Back, with Plenty to Say." *Atlanta Journal Constitution* (12 August 1990): N8.

Hiltbrand, David. "Picks and Pans: Pages—*Hocus Pocus*." *People Weekly* 34(13) (1990): 40–41.

Irving, John. "Vonnegut in Prison and Awaiting Trial." *Los Angeles Times* (2 September 1990): Book Reviews p.1.

Koning, Christina. "Life? It's a Dirty Joke." *Guardian* (18 October 1990): 22.

Lehmann-Haupt, Christopher. "Familiar Characters and Tricks of Vonnegut." *New York Times* (8 September 1990): A16.

Leonard, John. "Books & the Arts. Black Magic." *Nation* 251(12) (1990): 421–425.

Lescaze, Lee. "No Laughs, Not Much Magic." *Wall Street Journal* (7 August 1990): A17.

Matousek, Mark. "Book Bazaar: Gallows Humor." *Harper's Bazaar* 123(3345) (September 1990): 200–204.

McInery, Jay. "Still Asking the Embarrassing Questsions." *New York Times Book Review* (9 September 1990): 12.

Montrose, David. *Times Literary Supplemenet* (26 October 1990): 1146.

Phillips, Robert. "Fiction Chronicle—*Hocus Pocus* by Kurt Vonnegut." *Hudson Review* 44(1) (Spring 1991): 133–141.

Skow, John. "And So It Went." *Time* 136(10) 1990: CB4.

Steinberg, Sybil. "Fiction: *Hocus Pocus*." *Publishers Weekly* 237(27) (6 July 1990): 58.

Venant, Elizabeth. "A Doomsayer in Paradise." *Los Angeles Times* (26 August 1990): E1.

Wilson, Robert. "Vonnegut Conjures Up a Mad, Future Life." *USA Today* (31 August 1990): D5.

Zagst, Michael. "Grinning Through the Gloom." *Houston Post* (26 August 1990): C6.

Books and Articles

Abádi-Nagy, Zoltán. "An Original Look at 'Originals': Bokononism." In *The Origins and Originality of Amerian Culture*, ed. Frank Tabor, 601–608. Budapest: Akademiai Kiado, 1984.

Adams, Douglas. "'Hitchhiker' Novels as Mock Science Fiction." *Science Fiction Studies* 15 (March 1988): 61–70.

Allen, William Rodney. *Understanding Kurt Vonnegut*. Columbia: University of South Carolina, 1991.

Amerikanskaia Fantastika: V Chetyrnadtsati Tomakh. Moscow: Vse Dlia Vas, 1992.

Beidler, Phil. "Bad Business: Vietnam and Recent Mass-Market Fiction." *College English* 54(1) (January 1992): 64–75.

Berryman, Charles. "After the Fall: Kurt Vonnegut." *Critique: Studies in Modern Fiction* 26(2) (Winter 1985): 96–102.

——. "Vonnegut and Evolution: *Galápagos.*" In *Critical Essays on Kurt Vonnegut*, ed. Robert Merrill, 188–199. Boston: G.K. Hall & Co., 1990.

——. "Vonnegut's Comic Persona in *Breakfast of Champions* In *Critical Essays on Kurt Vonnegut*, ed. Robert Merrill, 162–170. Boston: G. K. Hall & Co., 1990.

Blackford, Russell. "Physics and Fantasy: Scientific Mysticism, Kurt Vonnegut and *Gravity's Rainbow.*" *Journal of Popular Culture* 19 (Winter 1985) 35–44.

Bly, William. *Kurt Vonnegut's* Slaughterhouse-Five. Woodbury, NY: Barron's Educational Series, 1985.

Broer, Lawrence R. "Kurt Vonnegut vs. Deadeye Dick: The Resolution of Vonnegut's Creative Schizophrenia." *Spectrum of the Fantastic*, ed. Donald Palumbo, 95–102. Westport, Conn.: Greenwood, 1988.

—— *Sanity Plea: Schizophrenia in the Novels of Kurt Vonnegut*. Ann Arbor: University of Michigan Research Press, 1988. Revised and reprinted by Tuscaloosa: University of Alabama Press, 1994.

Byun, Jong-Min. "Some Aspects of Confucianism in Vonnegut's *Cat's Cradle.*" *Journal of English Language and Literature* (JELL) 37(4) (Winter 1991): 973–981.

Campbell, Felicia. "Two Gurus—Vonnegut's Bokonon and Narayan's Raju: Teachers outside the Classroom." *West Virginia University Philological Papers* 36 (1990): 77–81.

Cohen-Safir, C. "Le Doute Chez Kurt Vonnegut, Jr." In *Société des Anglicistes de l'enseignement superieurs*, ed. Actes due Congres de Poitiers, Paris: Didier Erudition, 1984.

Cowart, David. "Culture and Anarchy: Vonnegut's Later Career." In *Critical Essays on Kurt Vonnegut*. ed. Robert Merrill, 170–188. Boston: G. K. Hall & Co., 1990. Boston: G.K. Hall & Co., 1990.

Crump, G. B. "Magic, Foma, Madness, and Art in the Fiction of Kurt Vonnegut, Jr." *Pleiades* 12(1) (Fall-Winter 1991): 64–82.

Dhar, T. N. "Vonnegut's Leap Within: *Slaughterhouse-Five* to *Slapstick.*" *Indian Journal of American Studies* 15 (Winter 1985): 57–63.

Dinsmore, John. "Kurt and Ollie." *Firsts: Collecting Modern First Editions* 2(10) (October 1992): 14–17.

Dorris, Michael, and Louise Erdrich. "Bangs and Whimplers, Novelists at Armageddon (Post-Apocalypse Worlds in Modern Fiction)," *New York Times Book Review* (13 March 1988): 1.

Dvin, E. "'Posle nas Khot' Potop?" *Literaturnaia Gazeta* 43 (1985): 15.

Faris, Wendy B. "Magic and Violence in Macondo and San Lorenzo." *Latin American Literary Review* 13 (January—June 1985): 44–54.

Fiene, Donald M. "Kurt Vonnegut in the USSR: A Bibliography." *Bulletin of Bibliography* 45(4) (1988): 223–232.

Freese, Peter. "Kurt Vonnegut: *Cat's Cradle* (1963)." In *Die Utopie in der Angloamerikanische Literatur: Interpretation*, ed. Bernd-Peter Lange. Dusseldorf: Bagel, 1984.

——. "Laurel and Hardy Versus the Self-Reflexive Artefact: Vonnegut's Novels between High Culture and Popular Culture." *High and Low in American Culture*, ed. Charlotte Kretzoi, 19–38. Budapest: Dept. of Eng., Lorand Eotvos University, 1986.

Gibson, David J. "Vonnegut's *Galpáagos*: The Myth of Art, Vice Versa, (or Something)." In *Draftings in Vonnegut: The Paradox of Hope*, ed. Loree Rackstraw, 33–48. Cedar Falls: University of Northern Iowa, 1988.

Greer, Creed. "Kurt Vonnegut and the Character of Words." *Journal of Narrative Technique* 19(3) 1989: 312–330.

Haas, Rudolf. "Form und Sinn bei Vonnegut: Vignetten zu *Cat's Cradle*," *Gottungsprobleme in der Anglo-Amerikanischen Literatur*, ed. Raimund Borgmeier, 230–238. Tubingen: Niemeyer, 1986.

Han, Chun-koong. "*Slaughterhouse-Five*: Dynamic Tension." *The Journal of English Language and Literature* 38(2) (Summer 1992): 295–314.

Hearron, Tom. "The Theme of Guilt in Vonnegut's Cataclysmic Novels." *The Nightmare Considered: Critical Essays on Nuclear War Literataure*, ed. Nancy Anisfield, 186–192. Bowling Green, Ohio: Popular Press, 1991.

Heger, Anders. ". . . to Poison Their Minds with Humanity: Kurt Vonnegut's Litteraere prosjekt." *Vinduet* 38(1) (1984): 32–36.

Horiachev, V., and O. I. Rudiachenko. "Z Tryvoholou za Mabulnie." *Vsesvit: Literaturno-Mystetss'kyi ta Hromads'ko-Politzchnyi' hurnal* (12 December 1984): 73–75.

Hou, Weirui. "From the Ladder to the Cobweb: Changes in the Structure of the Novel." *Waiguoyu* 2(84) (April 1993): 15–21.

Hutcheon, Linda. "Historiographic Metafiction: Parody and the Intertextuality of History." In *Intertextuality and Contemporary American Fiction*, ed. Patrick O'Donnell and Robert Con Davis, 3–32. Baltimore: Johns Hopkins University Press, 1989.

Jamosky, Edward, and Jerome Klinkowitz. "Kurt Vonnegut's Three Mother Nights." *Modern Fiction Studies* 34(2) (Summer 1988): 216–219.

Kaufman, Will. "Vonnegut's *Breakfast of Champions*—A Comedian's Primer." *Thalia: Studies in Literary Humor.* 13(1–2) (1993): 22–33.

Klinkowitz, Jerome. "Kurt Vonnegut's Ultimate." *The Nightmare Conisdered: Critical Essays on Nuclear War Literataure*, ed Nancy Anisfield, 193–198. Bowling Green, Ohio: Popular Press, 1991.

———. Slaughterhouse-Five: *Reforming the Novel and the World*. Boston: Twayne Masterworks Series, 1990.

Kopper, Edward A., Jr. "Abstract Expressionism in Vonnegut's *Bluebeard*." *Journal of Modern Literature* 17(4) (Spring, 1991): 583–584.

Langer, Freddy. "Das Grosse Ah-whumm: Uber Den Amerikanischen Schriftsteller Kurt Vonnegut." *Die Horen: Zeitschrift Fur Literatur*, Kunst und Kritik 38(2) (1993): 175–179.

Lazer, Mary. "Sam Johnson on Grub Street, Early Science Fiction Pulps, and Vonnegut." *Extrapolation: A Journal of Science Fiction and Fantasy* 32(2) (Fall 1991): 235–255.

Lee, Cremilda Toledo. "Fantasy and Reality in Kurt Vonnegut's *Slaughterhouse-Five*." *Journal of English Language and Literature* 37(4) (Winter 1991): 983–991.

Leeds, Marc. *The Vonnegut Encyclopedia: An Authorized Compendium*. Foreword by Kurt Vonnegut. Westport, Conn.: Greenwood Press, 1995.

Long, Marion. "Paradise Tossed: Personal Utopias of Elie Wiesel, Tammy Faye Bakker, Max Headroom, Hans Kung, Coretta Scott King, Stephen Jay Gould, Jesse Jackson, Grace Slick, David Rockefeller, Kurt Vonnegut, and Others." *Omni* 10(7) (April 1988): 27–42.

McBride, Vaughn. *Go Back to Your Precious Wife and Son: Based upon Kurt Vonnegut, Jr.'s, Welcome to the Monkey House*. Woodstock, Ill.: Dramatic Publishing Co., 1989.

McKinney, Devin. "Kurt Vonnegut and Nathanael West." In *Draftings in Vonnegut: The Paradox of Hope*, ed. Loree Rackstraw, 13–20. Cedar Falls: University of Northern Iowa, 1988.

"Marriage." *Lear's* 2(4) (June 1989): 71.

Martin, Robert A. "*Slaughterhouse-Five*." *Notes on Contemporary Literature* 15(4) (September 1985): 8–10.

———. "*Slaughterhouse-Five*: Vonnegut's Doomed Universe." *Notes on Contemporary Literature* 17(2) (March 1987): 5–8.

Mathiesen, Kenneth. "The Influence of Science Fiction in the Contemporary American Novel." *Science Fiction Studies* 12 (1985): 22–32.

Merrill, Robert. "Kurt Vonnegut as a German-American." In *Germany and German Thought in American Literature and Cultural Criticism*, ed. Peter Freese, 230–243. Essen: Blaue Eule, 1990.

———, ed. *Critical Essays on Kurt Vonnegut*. Boston: G. K. Hall & Co., 1990.

Meyer, William E. H., Jr. "Vonnegut, Kurt—The Man with Nothing to Say." *Critique—Studies in Modern Fiction* 29(2) (Winter 1988): 95–109.

Minehart, Jill. "Doctors in Spite of Themselves." In *Draftings in Vonnegut: The Paradox of Hope*, ed. Loree Rackstraw, 1–12. Cedar Falls: University of Northern Iowa, 1988.

Misra, Kalidas. "The American War Novel from World War II to Vietnam." *Indian Journal of American Studies* 14 (July 1984): 73–80.

Morse, Donald E. *Kurt Vonnegut*. San Bernardino, Calif.: Borgo Press; Mercer Island, WA: Starmont House, 1992.

———. "Kurt Vonnegut's *Jailbird* and *Deadeye Dick*: Two Studies of Defeat." *Hungarian Studies in English* 22 (1991): 109–119.

Muller, C. "Nuclear Disaster in the United States American Novel." *Weimarer Beitrage* 34(1) (1988): 17–28.

Mustazza, Leonard. *Forever Pursuing Genesis: The Myth of Eden in the Novels of Kurt Vonnegut*. Lewisburg, Pa.: Bucknell University Press, 1990.

———. "The Machine Within: Mechanization, Human Discontent, and the Genesis of Vonnegut's *Player Piano*." *Papers on Language and Literature: A Journal for Scholars and Critics of Language and Literature* 25(1) (Winter 1989): 99–113.

———. "Vonnegut's Tralfamadore and Milton's Eden." *Essays in Literature* 13(2) (1986): 299–312.

———, ed. *The Critical Response to Kurt Vonnegut*. Westport, Conn.: Greenwood Press, 1994.

Nuwer, Hank. "Kurt Vonnegut Close Up." *Saturday Evening Post* 258(4) (May 1986): 38–39.

Olson, Lynn. "Poo-tee-weet?" In *Draftings in Vonnegut: The Paradox of Hope*, ed. Loree Rackstraw, 21–32. Cedar Falls: University of Northern Iowa, 1988.

Orendain, Margarita R. "Confronting the Gods of Science: Kurt Vonnegut, Jr. in *Welcome to the Monkey House*." *Saint Louis University Research Journal of the Graduate School of Arts and Sciences* 18(1) (June 1987): 150–167.

Parschall, Peter F. "Meditations on the Philosophy of Tralfamadore: Kurt Vonnegut and George Roy Hill." *Literature/Film Quarterly* 15 (1987): 49–59.

Pieratt, Asa B., Jr., Julie Huffman-Klinkowitz, and Jerome Klinkowitz. *Kurt Vonnegut: A Comprehensive Bibliography*. Hamden, Conn: Shoe String Press, 1987.

Rackstraw, Loree, ed. *Draftings in Vonnegut: The Paradox of Hope*. Cedar Falls: University of Northern Iowa, 1988.

Rampton, David. "Into the Secret Chamber: Art and the Artist in Kurt Vonnegut's *Bluebeard.*" *Critique: Studies in Contemporary Fiction* 35(1) (Fall 1993): 16–26.

Rapf, Joanna E. "In the Beginning Was the Work: Steve Geller on *Slaughterhouse-Five.*" *PostScript: Essays in Film and the Humanities* 4 (Winter 1985): 19–31.

Reddy, K. Satyanaryana. "Structure of Consciousness in the Major Fiction of Kurt Vonnegut, Jr." *The Literary Endeavour: A Quarterly Journal Devoted to English Studies* 9(1–4) (1987–1988): 91–96.

Reed, Peter J. "Economic Neurosis: Kurt Vonnegut's *God Bless You, Mr. Rosewater.*" In *Critical Essays on Kurt Vonnegut*, ed. Robert Merill, 108–124. Boston: G. K. Hall & Co., 1990.

——. "Kurt Vonnegut." *Postmodern Fiction: A Bio Bibliographical Guide*, ed. Larry McCaffery, 533–535. Westport, Conn.: Greenwood Press, 1986.

——. "Kurt Vonnegut, Jr." In *The Concise Dictionary of American Literary Biography: Broadening Views, 1968–1988*, ed. Mary Bruccoli, 298–319. Detroit: Gale Research, 1989.

Saltzman, Arthur M. "The Aesthetic of Doubt in Recent Fiction." *Denver Quarterly* 20 (Summer 1985): 89–106.

Sandbank, Shimon. "Parable and Theme: Kafka and American Fiction." *Comparative Literature* 37(3) (Summer 1985): 252–268.

Schipp, Joseph C. "Science Fiction: The Struggle with a Form That Fails." *American Studies* 28(3) (1983): 335–345.

Schnackertz, Hermann Josef. *Darwinismus und literarischer Diskurs: der Dialog mit der Evolutionsbiologie in der englischen und amerikanischen Literatur: E. Bulwer-Lytton, S. Butler, J. Conrad, Ch. Darwin, Th. Dreiser, G. Gissing, H. Spencer, K. Vonnegut, H.G. Wells.* Munchen: W. Fink, 1992.

Sheldon, T. P. "*Galápagos.*" *Special Libraries* 78 (1987): 93.

Sheppeard, Sallye, "Kurt Vonnegut and the Myth of Scientific Progress." *Journal of the American Studies Association of Texas* 16 (1985): 14–19.

——. "Signposts in a Chaotic World: Naming Devices in Kurt Vonnegut's Dresden Books." *McNeese Review* 31 (1986): 14–22.

Sigman, Joseph. "Science and Parody in Kurt Vonnegut's *The Sirens of Titan.*" *Mosaic* 19 (Winter 1986): 15–32.

Simons, John L. "Tangled Up in You: A Playful Reading of *Cat's Cradle.*" In *Critical Essays on Kurt Vonnegut*, ed. Robert Merrill, 94–108. Boston: G. K. Hall & Co., 1990.

Singh, Jaidev, and Pankaj K. Singh. "Self-Reflexivity in Contemporary Fiction: A Note on Ideology." *Creative Forum: A Quarterly Journal of Contemporary Writing* 1(4) (1988): 1–11.

Singh, Sukhbir. "The Politics of Madness in Kurt Vonnegut's *God Bless You, Mr. Rosewater.*" *Punjab University Research Bulletin* 17 (April 1986): 19–27.

Singh, Sukhbir. *The Survivor in Contemporary American Fiction: Saul Bellow, Bernard Malamud, John Updike, Kurt Vonnegut, Jr.* Delhi: B. R. Publishing, 1991.

Smiley, Robin H. "Books into Film: *Slaughterhouse-Five.*" *Firsts: Collecting Modern First Editions* 2(10) (October 1992): 33–34.

Stownsend, Roy. "Eliot and Vonnegut: Modernism and Postmodernism?" *Journal of English* (Sana'a, Yemen Arab Republic) 16 (1988): 90–104.

"Super Author in Residence." Proceedings of the Vonnegut Symposium April 4–5, 1989; Davenport, Iowa: Davenport Public Library, 1989.

Szegedy-Maszak, Mihaly. "The Life and Times of the Autobiographical Novel." *Neo Helicon* 13(1) (1986): 83–104.

Tunnell, James R. "Kesey and Vonnegut: Preachers of Redemption." *A Casebook on Ken Kesey's One Flew Over the Cuckoo's Nest*, ed. George J. Searles, 127–133. Albuquerque: University of New Mexico Press, 1992.

"Vonnegut, Kurt, Jr." *Current Biography* 52(3) (March 1991): 52–56.

Watts, Philip. "Rewriting History: Céline and Kurt Vonnegut." *South Atlantic Quarterly* 93(2) (1994): 265–78.

Whitlark, James S. "Vonnegut's Anthropology Thesis." *Literature and Anthropology*, ed. Philip Dennis and Wendell Aycock, 77–86. Lubbock: Texas Tech University Press, 1989.

Wiedemann, Barbara. "American War Novels: Strategies for Survival." *War and Peace: Perspectives in the Nuclear Age*, ed. Ulrich Goebel and Otto Nelson. Lubbock: Texas Tech University Press, 1988: 127–144.

Wineapple, B. "God Bless You, Vonnegut." in *Current Perspectives in Social Theory*, ed S. G. McNall et al., vol. 2, 233–245. Greenwich, Conn.: JAI Press, 1981.

Zins, D. L. "Rescuing Science from Technocracy: *Cat's Cradle* and the Ploy of Apocalypse." *Science Fiction Studies* 13 (July 1986): 170–181.

Zvieriev, Oleski. "Skal pel Vonnekuta." *Vsesvit: Literaturno-Mustetskyita, Hromads'ko-Politzchunyi Zhurnal* 14 (1984): 140–142.

Profiles and Miscellany

Brown, Elizabeth A. "Too Much Love?" *Christian Science Monitor* (30 January 1989): 12.

Garcia, Chris. "Family Top Topic for Holidays." *Times-Picayune* (26 November 1992): OTT1.

Matousek, Mark. *Harper's Bazaar* 123(3345) (September 1990): 200–f204.

Outerbridge, Laura. "Vonnegut Says Censorship Problem Moot in Illiterate America." *Washington Times*, (1 March 1989): E5.

Persica, Dennis. "Vonnegut: Free Speech Rights Hard to Defend." *Times-Picayune* (9 March 1994): 3:5.

Streitfeld, David. "Footprints in the Cosmic Dust." *Washington Post* (20 July 1989): D1.

——. "Vonnegut from Cradle to Grave." *Washington Post* (29 August 1991): C1.

Volland, Victor. "How to Get a Job Like Vonnegut's? Be a Great Talker, He Discloses Here." *St. Louis Post-Dispatch* (3 September 1992): 4:1.

"Vonnegut in Poland: Spirit of Solidarity Lives On." *New York Times*, sec. 4, p.23 (9 June 1985). Translated and reprinted from newspaper *Tygodnik Mazowsze*.

Index

About the Contributors

ZOLTÁN ABÁDI-NAGY is President of Kossuth University in Debrecen, Hungary, Professor of English and American Studies, and the General Editor of the *Hungarian Journal of English and American Studies* (formerly *Hungarian Studies of English*). He served as an ACLS Fellow at Duke University and taught as a Fulbright Professor at the University of Minnesota, the University of Oklahoma, and the University of California, Irvine. His numerous books and articles consider a wide variety of material including Jonathan Swift; the American novel from the 1960s through the 1980s; black humor; entropic, postmodern and minimalist fiction; and interviews with contemporary American authors. Abádi-Nagy has translated contemporary American fiction and drama into Hungarian. Considered one of the leading Vonnegut scholars in Europe, Abádi-Nagy's contributions to Vonnegut scholarship include book chapters, critical essays, and interviews.

PAUL BAEPLER is writing his doctoral dissertation on the Barbary Captivity Narrative at the University of Minnesota. His work has appeared in *Early American Literature*, *Les Cahiers de la Nouvelle*, the *Walt Whitman Quarterly Review*, and the *Exquisite Corpse*.

LAWRENCE BROER is Professor of English at the University of South Florida and has authored over seventy articles and critical papers on modern and postmodern literature. His books include *Hemingway's Spanish Tragedy* and *Sanity Plea: Schizophrenia in the Novels of Kurt Vonnegut*. Broer twice served as a Fulbright lecturer at the University of Paris. In 1986 and 1993 he received the Faculty Award for Excellence in Teaching at USF, and in 1989 he received the Theodore and Benette Askounes-Ashford Distinguished Scholar Award.

PETER FREESE is President of the German Association for American Studies and Professor of American Studies at the University of Paderborn. Among the almost thirty books Freese has authored or edited are *"America": Dream or*

Nightmare? Reflections on a Composite Image; *Die amerikanische Kurzgeschichte nach 1945*; *Die Initiationsreise*; *From Melting Pot to Multiculturalism*; *Germany and German Thought in American Literature and Cultural Criticism*; *Growing up Black in America*; *Popular Culture in the United States*; *Postmodernism in American Literature*; *Religion and Philosophy in the United States of America*; *The Ethnic Detective*. Freese has published more than one hundred articles on American, English, and German literature, American popular culture, and ESL-methodology.

JEROME KLINKOWITZ is Professor of English and University Distinguished Scholar at the University of Northern Iowa. Among the many books Klinkowitz has authored or coedited are *Kurt Vonnegut: A Comprehensive Bibliography*; *Kurt Vonnegut*; *Slaughterhouse-Five: Reinventing the Novel and the World*; *The Vonnegut Statement*; and *Vonnegut in America*. His bibliography includes well over thirty books with topics as diverse as baseball, jazz, art, philosophy, and the narratology of World War II air combat memoirs.

MARC LEEDS authored *The Vonnegut Encyclopedia: An Authorized Compendium* and a number of articles on computer-assisted instruction. He is currently a freelance writer and hypertext developer in Boca Raton, Florida. Until recently he directed computer-assisted writing programs at Shawnee State University in Ohio and East Tennessee State University. His current projects include book-length considerations on narrative simultaneity and on Henry Adams' search for a unified field theory of history.

CLIFF MCCARTHY caught Kurt Vonnegut's attention in the early 1980s with a weekly radio program he was doing on the arts in Ohio. At the time, Vonnegut was looking for material for *Deadeye Dick*. Their correspondence about art, politics, and literature was so lively that Vonnegut made McCarthy a significant character in that book. McCarthy is a World War II veteran of the Army Air Corps photo reconnaissance squadron in the Pacific theater, a painter, and Professor Emeritus of Art at Ohio University. For the past six years he has made numerous trips to Nicaragua to photograph the development of its people.

ROBERT MERRILL is Foundation Professor of English and chair of the English Department at the University of Nevada, Reno. He is the author of books on Norman Mailer and Joseph Heller and is the editor of *Critical Essays on Kurt Vonnegut*. He has published essays on Shakespeare and various American writers, such as Vladimir Nabokov, F. Scott Fitzgerald, John Gardner, Thomas Pynchon, Ernest Hemingway, William Faulkner, and Norman Mailer, in journals such as *American Literature, Critique, Modern Fiction Studies, Modern Philology, Studies in American Fiction*, and *Texas Studies in Literature and Language*. He has also published essays on Vonnegut's *Slaughterhouse-Five* and *Breakfast of Champions*.

KAY HOYLE NELSON is Assistant Professor English and Humanities at Aurora University's Chicago Center. She recently coedited *The Critical Response to Tillie Olsen*.

LOREE RACKSTRAW is an Associate Professor of English at the University of Northern Iowa. She holds an M.F.A. from the University of Iowa where she studied with Kurt Vonnegut in the Writers Workshop. The former fiction editor of the *North American Review*, Rackstraw teaches fiction writing, mythology, and interdisciplinary courses in the humanities. She has published numerous articles on Vonnegut's career.

PETER J. REED, Professor of English and Associate Dean of the College of Liberal Arts at the University of Minnesota, wrote the first book-length treatment of Vonnegut in 1972, *Writers for the 70s: Kurt Vonnegut*. His biographical sketches of Vonnegut appear in such standard works as the *Concise Dictionary of American Literary Biography*; *Dictionary of Literary Biography*; *Magill's Survey of American Literature*; and *Postmodern Fiction: A Bio-Bibliographical Guide*. Like Vonnegut, Reed is a survivor of aerial bombardment—his childhood home in England was destroyed in the blitz.

ISBN 0-313-29719-3

90000>

9 780313 297199

EAN

HARDCOVER BAR CODE